The DLM Early Childhood EXPRESS

Teacher's Edition
Unit 4
Let's Investigate

Nell Duke • Douglas Clements • Julie Sarama • William Teale

McGraw Hill **Wright Group**

The McGraw-Hill Companies

Authors

Nell Duke
Professor of Teacher Education and Educational Psychology and Co-Director of the Literacy Achievement Research Center Michigan State University, East Lansing, MI

Douglas H. Clements
Professor of Early Childhood and Mathematics Education University at Buffalo, State University of New York, New York

Julie Sarama
Associate Professor of Mathematics Education University at Buffalo, State University of New York, New York

William Teale
Professor of Education University of Illinois at Chicago, Chicago, IL

Contributing Authors

Kim Brenneman, PhD
Assistant Research Professor of Psychology at Rutgers University, National Institute for Early Education Research Rutgers University, New Brunswick, NJ

Peggy Cerna
Early Childhood Consultant Austin, TX

Dan Cieloha
Educator and President of the Partnership for Interactive Learning Oakland, CA

Paula Jones
Early Childhood Consultant Lubbock, TX

Bobbie Sparks
Educator and K-12 Science Consultant Houston, TX

Image Credits: Cover (looking glass) CMCD/Getty Images, (wheels)felinda/istockphoto, (all other)The McGraw-Hill Companies; **5** blue jean images/Getty Images; **9** Seth Joel/Photographer's Choice RF/Getty Images; **18-19** Royalty-Free/Masterfile; **19** RubberBall/PunchStock; **24** Royalty-Free/Masterfile; **25** Daniel Cooper/Getty Images; **30** Royalty-Free/CORBIS; **36** TSI Graphics; **42** Dennis MacDonald/Alamy; **48** Steve Mack; **56-57** TSI Graphics; **57** Janis Christie/Getty Images; **62** Jake Curtis/Getty Images; **64** Blend Images/Alamy; **72** FoodCollection/SuperStock; **74** Daniel Griffo; **78** Mike Wesley; **80** Ross Anania/Getty Images; **82** Holli Conger; **84** Steve Mack; **86** The McGraw-Hill Companies Inc./Ken Cavanagh Photographer; **90** moodboard/CORBIS; **92** Melissa Iwai; **94-95** Christopher Gruver/Masterfile; **95** Image Source/Getty Images; **00** Royalty-Free/Masterfile; **102** RedChopsticks/Getty Images; **106** Tim Beaumont; **108** Eileen Hine; **112** The McGraw-Hill Companies, Inc.; **114** Mike Wesley; **118** Wayne R Bilenduke/Getty Images; **124** moodboard/CORBIS; **130** Hector Borlasca; **132-133** Don Mason/Getty Images; **133 138 139** Royalty-Free/Masterfile; **142** Glowimages/Getty Images; **146** Valeria Cis; **150** Comstock Images/Alamy; **152** (l r)The McGraw-Hill Companies, Inc.; **156** George Doyle/Getty Images; **162** Laura Gonzalez; **162** Melissa Iwai; **164** Jan Bryan-Hunt; **166** Royalty- Free/CORBIS; **171** The McGraw-Hill Companies, Inc./Ken Cavanagh photographer; **172** RubberBall/PunchStock; **178** D. Berry/PhotoLink/Getty Images; **181** (t)Steve Mack, (c)Ingram Publishing/Alamy, (b)Daniel Griffo; **183** (t)Susan LeVan/Getty Images, (b)Laura Gonzalez; **185** Mike Wesley; **186** (t)The McGraw-Hill Companies, Inc., (b)Eileen Hine; **192** Photodisc Collection/Getty Images; **BackCover** (all wheels)felinda/istockphoto, (pencil)Andy Crawford/Getty Images, (rust wicker)Comstock/CORBIS, (bell)Stockbyte/Getty Images, (webcam)Medioimages/Photodisc/Getty Images, (pencilmirror)Yasuhide Fumoto/Getty Images, (U3roof)Ryan McVay/Getty Images, (elephant)PhotoLink/Getty Images, (looking glass) CMCD/Getty Images, (alligator)Siede Preis/Getty Images, (alligatorbelly)Ryan McVay/Getty Images, (U5traincar)83owl/Getty Images, (toothbrush)Raimund Koch/Getty Images, (U8traincar)Ryan McVay/Getty Images, (brush)Brand X Pictures/PunchStock, (all other)The McGraw-Hill Companies.

The McGraw·Hill Companies

www.WrightGroup.com

Send all inquiries to:
Wright Group/McGraw-Hill
P.O. Box 812960
Chicago, IL 60681

ISBN 978-0-07-658082-8
MHID 0-07-658082-2

2 3 4 5 6 7 8 9 WEB 16 15 14 13 12 11 10

Acknowledgment

Building Blocks was supported in part by the National Science Foundation under Grant No. ESI-9730804, "Building Blocks— Foundations for Mathematical Thinking, Pre-Kindergarten to Grade 2: Research-based Materials Development" to Douglas H. Clements and Julie Sarama. The curriculum was also based partly upon work supported in part by the Institute of Educational Sciences (U.S. Dept. of Education, under the Interagency Education Research Initiative, or IERI, a collaboration of the IES, NSF, and NICHHD) under Grant No. R305K05157, "Scaling Trajectories and Technologies" and by the IERI through a National Science Foundation NSF Grant No. REC-0228440, "Scaling Up the Implementation of a Pre-Kindergarten Mathematics Curricula: Teaching for Understanding with Trajectories and Technologies." Any opinions, findings, and conclusions or recommendations expressed in this material are those of the authors and do not necessarily reflect the views of the funding agencies.

Reviewers

Tonda Brown, *Pre-K Specialist*, Austin ISD; Deanne Colley, *Family Involvement Facilitator*, Northwest ISD; Anita Uphaus, *Retired Early Childhood Director*, Austin ISD; Cathy Ambridge, *Reading Specialist*, Klein ISD; Margaret Jordan, *PreK Special Education Teacher*, McMullen Booth Elementary; Niki Rogers, *Adjunct Professor of Psychology/ Child Development*, Concordia University Wisconsin

Table of Contents

Getting Started

Getting Started with *The DLM Early Childhood Express*

The DLM Early Childhood Express is a holistic, child-centered program that nurtures each child by offering carefully selected and carefully sequenced learning experiences. It provides a wealth of materials and ideas to foster the social-emotional, intellectual, and physical development of children. At the same time, it nurtures the natural curiosity and sense of self that can serve as the foundation for a lifetime of learning.

The lesson format is designed to present information in a way that makes it easy for children to learn. Intelligence is, in large part, our ability to see patterns and build relationships out of those patterns, which is why *DLM* is focused on helping children see the patterns in what they are learning. It builds an understanding of how newly taught material resembles what children already know. Then it takes the differences in the new material and helps the children convert them into new understanding.

Each of the eight Teacher Edition Unit's in *DLM* are centered on an Essential Question relating to the unit's theme. Each week has its own more specific focus question. By focusing on essential questions, children are better able to connect their existing knowledge of the world with the new concepts and ideas they are learning at school. Routines at the beginning and end of each day help children focus on the learning process, reflect on new concepts, and make important connections. The lessons are designed to allow children to apply what they have learned.

Social and Emotional Development

Social-emotional development is addressed everyday through positive reinforcement, interactive activities, and engaging songs.

Language and Communication

All lessons are focused on language acquisition, which includes oral language development and vocabulary activities.

Emergent Literacy: Reading

Children develop literacy skills for reading through exposure to multiple read-aloud selections each day and through daily phonological awareness and letter recognition activities.

Emergent LIteracy: Writing

Children develop writing skills through daily writing activities and during Center Time.

Mathematics

The math strand is based on **Building Blocks,** the result of NSF-funded research, and is designed to develop children's early mathematical knowledge through various individual and group activities.

Science

Children explore scientific concepts and methods during weekly science-focused, large-group activities, and Center Time activities.

Social Studies

Children explore Social Studies concepts during weekly social studies-focused, large-group activities, and Center Time activities.

Fine Arts

Children are exposed to art, dance, and music through a variety of weekly activities and the Creativity Center.

Physical Development

DLM is designed to allow children active time for outdoor play during the day, in addition to daily and weekly movement activities.

Technology Applications

Technology is integrated throughout each week with the use of online math activities, computer time, and other digital resources.

English Language Learners

Today's classrooms are very diverse. *The DLM Early Childhood Express* addresses this diversity by providing lessons in both English and Spanish. The program also offers strategies to assist English Language Learners at multiple levels of proficiency.

Flexible Scheduling

With *The DLM Early Childhood Express*, it's easy to fit lessons into your day.

Typical Full-Day Schedule

10 min	Opening Routines
15 min	Language Time
60-90 min	Center Time
15 min	Snack Time
15 min	Literacy Time
20 min	Active Play (outdoors if possible)
30 min	Lunch
15 min	Math Time
	Rest
15 min	Circle Time: Social and Emotional Development
20 min	Circle Time: Content Connection
30 min	Center Time
25 min	Active Play (outdoors if possible)
15 min	Let's Say Good-Bye

Typical Half-Day Schedule

10 min	Opening Routines
15 min	Language Time
60 min	Center Time
15 min	Snack Time
15 min	Circle Time (Literacy, Math, or Social and Emotional Development)
30 min	Active Play (outdoors if possible)
20 min	Circle Time (Content Connection, Literacy, Math, or Social and Emotional Development)
15 min	Let's Say Good-Bye

Welcome to *The DLM Early Childhood Express.*

Add your own ideas. Mix and match activities. Our program is designed to offer you a variety of activities on which to build a full year of exciting and creative lessons.

Happy learning to you and the children in your care!

Themes and Literature

With *The DLM Early Childhood Express,* children develop concrete skills through experiences with music, art, storytelling, hands-on activities and teacher-directed lessons that, in addition to skills development, emphasize practice and reflection. Every four weeks, children are introduced to a new theme organized around an essential question.

Literature selections and cross-curricular content are linked to the theme to help children reinforce lesson concepts. Children hear and discuss an additional read-aloud selection from the *Teacher Treasure Book* at the beginning and end of each day. At the end of each unit, children take home a *My Theme Library Book* reader of their own.

Unit 1: All About Pre-K
Why is school important?

	Focus Question	Literature
Week 1	What happens at school?	Welcome to School Bienvenidos a la escuela
Week 2	What happens in our classroom?	Yellowbelly and Plum Go to School Barrigota y Pipón van a la escuela
Week 3	What makes a good friend?	Max and Mo's First Day at School Max y Mo van a la escuela
Week 4	How can we play and learn together?	Amelia's Show and Tell Fiesta/Amelia y la fiesta de "muestra y cuenta"
Unit Wrap-Up	My Library Book	How Can I Learn at School? ¿Cómo puedo aprender en la escuela?

Unit 2: All About Me
What makes me special?

	Focus Question	Literature
Week 1	Who am I?	All About Me Todo sobre mí
Week 2	What are my feelings?	Lots of Feelings Montones de sentimientos
Week 3	What do the parts of my body do?	Eyes, Nose, Fingers, and Toes Ojos, nariz, dedos y pies
Week 4	What is a family?	Jonathan and His Mommy Juan y su mamá
Unit Wrap-Up	My Library Book	What Makes Us Special? ¿Qué nos hace especiales?

Unit 3: My Community
What is a community?

	Focus Question	Literature
Week 1	What are the parts of a community?	In the Community En la comunidad
Week 2	Hoe does a community help me?	Rush Hour, Hora pico
Week 3	Who helps the community?	Quinito's Neighborhood
Week 4	How can I help my community?	Flower Garden Un jardín de flores
Unit Wrap-Up	My Library Book	In My Community Mi comunidad

Unit 4: Let's Investigate
How can I learn more about things?

	Focus Question	Literature
Week 1	How can I learn by observing?	Let's Investigate Soy detective
Week 2	How can I use tools to investiagte?	I Like Making Tamales Me gusta hacer tamales
Week 3	How can I compare things?	Nature Spy Espía de la naturaleza
Week 4	How do objects move?	What Do Wheels Do All Day? ¿Qué hacen las ruedas todo el día?
Unit Wrap-Up	My Library Book	How Can We Investigate? ¿Cómo podemos investigar?

Unit 5: Amazing Animals
What is amazing about animals?

	Focus Question	Literature
Week 1	What are animals like?	Amazing Animals Animales asombrosos
Week 2	Where do animals live and what do they eat?	Castles, Caves, and Honeycombs Castillos, cuevas y panales
Week 3	How are animals the same and different?	Who Is the Beast? Quien es la bestia?
Week 4	How do animals move?	Move! ¡A moverse!
Unit Wrap-Up	My Library Book	Hello, Animals! ¡Hola, animales!

Unit 6: Growing and Changing
How do living things grow and change?

	Focus Question	Literature
Week 1	How do animals grow and change?	Growing and Changing Creciendo y cambiando
Week 2	How do plants grow and change?	I Am a Peach Yo soy el durazno
Week 3	How do people grow and change?	I'm Growing! Estoy creciendo!
Week 4	How do living things grow and change?	My Garden Mi jardin
Unit Wrap-Up	My Library Book	Growing Up Creciendo

Unit 7: The Earth and Sky
What can I learn about the earth and the sky?

	Focus Question	Literature
Week 1	What can I learn about the earth and the sky?	The Earth and Sky La Tierra y el cielo
Week 2	What weather can I observe each day?	Who Likes Rain? ¿A quién le gusta la lluvia?
Week 3	What can I learn about day and night?	Matthew and the Color of the Sky Matias y el color del cielo
Week 4	Why is caring for the earth and sky important?	Ada, Once Again! ¡Otra vez Ada!
Unit Wrap-Up	My Library Book	Good Morning, Earth! ¡Buenos días, Tierra!

Unit 8: Healthy Food/Healthy Body
Why is healthy food and exercise good for me?

	Focus Question	Literature
Week 1	What are good healthy habits?	Staying Healthy Mantente sano
Week 2	What kinds of foods are healthy?	Growing Vegetable Soup A sembrar sopa de verduras
Week 3	Why is exercise important?	Rise and Exercise! A ejercitarse, ¡uno, dos, tres!
Week 4	How can I stay healthy?	Jamal's Busy Day El intenso día de Jamal
Unit Wrap-Up	My Library Book	Healthy Kids Niños sanos

Tools for Teaching

The *DLM Early Childhood Express* is packed full of the components you'll need to teach each theme and enrich your classroom. The *Teacher Treasure Package* is the heart of the program, because it contains all the necessary materials. Plus, the *Teacher's Treasure Book* contains all the fun components that you'll love to teach. The *Literature Package* contains all the stories and books you need to support children's developing literacy. You'll find letter tiles, counters, and puppets in the *Manipulative Package* to connect hands-on learning skills with meaningful play.

ABC Picture Cards
(English and Spanish)

Alphabet Wall Cards
(English and Spanish)

Teacher Treasure Package

This package contains all the essential tools for the teacher such as the *Teacher's Treasure Book, Teacher's Editions*, technology, and other resources no teacher would want to be without!

Sequence Cards
(English and Spanish)

Oral Language Development Cards
(English and Spanish)

Photo Library
CD-ROM

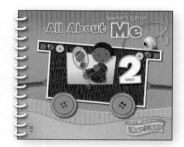

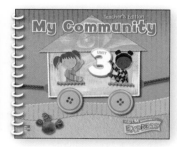

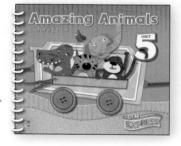

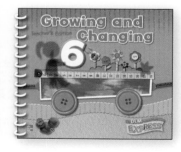

▲ Each lesson's instruction uses a variety of cards to help children learn. **Alphabet Wall Cards** and **ABC Picture Cards** help build letter recognition and phonemic awareness. **Oral Language Development Cards** teach new vocabulary, and are especially helpful when working with English Language Learners. **Sequencing Cards** help children learn how to order events and the vocabulary associated with time and sequence.

▲ There is one bilingual **Teacher's Edition** for each four-week theme. It provides the focus questions for each lesson as well as plans for centers and suggestions for classroom management.

▶ The bilingual **Teacher's Treasure Book** features 500+ pages of the things you love most about teaching Early Childhood, such as songs, traditional read alouds, folk tales, finger plays, and flannelboard stories with patterns.

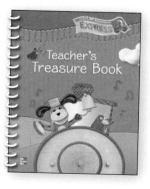

▶ An **ABC Take-Home Book** with blackline masters is provided for each letter of the English and Spanish alphabets.

ABC Take-Home Book
(English and Spanish)

▶ Flip charts and their Audio CDs support the activities in each lesson. Children practice literacy and music skills using the **Rhymes and Chants Flip Chart,** which supports oral language development and phonological awareness in both English and Spanish. An Audio CD is included and provides a recording of every rhyme or chant. The **Making Good Choices Flip Chart** provides illustrations to allow students to explore social and emotional development concepts while facilitating classroom activities and discussion. 15 lively songs recorded in both English and Spanish address key social emotional development themes such as: joining in, helping others, being fair, teasing, bullying, and much more. The **Math and Science Flip Chart** is a demonstration tool that addresses weekly math and science concepts through photos and illustrations.

▶ Other key resources include a **Research & Professional Development Guide,** and a bilingual **Home Connections Resource Guide** which provides weekly letters home and take-home story books.

Building Blocks

Building Blocks, the result of NSF-funded research, develops young children's mathematical thinking using their bodies, manipulatives, paper, and computers.

Building Blocks online management system guides children through research-based learning trajectories. These activities-through-trajectories connect children's informal knowledge to more formal school mathematics. The result is a mathematical curriculum that is not only motivating for children but also comprehensive.

▶ **DLMExpressOnline.com** includes the following:

● e-Books of student and teacher materials

● Audio recordings of the **My Library** and **Literature Books** (Big/Little) in English and Spanish

● Teacher planning tools and assessment support

Tools for Teaching

Literature Package

This package contains the literature referenced in the program. Packages are available in several variations so you can choose the package that best meets the needs of your classroom. The literature used in the program includes expository selections, traditional stories, and emergent readers for students. All literature is available in English or Spanish.

▶ **Concept Big Books** are nonfiction selections that introduce the essential questions for each unit and help children make connections between their background knowledge and unit themes. (English and Spanish)

▶ **My Library Books** are take-home readers for children to continue their exploration of unit themes. (English and Spanish)

▶ The **ABC Big Book** helps children develop phonemic awareness and letter recognition. (English and Spanish)

▶ The *Big Books* and *Little Books* reinforce each week's theme and the unit theme. Selections include stories originally written in Spanish, as well as those written in English.

▶ The stories in the *Big Books and Little Books* are recorded on the *Listening Library Audio CDs*. They are available in English and Spanish.

Manipulative Package

This package contains fun tools for children to play and learn with in the classroom.

Two Puppets

Alphabet Letter Tiles (in English and Spanish)

Transportation and Farm Animal Counters

Two-Color Counters

Step-by-Step Number Line

Balance Scale

Pattern Blocks

Shape Sets

Connecting Cubes

Jumbo Hand Lenses

Magnetic Wands

A Typical Weekly Lesson Plan

Each week of *The DLM Early Childhood Express* is organized the same way to provide children with the structure and routines they crave. Each week begins with a weekly opener that introduces the focus question for the week and includes a review of the week's Learning Goals, the Materials and Resources needed for the week, a Daily Planner, and a plan for the Learning Centers children will use throughout the week.

Each day's lesson includes large-group Circle Time and small-group Center Time. Each day includes Literacy, Math, and Social and Emotional Development activities during Circle Time. On Day 1, children explore Science. On Days 2 and 4, they work on more in-depth math lessons. On Day 3, Social Studies is the focus. Fine Art or Music/Movement activities take place during Circle Time on Day 5.

You will find the **Program Materials** and **Other Materials** needed for each day on the Materials and Resources page.

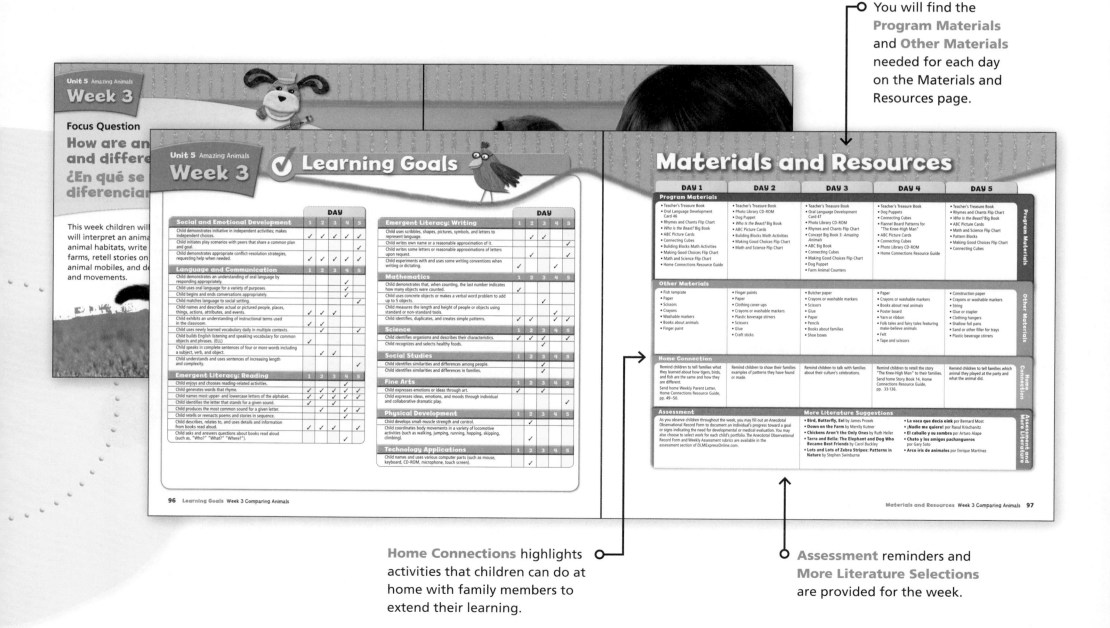

Home Connections highlights activities that children can do at home with family members to extend their learning.

Assessment reminders and **More Literature Selections** are provided for the week.

The **Daily Planner** provides a Week-at-a-Glance view of the daily structure and lesson topics for each week.

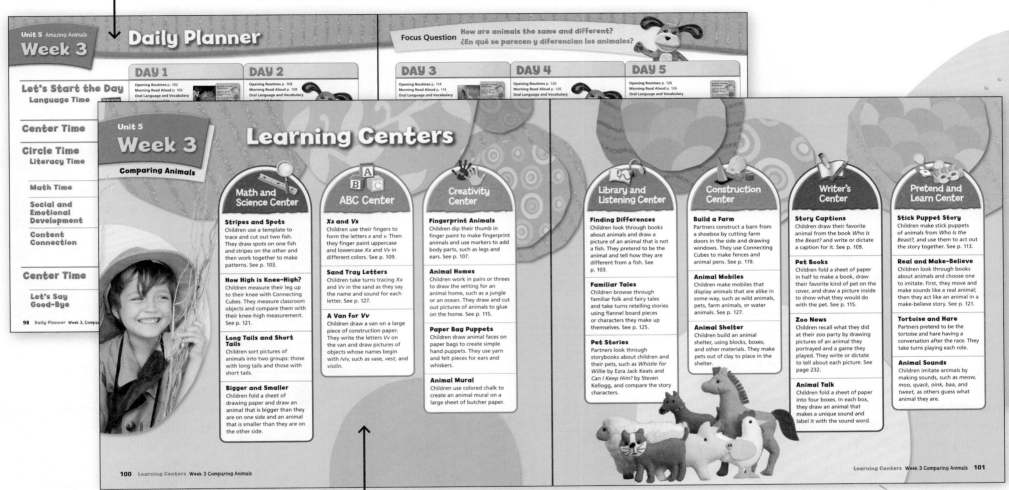

Learning Centers should be used throughout the week during Center Time. This page provides an overview of center activities to set up for children. Additional information about some center activities is provided in the daily lessons. The Learning Centers are intended to remain open for the entire week. These centers provide the opportunity for children to explore a wide range of curricular areas.

Lesson Overview

Our **Teacher's Editions** are organized by theme, week, and day. Each day's lesson is covered in six page spreads. The lessons integrate learning from the skill domain areas of: Social Emotional Development, Language and Communication, Emergent Literacy Reading and Writing, Mathematics, Science, Social Studies, Fine Arts, Physical Development, and Technology.

Each day begins with **Opening Routines** and a **Read Aloud** selection. This structured time helps children settle into their day.

The **Learning Goals** met by the lesson are listed on each page.

Observational Checks at point of use help to focus learning. These informal assessment questions help to ensure children are meeting lesson objectives.

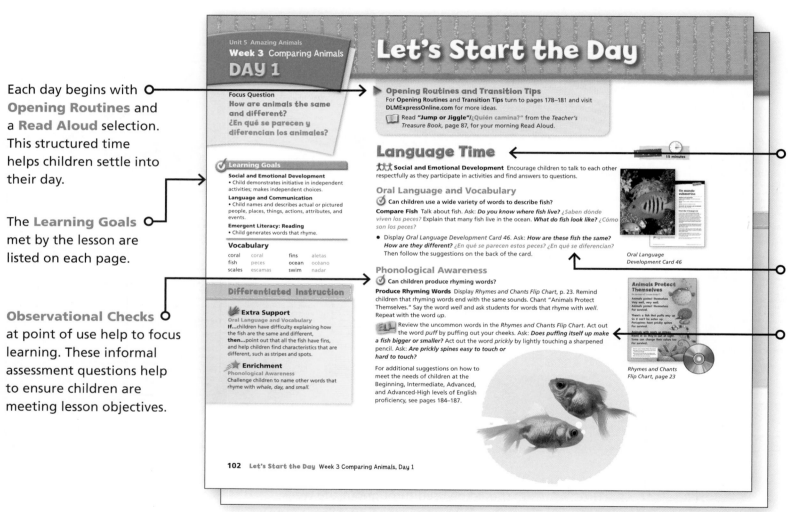

Language Time is the first large-group activity of the day. It includes Oral Language and Vocabulary Development as well as Phonological Awareness activities.

Instructional questions are provided in both **English and Spanish**.

Tips for working with **English Language Learners** are shown at point of use throughout the lessons. Teaching strategies are provided to help children of of all language backgrounds and abilities meet the lesson objectives.

Center Time provides additional information for teacher-guided small-group activities and suggestions for independent activities children will complete during weekly Center Rotation.

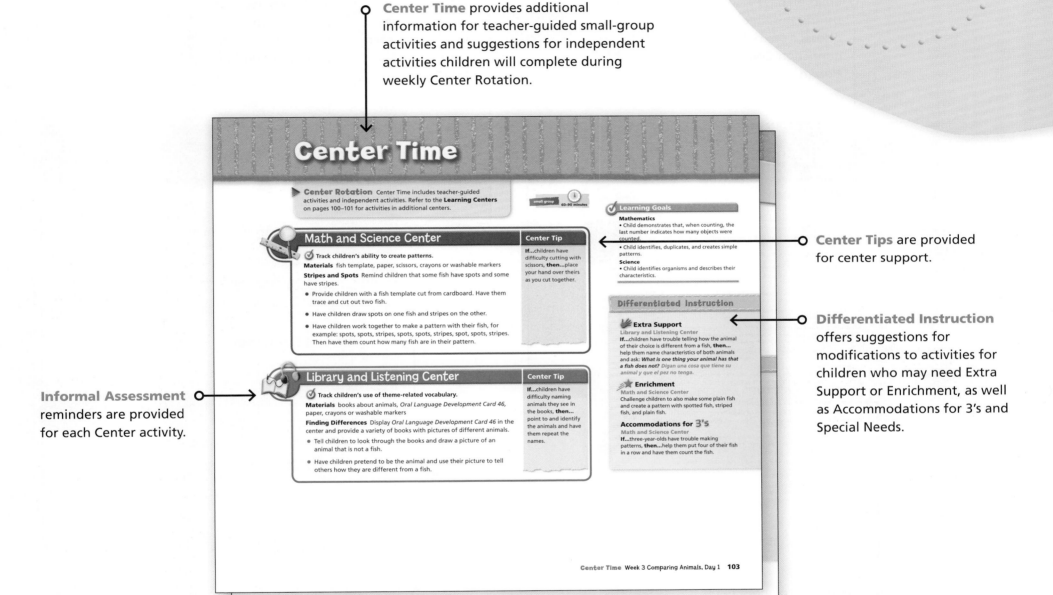

Center Time

▶ **Center Rotation** Center Time includes teacher-guided activities and independent activities. Refer to the **Learning Centers** on pages 100–101 for activities in additional centers.

small group 60–90 minutes

Math and Science Center

☑ Track children's ability to create patterns.

Materials fish template, paper, scissors, crayons or washable markers

Stripes and Spots Remind children that some fish have spots and some have stripes.

● Provide children with a fish template cut from cardboard. Have them trace and cut out two fish.

● Have children draw spots on one fish and stripes on the other.

● Have children work together to make a pattern with their fish, for example: spots, spots, stripes, spots, spots, stripes, spot, spots, stripes. Then have them count how many fish are in their pattern.

Center Tip

If...children have difficulty cutting with scissors, **then...**place your hand over theirs as you cut together.

Library and Listening Center

☑ Track children's use of theme-related vocabulary.

Materials books about animals, *Oral Language Development Card 46,* paper, crayons or washable markers

Finding Differences Display *Oral Language Development Card 46* in the center and provide a variety of books with pictures of different animals.

● Tell children to look through the books and draw a picture of an animal that is not a fish.

● Have children pretend to be the animal and use their picture to tell others how they are different from a fish.

Center Tip

If...children have difficulty naming animals they see in the books, **then...**point to and identify the animals and have them repeat the names.

🗹 Learning Goals

Mathematics
● Child demonstrates that, when counting, the last number indicates how many objects were counted.
● Child identifies, duplicates, and creates simple patterns.

Science
● Child identifies organisms and describes their characteristics.

Differentiated Instruction

✋ Extra Support
Library and Listening Center
If...children have trouble telling how the animal of their choice is different from a fish, **then...** help them name characteristics of both animals and ask: *What is one thing your animal has that a fish does not? Digan una cosa que tiene su animal y que el pez no tenga.*

★ Enrichment
Math and Science Center
Challenge children to also make some plain fish and create a pattern with spotted fish, striped fish, and plain fish.

Accommodations for 3's
Math and Science Center
If...three-year-olds have trouble making patterns, **then...**help them put four of their fish in a row and have them count the fish.

Center Tips are provided for center support.

Differentiated Instruction offers suggestions for modifications to activities for children who may need Extra Support or Enrichment, as well as Accommodations for 3's and Special Needs.

Informal Assessment reminders are provided for each Center activity.

Lesson Overview

Children have **Literacy Time** every day. During this time, children listen to and discuss a second Read Aloud from a nonfiction *Concept Big Book* or a *Big Book/Little Book* literature selection

Building Blocks online activities are provided each week during Math Time.

Children work in large groups on 15 minute math activities during daily **Math Time**.

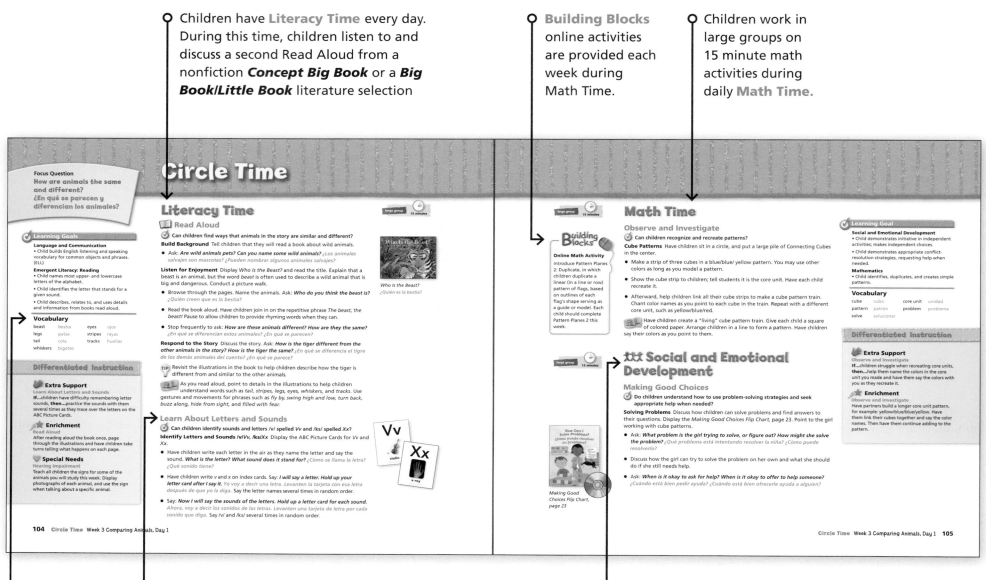

Focus Question
How are animals the same and different?
¿En qué se parecen y diferencian los animales?

Circle Time

Literacy Time

large group 15 minutes

📖 Read Aloud

✓ Can children find ways that animals in the story are similar and different?

Build Background Tell children that they will read a book about wild animals.

• Ask: *Are wild animals pets? Can you name some wild animals?* ¿Los animales salvajes son mascotas? ¿Pueden nombrar algunos animales salvajes?

Listen for Enjoyment Display *Who Is the Beast?* and read the title. Explain that a beast is an animal, but the word *beast* is often used to describe a wild animal that is big and dangerous. Conduct a picture walk.

• Browse through the pages. Name the animals. Ask: *Who do you think the beast is?* ¿Quién creen que es la bestia?

• Read the book aloud. Have children join in on the repetitive phrase *The beast, the beast!* Pause to allow children to provide rhyming words when they can.

• Stop frequently to ask: *How are these animals different? How are they the same?* ¿En qué se diferencian estos animales? ¿En qué se parecen?

Respond to the Story Discuss the story. Ask: *How is the tiger different from the other animals in the story? How is the tiger the same?* ¿En qué se diferencia el tigre de los demás animales del cuento? ¿En qué se parece?

TIP Revisit the illustrations in the book to help children describe how the tiger is different from and similar to the other animals.

As you read aloud, point to details in the illustrations to help children understand words such as *tail, stripes, legs, eyes, whiskers,* and *tracks.* Use gestures and movements for phrases such as *fly by, swing high and low, turn back, buzz along, hide from sight,* and *filled with fear.*

Learn About Letters and Sounds

✓ Can children identify sounds and letters /v/ spelled *Vv* and /ks/ spelled *Xx*?

Identify Letters and Sounds /v/Vv, /ks/Xx Display the ABC Picture Cards for *Vv* and *Xx.*

• Have children write each letter in the air as they name the letter and say the sound. *What is the letter? What sound does it stand for?* ¿Cómo se llama la letra? ¿Qué sonido tiene?

• Have children write *v* and *x* on index cards. Say: *I will say a letter. Hold up your letter card after I say it.* Yo voy a decir una letra. Levanten la tarjeta con esa letra después de que yo la diga. Say the letter names several times in random order.

• Say: *Now I will say the sounds of the letters. Hold up a letter card for each sound.* Ahora, voy a decir los sonidos de las letras. Levanten una tarjeta de letra por cada sonido que diga. Say /v/ and /ks/ several times in random order.

Who Is the Beast?
¿Quién es la bestia?

Vv violin
Xx x-ray

104 Circle Time Week 3 Comparing Animals, Day 1

Learning Goals

Language and Communication
• Child builds English listening and speaking vocabulary for common objects and phrases. (ELL)

Emergent Literacy: Reading
• Child names most upper- and lowercase letters of the alphabet.
• Child identifies the letter that stands for a given sound.
• Child describes, relates to, and uses details and information from books read aloud.

Vocabulary

beast	bestia	eyes	ojos
legs	patas	stripes	rayas
tail	cola	tracks	huellas
whiskers	bigotes		

Differentiated Instruction

★ **Extra Support**
Learn About Letters and Sounds
If...children have difficulty remembering letter sounds, then...practice the sounds with them several times as they trace over the letters on the ABC Picture Cards.

★ **Enrichment**
Read Aloud
After reading aloud the book once, page through the illustrations and have children take turns telling what happens on each page.

♥ **Special Needs**
Hearing Impairment
Teach all children the signs for some of the animals you will study this week. Display photographs of each animal, and use the sign when talking about a specific animal.

Math Time

large group 15 minutes

Observe and Investigate

✓ Can children recognize and recreate patterns?

Cube Patterns Have children sit in a circle, and put a large pile of Connecting Cubes in the center.

• Make a strip of three cubes in a blue/blue/ yellow pattern. You may use other colors as long as you model a pattern.

• Show the cube strip to children; tell students it is the core unit. Have each child recreate it.

• Afterward, help children link all their cube strips to make a cube pattern train. Chant color names as you point to each cube in the train. Repeat with a different core unit, such as yellow/blue/red.

Have children create a "living" cube pattern train. Give each child a square of colored paper. Arrange children in a line to form a pattern. Have children say their colors as you point to them.

Building Blocks

Online Math Activity
Introduce Pattern Planes 2: Duplicate, in which children duplicate a linear (in a line or row) pattern of flags, based on outlines of each flag's shape serving as a guide or model. Each child should complete Pattern Planes 2 this week.

large group 15 minutes

⚤ Social and Emotional Development

Making Good Choices

✓ Do children understand how to use problem-solving strategies and seek appropriate help when needed?

Solving Problems Discuss how children can solve problems and find answers to their questions. Display the *Making Good Choices Flip Chart*, page 23. Point to the girl working with cube patterns.

• Ask: *What problem is the girl trying to solve, or figure out? How might she solve the problem?* ¿Qué problema está intentando resolver la niña? ¿Cómo puede resolverlo?

• Discuss how the girl can try to solve the problem on her own and what she should do if she still needs help.

• Ask: *When is it okay to ask for help? When is it okay to offer to help someone?* ¿Cuándo está bien pedir ayuda? ¿Cuándo está bien ofrecerle ayuda a alguien?

Making Good Choices Flip Chart, page 23

Learning Goal

Social and Emotional Development
• Child demonstrates initiative in independent activities; makes independent choices.
• Child demonstrates appropriate conflict-resolution strategies, requesting help when needed.

Mathematics
• Child identifies, duplicates, and creates simple patterns.

Vocabulary

cube	cubo	core unit	unidad
pattern	patrón	problem	problema
solve	solucionar		

Differentiated Instruction

★ **Extra Support**
Observe and Investigate
If...children struggle when recreating core units, then...help them name the colors in the core unit you made and have them say the colors with you as they recreate it.

★ **Enrichment**
Observe and Investigate
Have partners build a longer core unit pattern, for example: yellow/blue/blue/yellow. Have them link their cubes together and say the color names. Then have them continue adding to the pattern.

Circle Time Week 3 Comparing Animals, Day 1 105

Vocabulary is provided in English and Spanish to help expand children's ability to use both languages.

Children learn about **Letters and Sounds** every day. The sound is introduced with the letter. Children also practice letter formation.

Social and Emotional Development concepts are addressed every day to help children better express their emotions and needs, and establish positive relationships.

Circle Time is devoted to longer activities focusing on different cross-curricular concepts each day. Day 1 is Science Time. Days 2 and 4 are Math Time. On Day 3, children have Social Studies Time. Fine arts are covered in Art Time or Music and Movement Time on Day 5.

An end-of-the-day **Writing** activity is provided each day.

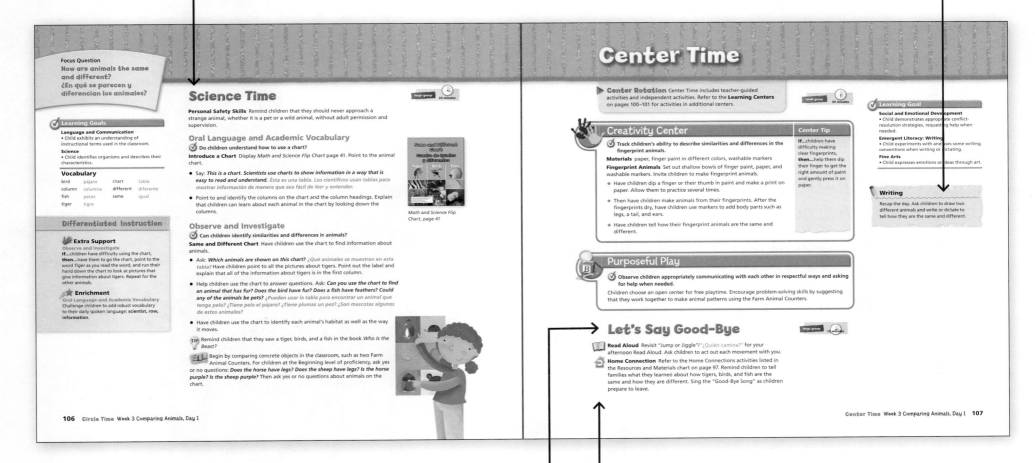

Focus Question
How are animals the same and different?
¿En qué se parecen y diferencian los animales?

Learning Goals

Language and Communication
• Child exhibits an understanding of instructional terms used in the classroom.
Science
• Child identifies organisms and describes their characteristics.

Vocabulary

bird	pájaro	chart	tabla
column	columna	different	diferente
fish	peces	same	igual
tiger	tigre		

Differentiated Instruction

Extra Support
Observe and Investigate
If...children have difficulty using the chart, then...have them to go the chart, point to the word *Tiger* as you read the word, and run their hand down the chart to look at pictures that give information about tigers. Repeat for the other animals.

Enrichment
Oral Language and Academic Vocabulary
Challenge children to add robust vocabulary to their daily spoken language: **scientist, row, information**.

Science Time

Personal Safety Skills Remind children that they should never approach a strange animal, whether it is a pet or a wild animal, without adult permission and supervision.

Oral Language and Academic Vocabulary
☑ Do children understand how to use a chart?
Introduce a Chart Display *Math and Science Flip Chart* page 41. Point to the animal chart.

• Say: *This is a chart. Scientists use charts to show information in a way that is easy to read and understand. Ésta es una tabla. Los científicos usan tablas para mostrar información de manera que sea fácil de leer y entender.*

• Point to and identify the columns on the chart and the column headings. Explain that children can learn about each animal in the chart by looking down the columns.

Observe and Investigate
☑ Can children identify similarities and differences in animals?
Same and Different Chart Have children use the chart to find information about animals.

• Ask: *Which animals are shown on this chart? ¿Qué animales se muestran en esta tabla?* Have children point to all the pictures about tigers. Point out the label and explain that all of the information about tigers is in the first column.

• Help children use the chart to answer questions. Ask: *Can you use the chart to find an animal that has fur? Does the bird have fur? Does a fish have feathers? Could any of the animals be pets? ¿Pueden usar la tabla para encontrar un animal que tenga pelo? ¿Tiene pelo el pájaro? ¿Tiene plumas un pez? ¿Son mascotas algunos de estos animales?*

• Have children use the chart to identify each animal's habitat as well as the way it moves.

TIP Remind children that they saw a tiger, birds, and a fish in the book *Who Is the Beast?*

Begin by comparing concrete objects in the classroom, such as two Farm Animal Counters. For children at the Beginning level of proficiency, ask yes or no questions: *Does the horse have legs? Does the sheep have legs? Is the horse purple? Is the sheep purple?* Then ask yes or no questions about animals on the chart.

Math and Science Flip Chart, page 41

Center Time

Center Rotation Center Time includes teacher-guided activities and independent activities. Refer to the **Learning Centers** on pages 100–101 for activities in additional centers.

Creativity Center

☑ Track children's ability to describe similarities and differences in the fingerprint animals.

Materials paper, finger paint in different colors, washable markers

Fingerprint Animals Set out shallow bowls of finger paint, paper, and washable markers. Invite children to make fingerprint animals.

• Have children dip a finger or their thumb in paint and make a print on paper. Allow them to practice several times.

• Then have children make animals from their fingerprints. After the fingerprints dry, have children use markers to add body parts such as legs, a tail, and ears.

• Have children tell how their fingerprint animals are the same and different.

Center Tip
If...children have difficulty making clear fingerprints, then...help them dip their finger to get the right amount of paint and gently press it on paper.

Purposeful Play

☑ Observe children appropriately communicating with each other in respectful ways and asking for help when needed.

Children choose an open center for free playtime. Encourage problem-solving skills by suggesting that they work together to make animal patterns using the Farm Animal Counters.

Learning Goal

Social and Emotional Development
• Child demonstrates appropriate conflict-resolution strategies, requesting help when needed.
Emergent Literacy: Writing
• Child experiments with and uses some writing conventions when writing or dictating.
Fine Arts
• Child expresses emotions or ideas through art.

Writing
Recap the day. Ask children to draw two different animals and write or dictate to tell how they are the same and different.

Let's Say Good-Bye

Read Aloud Revisit "Jump or Jiggle"/"¿Quién camina?" for your afternoon Read Aloud. Ask children to act out each movement with you.

Home Connection Refer to the Home Connections activities listed in the Resources and Materials chart on page 97. Remind children to tell families what they learned about how tigers, birds, and fish are the same and how they are different. Sing the "Good-Bye Song" as children prepare to leave.

Let's Say Good-Bye includes the closing routines for each day. The Read Aloud from the beginning of the day is revisited with a focus on skills practiced during the day.

Each day provides a **Home Connection**. At the start of each week, a letter is provided to inform families of the weekly focus and offer additional literature suggestions to extend the weekly theme focus.

Focus Question

How can I learn by observing?
¿Qué puedo aprender observando las cosas?

This week children will use their senses to sort common objects. They will explore their world as they pretend to be detectives, look at objects up close, and draw pictures of a favorite food. They will also listen to stories about an adventurous worm and a little girl who goes to visit her grandmother.

Social and Emotional Development	1	2	3	4	5
Child is aware of self in terms of abilities, characteristics and preferences, and respects personal boundaries.		✓		✓	
Child identifies self by categories (such as gender, age, family member, cultural group).					✓
Child demonstrates initiative in independent activities; makes independent choices.	✓	✓	✓	✓	✓
Child initiates play scenarios with peers that share a common plan and goal.	✓		✓	✓	✓
Child demonstrates appropiate conflict-resolution strategies, requesting help when needed.				✓	

Language and Communication	1	2	3	4	5
Child follows two- and three-step oral directions.		✓	✓		
Child begins and ends conversations appropriately.		✓	✓	✓	✓
Child names and describes actual or pictured people, places, things, actions, attributes, and events.	✓				
Child uses newly learned vocabulary daily in multiple contexts.	✓	✓	✓	✓	✓

Emergent Literacy: Reading	1	2	3	4	5
Child independently engages in pre-reading behaviors and activities (such as, pretending to read, turning one page at a time).	✓				
Child blends onset and rime to form a word with pictoral support.	✓	✓	✓	✓	✓
Child names most upper- and lowercase letters of the alphabet.	✓			✓	
Child identifies the letter that stands for a given sound.	✓	✓		✓	
Child produces the most common sound for a given letter.			✓	✓	✓
Child describes, relates to, and uses details and information from books read aloud.				✓	✓
Child asks and answers questions about books read aloud (such as, "Who?" "What?" "Where?").	✓	✓	✓	✓	✓

Emergent Literacy: Writing	1	2	3	4	5
Child uses scribbles, shapes, pictures, symbols, and letters to represent language.			✓		
Child writes some letters or reasonable approximations of letters upon request.				✓	✓
Child experiments with and uses some writing conventions when writing or dictating.	✓	✓			

Mathematics	1	2	3	4	5
Child tells how many are in a group of up to 5 objects without counting.					✓
Child recognizes, names, describes, matches, compares, sorts common two-dimensional shapes (such as circle, square, rectangle, triangle, rhombus).	✓	✓	✓	✓	✓
Child understands and uses words that describe position/location in space (such as under, over, beside, between, on, in, near, far away).		✓	✓	✓	
Child sorts objects and explains how the sorting was done.		✓		✓	✓

Science	1	2	3	4	5
Child uses senses to observe, classify, investigate, and collect data.	✓				✓

Social Studies	1	2	3	4	5
Child identifies similarities and differences in families.			✓		
Child participates in voting for group decision-making.					✓
Child respects/appreciates the differing interests, skills, abilities, cultures, languages, and family structures of people.			✓		

Fine Arts	1	2	3	4	5
Child uses and experiments with a variety of art materials and tools in various art activities.					✓

Physical Development	1	2	3	4	5
Child develops small-muscle strength and control.					✓

Materials and Resources

DAY 1	DAY 2	DAY 3	DAY 4	DAY 5

Program Materials

DAY 1	DAY 2	DAY 3	DAY 4	DAY 5
• Teacher's Treasure Book • Oral Language Development Card 31 • Rhymes and Chants Flip Chart • Concept Big Book 2: *Let's Investigate* • ABC Big Book • ABC Picture Cards • Alphabet Wall Cards • Shape Sets • Building Blocks Online Math Activities • Making Good Choices Flip Chart • Math and Science Flip Chart • Home Connections Resource Guide	• Teacher's Treasure Book • Concept Big Book 2: *Let's Investigate* • Hand Lens, Shape Sets, Pattern Blocks, Balance Scale • Dog Puppets • Oral Language Development Card 39 • Rhymes and Chants Flip Chart • ABC Big Book • ABC Picture Cards • Alphabet Wall Cards • Building Blocks Online Math Activities • Making Good Choices Flip Chart	• Teacher's Treasure Book • Oral Language Development Card 32 • Rhymes and Chants Flip Chart • ABC Big Book • ABC Picture Cards • Alphabet Wall Cards • Dog Puppets • Building Blocks Online Math Activities • Shape Sets • Photo Library CD-ROM • Making Good Choices Flip Chart	• Teacher's Treasure Book • Flannel Board and Characters for "Little Red Riding Hood" • Oral Language Development Card 40 • Dog Puppets • ABC Big Book, ABC Picture Cards • Alphabet Wall Cards • Shape Sets • Building Blocks Online Math Activities • Math and Science Flip Chart • Photo Library CD-ROM • Concept Big Book 2: *Let's Investigate*	• Teacher's Treasure Book • Rhymes and Chants Flip Chart • Concept Big Book 2: *Let's Investigate* • Connecting Cubes • ABC Big Book • ABC Picture Cards • Alphabet Wall Cards • Building Blocks Online Math Activities • Making Good Choices Flip Chart • Jumbo Hand Lens

Other Materials

DAY 1	DAY 2	DAY 3	DAY 4	DAY 5
• books about caterpillars, insects • onset/rime cards with pictures of one-syllable objects • two different shoes • objects to compare: heavy/light, rough/smooth, big/small, etc. • objects of different materials (wood, metal, plastic, stone, foam) and images of the same objects • water table, glue, chart paper	• objects of different textures • items for measuring weight • masking or colored tape • paper, pencils, markers, crayons	• sponge or paper towel • paper plates • masking or colored tape • food photos • pencils, markers, crayons, glue • paper, chart paper	• small paper bag • various items w/ scent, texture, sound (bar of soap, rock, cotton ball, bell, block, etc) • boxes, pillows, blocks for building • images of one-syllable items children can build (car, bus, dog, road, etc.) • tracings of shapes • large sheet of paper	• half sheets of paper folded in quarters • dress-up clothes and props • full paint bottle • numeral cards • books of paintings and photographs of shapes; cutouts of similar shapes • objects of different shapes • crayons, yarn, scissors

Home Connection

DAY 1	DAY 2	DAY 3	DAY 4	DAY 5
Have children describe to their families the materials they observed in class. Send home the following materials: Weekly Parent Letter, Home Connections Resource Guide, pp. 37–38; ABC Take-Home Book for *Bb*, p. 8 (English), *Bb*, p. 36 (Spanish)	Encourage children to tell their families what different shapes look like. Send home the following materials: ABC Take-Home Book for *Ii*, p. 15 (English) *Ii*, p. 44 (Spanish)	Invite children to ask their families about their special language, culture, and traditions. Send home the following: ABC Take-Home Book for *Nn*, p. 20 (English), *Nn*, p. 50 (Spanish)	Send home the following materials: ABC Take-Home Book for *Kk*, p 17 (English), *Kk*, p. 46 (Spanish)	Encourage children to point out different shapes in paintings and photographs at home.

Assessment

As you observe children throughout the week, you may fill out an Anecdotal Observational Record Form to document an individual's progress toward a goal or signs indicating the need for developmental or medical evaluation. You may also choose to select work for each child's portfolio. The Anecdotal Observational Record Form and Weekly Assessment rubrics are available in the assessment section of DLMExpressOnline.com.

More Literature Suggestions

• **Toot and Puddle: Top Of The World** (Choni y Chano en la cima del mundo) by Holly Hobbie
• **Snowmen At Night** by Caralyn Buehner
• **Lots and Lots of Zebra Stripes: Patterns in Nature** by Stephen Swinburne
• **Watch Out, Little Wombat!** by Charles Fuge
• **Shapes, Shapes, Shapes** by Tana Hoban
• **Patito, ¿dónde estás?** por Margarita Robleda
• **Oye al desierto** por Pat Morah

Daily Planner

	DAY 1	**DAY 2**
Let's Start the Day **Language Time** `large group`	Opening Routines p. 26 **Morning Read Aloud** p. 26 **Oral Language and Vocabulary** p. 26 Caterpillars **Phonological Awareness** p. 26 Blend Onset and Rime	Opening Routines p. 32 **Morning Read Aloud** p. 32 **Oral Language and Vocabulary** p. 32 Being a Detective **Phonological Awareness** p. 32 Blend Onset and Rime
Center Time `small group`	**Focus On:** **Library and Listening Center** p. 27 **ABC Center** p. 27	**Focus On:** **Creativity Center** p. 33 **Library and Listening Center** p. 33
Circle Time **Literacy Time** `large group`	**Read Aloud** *Let's Investigate/Soy detective* p. 28 **Learn About Letters and Sounds: Learn About** *Bb* p. 28	**Read Aloud** *Let's Investigate/Soy detective* p. 34 **Learn About Letters and Sounds: Learn about** *Ii* p. 34
Math Time `large group`	**Observe and Investigate** I Spy p. 29	**Observe and Investigate** Shhh...Watch Carefully p. 35
Social and Emotional Development `large group`	**Solving a Problem** p. 29	**Working Together** p. 35
Content Connection `large group`	**Science:** **Oral Language and Academic Vocabulary** p. 30 **Observe and Investigate** p. 30	**Math:** **Step on that Shape!** p. 36
Center Time `small group`	**Focus On:** **Math and Science Center** p. 31 **Purposeful Play** p. 31	**Focus On:** **Math and Science Center** p. 37 **Purposeful Play** p. 37
Let's Say Good-Bye `large group`	**Read Aloud** p. 31 **Writing** p. 31 **Home Connection** p. 31	**Read Aloud** p. 37 **Shared Writing** p. 37 **Home Connection** p. 37

Focus Question How can I learn by observing?
¿Qué puedo aprender observando las cosas?

DAY 3

Opening Routines p. 38
Morning Read Aloud p. 38
Oral Language and Vocabulary
p. 38 Good Tastes and Smells
Phonological Awareness
p. 38 Blend Onset and Rime

Focus On:
Writer's Center p. 39
ABC Center p. 39

Read Aloud
"Wally Worm's World"/
"El mundo del gusano Wally"
p. 40
Learn About Letters and Sounds: Learn About *Nn* p. 40

Observe and Investigate
Step on that Shape! p. 41

Asking for Help p. 41

Social Studies:
Oral Language and Academic Vocabulary p. 42
Understand and Participate p. 42

Focus On:
Creativity Center p. 43
Purposeful Play p. 43

Read Aloud p. 43
Shared Writing p. 43
Home Connection p. 43

DAY 4

Opening Routines p. 44
Morning Read Aloud p. 44
Oral Language and Vocabulary
p. 44 The Senses
Phonological Awareness
p. 44 Blend Onset and Rime

Focus On:
Pretend and Learn Center p. 45
Construction Center p. 45

Read Aloud "Little Red Riding Hood"/
"Caperucita Roja" p. 46
Learn About Letters and Sounds:
Learn About *Kk* p. 46

Observe and Investigate
Shhh...Watch Carefully p. 47

Act It Out p. 47

Math:
I Spy p. 48

Focus On:
Math and Science Center p. 49
Purposeful Play p. 49

Read Aloud p. 49
Writing p. 49
Home Connection p. 49

DAY 5

Opening Routines p. 50
Morning Read Aloud p. 50
Oral Language and Vocabulary
p. 50 Snowflakes
Phonological Awareness
p. 50 Blend Onset and Rime

Focus On:
Construction Center p. 51
Pretend and Learn Center p. 51

Read Aloud
Let's Investigate/Soy detective p. 52
Learn About Letters and Sounds: Learn About *Bb, Ii, Nn, Kk*
p. 52

Observe and Investigate
Compare Game p. 53

Talking with Peers p. 53

Art:
Oral Language and Academic Vocabulary p. 54
Observe and Investigate p. 54

Focus On:
Library and Listening Center p. 55
Purposeful Play p. 55

Read Aloud p. 55
Shared Writing p. 55
Home Connection p. 55

Learning Centers

Math and Science Center

What Floats?
Children experiment to see what floats, p. 31

Shape Patterns
Children make shapes by arranging pattern blocks, p. 37

Match the Shape
Children match shapes to their outlines, p. 49

Examine Sand
Children use a hand lens to examine a scoop of sand and then work with a partner to ask and answer questions about it.

ABC Center

Color Matching
Children make words by matching colors, p. 27

Beginning Sounds
Children think of words that begin with the same sound, p. 39

Letter Designs
Children choose a letter B, I, N, or K and create a design by drawing the letter using various positions, weights, and treatments.

Favorite Colors
Children choose their favorite color. Then they identify the first letter in the name of that color and trace it in that color on a piece of paper.

Letter Names
Hang several sets of letter cards on a clothesline. Children take letters from the line and use them to spell out their names.

Creativity Center

Smooth or Rough?
Children explore objects that are smooth or rough, p. 33

Our Families' Foods
Children draw a favorite food, p. 43

Examine Children
Children make handprints by dipping their palms in poster paint and pressing them on paper. Line up the prints for children to examine and compare.

Let's Celebrate
Provide children with paper outlines of people. Children create clothes and accessories they would wear to a celebration or festival their family attends. Allow children to share the figures.

Shape People
Distribute geometric shapes cut from construction paper. Pairs make a "shape person" out of shape pieces. Then they give their person a silly name. (Stella Squarehead)

Library and Listening Center

Browsing Insect Books
Children look for pictures of insects, p. 27

Use Your Senses
Children notice how they use their senses, p. 33

Look for Shapes
Children look through books to find a favorite shape and match that shape to objects in the classroom. p. 55

Stop and Wonder
Children browse books about exploring nature and objects in nature. Encourage them to pause and ask a question whenever they wonder about a picture.

Languages
Children listen to classmates or adults speak in a language other than English.

Listen to Big Book
Children listen in pairs to *Let's Investigate* as they ask and answer each other's questions about the book.

Construction Center

Building Onset and Rime
Children build words out of blocks, p. 45

My Snowflake
Children fold paper and cut out snowflakes, p. 51

Build Grandma's House
Children build Red Riding Hood's grandma's house using various building materials.

Shape Keepers
Children work in small groups, and each child chooses one shape and becomes the keeper of those shapes. They work together to build a house out of many shapes and solve problems along the way.

Build It!
Have children choose a building from a folktale or fairy tale and build a clay model or block structure to represent the building. Provide picture books as inspiration if necessary.

Writer's Center

Foods We Like
Children use sensory language to describe favorite foods, p. 39

Add-On Story
Have one child begin a story as you write it on the board. Have other children add to the story. Read the completed story aloud, pointing to each word as you do so.

I'm Curious
Children think of something they want to learn more about and draw a picture of it. Then have them write to complete the following sentence frame: I want to learn all about _____.

Fingers or Nose
Put objects in paper bags (lemon slices, pom poms, soap, crayons, etc.). Children smell or feel each item to identify it and then put a sticker on a chart to show the sense they used— smell or touch.

Pretend and Learn Center

What Is It?
Children use their senses to identify hidden objects, p. 45

Act Out Onset and Rime
Children act out words for others to guess, p. 51

I'm a Square
Children work together to determine how many children are needed to make each shape. They lie on the floor to make the shape and make up a story about the shape. Each person adds a sentence to the story.

Festivities!
Children dress up and use props to partake in a festival or celebration. They work together to determine which celebration they will attend.

Nature Center Guide!
Children act out being a confident nature guide and a curious visitor at a nature center or park. Encourage them to ask and answer questions about wildlife, plants, and other natural features.

Focus Question

How can I learn by observing?

¿Qué puedo aprender observando las cosas?

Learning Goals

Social and Emotional Development
• Child demonstrates initiative in independent activities; makes independent choices.

Language and Communication
• Child uses newly learned vocabulary daily in multiple contexts.

Emergent Literacy: Reading
• Child blends onset and rime to form a word with pictoral support.

Vocabulary

caterpillar	oruga	finger	dedo
insect	insecto	living	vivo

Differentiated Instruction

 Extra Support
Oral Language and Vocabulary
If...children have not seen a caterpillar, **then**... provide additional visuals from your classroom library so children become more familiar with the insect.

 Enrichment
Phonological Awareness
Challenge pairs of children to blend more one-syllable words: *bug, we, tug, top, be, mop.*

Accommodations for 3's
Phonological Awareness
If...children have difficulty blending onset and rime, **then**...have them stand near a partner. One child says the onset /g/, and the other says the rime /irl/. As they blend the two sounds, have them move next to each other.

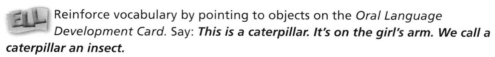

Let's Start the Day

▶ **Opening Routines and Transition Tips**
For **Opening Routines** and **Transition Tips** turn to pages 178–181 and visit DLMExpressOnline.com for more ideas.

📖 Read **"The Crow and the Fox"/**"El cuervo y el zorro" from the *Teacher's Treasure Book,* page 268, for your morning Read Aloud.

Language Time

 large group 15 minutes

🧍🧍🧍 **Social and Emotional Development** Support initiative and creativity by occasional prompting: *Do you have another idea? How else could we do it? ¿Tienen alguna otra idea? ¿De qué otra manera podríamos hacerlo?*

Oral Language and Vocabulary

✓ **Can children use newly learned vocabulary to describe an insect?**

Caterpillars Talk about caterpillars. Ask: *Have you ever seen a caterpillar? ¿Alguna vez han visto una oruga?* Explain that caterpillars are small living things that live outside. *What does a caterpillar look like? Can a caterpillar crawl on your arm? ¿Qué aspecto tiene una oruga? ¿Una oruga puede arrastrarse por tu brazo?*

● Display *Oral Language Development Card 31.* Point to the caterpillar on the girl's arm. Then follow the suggestions on the back of the card.

ELL Reinforce vocabulary by pointing to objects on the *Oral Language Development Card.* Say: *This is a caterpillar. It's on the girl's arm. We call a caterpillar an insect.*

Oral Language Development Card 31

Phonological Awareness

✓ **Can children blend onset and rime with pictorial support to make the word *girl*?**

Blend Onset and Rime Display *Rhymes and Chants Flip Chart, page 17,* "I'm a Detective." Read the rhyme aloud.

● Point to the picture of the girl. Say: *I see a girl in this picture. Listen to the sounds in this word: /g/ -irl. When we blend the sounds together, we can make the word girl. Veo una niña en esta ilustración. Escuchen los sonidos en esta palabra: /g/ -irl. Cuando mezclamos los sonidos, podemos formar la palabra girl.*

● Say the complete word. Then point to yourself, and tell children you will start the word. Say: */g/.* Point to the children so they can finish the word by saying *-irl.* Have children blend the sounds with you.

● Divide the group in two. One group says /g/, and the other says *-irl.* Then have children blend the sounds.

I'm a Detective

I'm a detective.
What do I see?
I see a snowflake
In front of me.

So soft and white,
It floats like a feather
And falls to the ground
In cold winter weather.

Detectives write down
What is seen and is felt.
But I must look quickly,
Because snowflakes melt!

Rhymes and Chants Flip Chart, p. 17

Center Time

▶ **Center Rotation** Center time includes teacher-guided activities and independent activities. Refer to the **Learning Centers** on pages 24–25 for independent activity ideas.

small group · 60–90 minutes

Library and Listening Center

✓ **Can children use the new vocabulary from instruction?**

✓ **Can children use books for browsing?**

Materials Books about caterpillars or other insects

Browsing Insect Books Have children browse several books about insects. Encourage them to describe the insects they see. Ask: *How many legs does the insect have? What color is it?* ¿Cuántas patas tiene ese insecto? ¿De qué color es?

● Remind children that insects have six legs and three body parts.

● Have each child choose an insect and tell a friend about it. Encourage use of new vocabulary in their descriptions.

Center Tip

If...children cannot describe the insects accurately, **then...**help them count the legs or compare the sizes of the insects.

ABC Center

✓ **Can children form one-syllable words?**

Materials onset/rime index cards, pictures representing one-syllable words, colored markers

Color Matching Prepare color-matching cards. For example, for *bee*, use two cards of matching color: On the onset card glue a picture of the head of a bee; on the the rime card, a picture of the body of a bee. Prepare different color cards for each word.

● Explain to children they will be making words by looking at pictures and matching colors. Tell them the card with the head is the first part of the word.

● Model holding up the onset *bee* card. Say **/b/** as you hold it up. Then hold up the rime card, and say: **-ee**. Put the cards together, and say: **bee**

● Have a child repeat, using the same cards.

● Have children continue with other color-matching cards/pictures.

Center Tip

If...children have difficulty saying the letter sounds, **then...** say a word that begins with the same sound, and stress the sound, /s/, /s/, /s/, *snow*.

Learning Goals

Social and Emotional Development
• Child demonstrates initiative in independent activities; makes independent choices.

Language and Communication
• Child uses newly learned vocabulary daily in multiple contexts.

Emergent Literacy: Reading
• Child independently engages in pre-reading behaviors and activities (such as, pretending to read, turning one page at a time).

• Child blends onset and rime to form a word with pictoral support.

Differentiated Instruction

 Extra Support
Library and Listening Center
If...children have difficulty choosing from a variety of books, **then...**limit their choices. Ask: *Would you like to read this book or this one?* ¿Les gustaría leer este libro o aquel otro?

 Enrichment
ABC Center
Challenge children to use the words they make in full sentences.

Accommodations for 3's
Library and Listening Center
If...children are not ready to browse through books by themselves, **then...**help them choose one book, and read it aloud.

Circle Time

Focus Question

How can I learn by observing?

¿Qué puedo aprender observando las cosas?

Learning Goals

Emergent Literacy: Reading

• Child names most upper- and lowercase letters of the alphabet.

• Child identifies the letter that stands for a given sound.

• Child asks and answers questions about books read aloud (such as, "Who?" "What?" "Where?").

Vocabulary

answers	respuestas	compare	comparar
detective	detective	observe	observar
scale	balanza	tools	instrumentos

Differentiated Instruction

 Extra Support

Read Aloud

If...children have difficulty understanding comparisons, **then...**compare common characteristics, such as tall/short; hot/cold.

Enrichment

Read Aloud

List items children wonder about. Then challenge children to suggest how they might find out about these items.

Accommodations for 3's

Read Aloud

If...children have difficulty with the concepts, **then...**read the book in sections, discussing each section as you go.

Special Needs

Behavioral Social/Emotional

As you present items with various textures, keep in mind that children with behavior/emotional issues may be sensitive to certain materials. Try offering items covered in soft material, hard plastic, rough material such as sandpaper, and smooth paper such as matte board.

Literacy Time

large group — *15 minutes*

📖 Read Aloud

☑ **Do children exhibit and express curiosity about the questions raised in the book?**

Build Background Tell children you will read a book about becoming a detective. Say: *A detective's job is to find information and answers to questions.* *El trabajo de un detective es encontrar información y responder preguntas.*

• Ask: *Have you ever wondered about something? How did you find out about it?* *¿Alguna vez han investigado algo? ¿Qué hicieron para obtener información?*

Listen for Enjoyment Display *Let's Investigate/ Soy detective.* Explain that tools can help people find answers to questions.

• Browse the illustrations, pointing out the scale and the hand lens. Ask: *Have you ever seen these tools? Where? ¿Alguna vez han visto estos instrumentos? ¿Dónde?*

• Explain that looking at, or observing, things is a way to find answers. Say: *Let's compare our hands. Whose hand is bigger? Smaller? Comparemos nuestras manos. ¿Cuáles son más grandes? ¿Cuáles son más pequeñas?*

• Read the book aloud, pointing out specific tools used to gather information.

Respond to the Story Discuss the book. Help children recall the different ways they can get information. Ask: *What do you wonder about? How might you find out about it? ¿Sobre qué cosas se hacen preguntas? ¿Cómo pueden investigar acerca de eso?*

TIP Have several items for comparison activities: two different shoes, items that are smooth and rough, items that are heavy and light.

ELL Help children grasp the concept of what a scale is. Hold a heavy book in one hand and a marker in the other. Explain that a scale shows which items are heavy, like the book.

Learn About Letters and Sounds

☑ **Can children identify the letters *Bb* and the sound /b/?**

Learn About Bb Display the *Bb* page of the *ABC Big Book*, and point to the ball. Ask: *What do you see?* Repeat *ball*, emphasizing the /b/ sound. Continue with *bee* and *bed*. Then say the following words one at a time: *cat, book, dog, button, goat, fish, big, bear* Have children clap when they hear a word that begins with /b/.

• Say the /b/ sound, and have children repeat it several times. Then point to the uppercase *B*, name it, and say its sound. Have children repeat several times. Slowly trace uppercase *B*, demonstrating how it is formed. Using the picture card *Bb*, have volunteers repeat the process. Repeat for lowercase *b*.

• Conclude by reciting the alphabet together as you point to the corresponding *Alphabet Wall Cards*.

Let's Investigate
Soy detective

ABC Big Book

Math Time

Observe and Investigate

✓ **Can children correctly identify shapes?**

I Spy Invite children to play a detective game with you. Tell them they are going to be detectives. Discuss what detectives do.

- Before children arrive, place various Shape Set shapes in plain view throughout the classroom.

- Choose an object in the room, and name its shape. Say: *I spy something that is a big rectangle. What do I spy?* *Veo algo con forma de rectángulo grande. ¿Qué es?* Allow children time to look around the room.

- When a child guesses the object correctly, say: *Yes! I spied a [object]. Tell me again. What is its shape?* *¡Sí! Veo un/una [objeto]. Díganme nuevamente. ¿Qué forma tiene?* Ask the child to whisper another shape to you, and then have the class guess what object has that shape.

 Provide support by giving a "shape show" to review the names of shapes.

✗✗✗ Social and Emotional Development

Making Good Choices

✓ **Can children attempt to solve a problem in a positive way on their own?**

✓ **Can children communicate and interact with peers?**

Solving a Problem Discuss problems that arise in the classroom. Encourage children to talk about a problem they have had during school.

- Ask: *How did you fix, or solve, the problem? Did you ask for help, or were you able to work it out with a friend?* *¿Cómo resolvieron el problema? ¿Pidieron ayuda o pudieron resolverlo solos?* Talk about how you can sometimes take care of a problem by yourself, but sometimes you might need to ask for help.

- Show the *Making Good Choices Flip Chart, page 17.* Focus on the children in the block area. Ask: *What problem are the children having? Are the children trying to solve the problem on their own or asking for help?* *¿Qué problema tienen los niños? ¿Intentan los niños resolver el problema por sí mismos o piden ayuda?* Encourage children to describe the different behaviors each child is using. Ask: *Why do you think the girl in the picture is angry? Do you think it helps to get angry?* *¿Creen que la niña de la ilustración está enojada? ¿Creen que enojarse ayuda a resolver un problema?* Elicit children's reactions to the various emotions in the picture.

Building Blocks

Online Math Activity

Introduce Mystery Pictures 2: Name Shapes. In this activity, children identify shapes to construct each mystery picture. Encourage children to guess what each picture will be.

Making Good Choices Flip Chart, p. 17

Learning Goals

Social and Emotional Development
- Child demonstrates initiative in independent activities; makes independent choices.
- Child initiates play scenarios with peers that share a common plan and goal.

Mathematics
- Child recognizes, names, describes, matches, compares, sorts common two-dimensional shapes (such as circle, square, rectangle, triangle, rhombus).

Vocabulary

angry	enojarse	detective	detective
help	ayudar	spy	veo veo
problem	problema	solve	resolver

Differentiated Instruction

 Extra Support

Making Good Choices

If...children have difficulty identifying the angry emotion the child might be feeling when she noticed the other children's large pile of blocks, **then**...have small groups act out the scenario.

★ **Enrichment**

Observe and Investigate

Consider using more difficult shapes, like circles or isosceles triangles or shapes that are in different orientations.

Accommodations for 3's

Making Good Choices

If...children are unsure when to ask for help with a project, **then**...highlight instances when help is offered, and praise children who ask for help.

How can I learn by observing?

¿Qué puedo aprender observando las cosas?

Learning Goals

Language and Communication
• Child names and describes actual or pictured people, places, things, actions, attributes, and events.

Science
• Child uses senses to observe, classify, investigate, and collect data.

Vocabulary

material	material	paper	papel
plastic	plástico	senses	sentidos
wood	madera		

Differentiated Instruction

 Extra Support

Observe and Investigate

If...children have difficulty describing the materials, **then...**suggest two words, and have the child choose the appropriate word.

Enrichment

Observe and Investigate

Challenge children to think of a variety of descriptive words for each sense: touch, taste, sound.

Accommodations for 3's

Oral Language and Academic Vocabulary

If...children have difficulty understanding the meanings of useful descriptive words, **then...**help them by associating the words with materials that illustrate them.

Science Time

large group | 20 minutes

Personal Safety Skills Model safety procedures by cleaning up water spills quickly and carefully.

Oral Language and Academic Vocabulary

✓ **Can children identify materials used to make various items?**

Point to the shelves on the *Math and Science Flip Chart, page 29.* Say: ***There are things made of many different materials in this picture.*** *Hay cosas hechas de muchos materiales diferentes en esta imagen.*

● Point to the various objects, and discuss what they are made of.

● Ask: ***What are the shelves made of? (wood) There are many things to play with in this picture. What are the toys made of? (plastic, metal, fabric)*** *¿De qué están hehos los estantes? (madera) En esta imagen podemos ver muchas cosas para jugar. ¿De qué están hechos los juguetes? (plástico, metal, tela)*

● Point to an object, and discuss what it is made of. Say: ***I see a truck. Do you know what material people used to make the truck? The truck is made of metal.*** Challenge children to identify where metal comes from. Explain that some materials, such as wood, can be found in nature, and other things, such as plastic, are made by people. Help children name some other materials from nature.

Observe and Investigate

✓ **Can children identify and describe common materials using their senses?**

Provide children with small objects made of wood, stone, plastic, plastic foam, and metal. Say: ***You can use your senses to find out about different materials.*** *Pueden usar sus sentidos para conocer los distintos materiales.*

● Have children work in pairs or small groups to look at and touch the different objects. Encourage children to name both the object and the material it is made from.

● Encourage children to use descriptive language to talk about what they feel and see.

💡 **TIP** Tell children they will have another chance to use these materials in the Science Center.

ELL Hold up your hands, and say: ***I touch with my hands and skin.*** Touch an item. Then point to your nose, and say: ***I smell with my nose.*** Model smelling an object.

● For additional suggestions on how to meet the needs of children at the Beginning, Intermediate, Advanced, and Advanced-High levels of English proficiency, see pages 184–187.

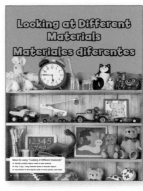

Math and Science Flip Chart, p. 29

Center Time

> **Center Rotation** Center Time includes teacher-guided activities and independent activities. Refer to the **Learning Centers** on pages 24–25 for independent activity ideas.

  small group   30 minutes

Math and Science Center

✓ **Can children test, describe, and record whether objects and materials sink or float?**

Materials small objects made of wood, stone, plastic, plastic foam, and metal; water; container; table; pictures of items; chart paper; glue

What Floats? Ask children to think about materials that float, or stay on top of water. Say: *Let's see what sinks, or goes down in the water, and what floats, or stays on top of the water. Veamos qué se hunde, o se sumerge en el agua, y qué flota, o se mantiene sobre el agua.*

- Prepare a container of water. Ask children to place each object on top of the water. Ask: *Did it stay on top of the water, or did it sink to the bottom? ¿Se hundió o flotó?*

- Create a chart with two columns: "Floats" and "Sinks." Have children glue a picture onto the chart for each item they test.

- When you have completed the chart, guide children to review it with you and summarize their findings.

Center Tip

If...children have trouble getting objects to float, **then...**demonstrate how to carefully slide the object into the water.

Learning Goals

Language and Communication
- Child names and describes actual or pictured people, places, things, actions, attributes, and events.

Emergent Literacy: Writing
- Child experiments with and uses some writing conventions when writing or dictating.

Science
- Child uses senses to observe, classify, investigate, and collect data.

 Writing

Recap the day by reviewing a situation when a child needed help. Whom did the child ask? Who helped? Write this sentence frame for children on the board: _____ helped me. Assist children in copying the sentence and filling in the blank. Ask children to draw a picture to go with the sentence.

Purposeful Play

✓ **Can children describe an object and identify what material(s) it is made from?**

Children choose an open center for free playtime. Challenge them to use words to describe a certain classroom object and have a partner guess what the object is.

Let's Say Good-Bye

 large group   15 minutes

 Read Aloud Reread "The Crow and the Fox"/"El cuervo y el zorro" for your afternoon Read Aloud. Remind children to listen for the /b/ sound in words.

 Home Connection Refer to the Home Connections activities listed in the Resources and Materials chart on page 21. Remind children to tell families about some of the materials they see at home. Sing the "Good-Bye Song"/"Hora de ir a casa" as children prepare to leave.

Focus Question

How can I learn by observing?

¿Qué puedo aprender observando las cosas?

 Learning Goals

Language and Communication
• Child begins and ends conversations appropriately.
• Child uses newly learned vocabulary daily in multiple contexts.

Emergent Literacy: Reading
• Child blends onset and rime to form a word with pictoral support.

Vocabulary

compare	comparan	detective	detective
observe	observar	rough	áspero
scale	balanza	smooth	suave
tools	instrumentos		

Differentiated Instruction

 Extra Support

Oral Language and Vocabulary
If...children do not remember words that describe the characteristics of things, **then...**give them a classroom object and say: *Tell me what this object is like. How does it look? How does it feel? Díganme cómo es este objeto. ¿Cómo se ve? ¿Cómo se siente cuando lo tocan?*

⭐ **Enrichment**

Phonological Awareness
Challenge pairs of children to blend one-syllable words that begin with the /b/ sound: *bug, bat, book, bang, bee, ball.*

Accommodations for 3's

Oral Language and Vocabulary
If...children need visual reinforcement, **then...** show real examples of the tools mentioned in the book.

Let's Start the Day

▶ **Opening Routines and Transition Tips**
For **Opening Routines** and **Transition Tips** turn to pages 178–181 and visit DLMExpressOnline.com for more ideas.

📖 Read **"Going on Safari"/**"Ir de safari" from the *Teacher's Treasure Book*, page 209, for your morning Read Aloud.

Language Time

large group 15 minutes

👥👥 **Social and Emotional Development** Encourage peer conversation. Have children compare various classroom objects. Ask: *Can you compare these objects? Which objects are rough? Which objects are smooth? ¿Pueden comparar estos objetos? ¿Qué objetos son ásperos? ¿Cuáles son suaves?*

Oral Language and Vocabulary

✓ **Can children use new vocabulary to name tools used for observation and to describe what they observe?**

Being a Detective Discuss some tools detectives use to observe things and learn more about them. Ask children to tell you what each tool measures or compares. Ask: *How can you tell if something is smooth or rough? ¿Cómo se dan cuenta de que algo es suave o áspero?*

● Display *Let's Investigate/Soy Detective*, page 21. Say: *What tool do we use to measure how heavy something is? How can we describe something that is not heavy? ¿Qué instrumento usamos para saber cuánto pesa algo? ¿Cómo podemos describir algo que no es pesado?*

● Display *Let's Investigate*, page 25. Say: *Can we tell with our eyes if something is smooth or rough? Our hands? What tools can help us? ¿Cómo nos damos cuenta de que algo es suave o áspero? ¿Podemos hacerlo con nuestros ojos? ¿Y con nuestras manos? ¿Qué instrumentos nos pueden ayudar a saberlo?*

Phonological Awareness

✓ **Can children blend onset and rime with pictorial support?**

Blend Onset and Rime Use the Dog Puppets to introduce a game. Use the images on the *Oral Language Development Card* to find simple words for the children to blend. Use the puppets to hold the card and direct children in the blending.

● Have one puppet hold up *Oral Language Development Card 39*. The puppet says: *The children in this picture are at the zoo. Listen to the sounds in this word: /z/ /oo/. When we blend the sounds together, we can make the word* zoo. *Los niños de esta foto están en el zoo. Escuchen los sonidos de esta palabra: /z/ /oo/. Cuando combinamos los sonidos, podemos formar la palabra* zoo. Use the other puppet to demonstrate how to blend the onset and rime in the word *zoo*. Have children repeat what the second puppet says. Use the puppets to help children practice other one-syllable words.

Let's Investigate
Soy detective

Oral Language Development Card 39

Center Time

Center Rotation Center Time includes teacher-guided activities and independent activities. Refer to the **Learning Centers** on pages 24–25 for independent activity ideas.

 small group | 60–90 minutes

Creativity Center

	Center Tip

 Can children observe characteristics and draw them?

Materials hand lenses, objects of different textures, crayons, markers, paper

Smooth or Rough? Place children into pairs, and give each pair one object with a smooth texture and one with a rough texture.

- Have children use hand lenses to observe the objects and identify which is smooth and which is rough. Allow them to use their skin to feel the textures of the objects. Ask: *Did it feel the way you expected it to feel? ¿Se siente cómo esperaban o se siente diferente?*

- Have each child draw one of the objects, clearly demonstrating the smooth or rough texture in the drawing, and have them describe the object and how it felt.

Center Tip

If...children do not know how to show the texture in the drawing, **then...** suggest they use straight lines for smooth and zigzag or squiggly lines for rough.

Library and Listening Center

	Center Tip

 Can children work cooperatively to blend onset and rime?

Materials CD player, *Rhymes and Chants CD*, *Rhymes and Chants Flip Chart*, p. 17

Use Your Senses Place children into pairs. Discuss with children what senses they use to observe.

- Ask: *What do you do with your eyes? ¿Qué hacen con sus ojos?* (see)

- Tell children to listen and raise their hands when they hear the word *see*. Play the audio version of the *Rhymes and Chants CD* once through, and point to the girl observing on the *Rhymes and Chants Flip Chart*, page 17.

- Model for children the onset and rime: /s/ /ee/. Encourage pairs to divide the onset and rime and then say the word aloud together.

Center Tip

If...children have difficulty hearing the word *see*, **then...**play that part back several times.

Learning Goals

Language and Communication
- Child uses newly learned vocabulary daily in multiple contexts.

Emergent Literacy: Reading
- Child blends onset and rime to form a word with pictoral support.

Differentiated Instruction

Extra Support
Creativity Center
If...children cannot tell which object is rough and which is smooth using the hand lens, **then...**have them use their skin to feel the texture.

Enrichment
Library and Listening Center
Encourage children to listen for the other words on the *Rhymes and Chants Flip Chart* that begin with the /s/ sound (*see, soft, seen*).

Accommodations for 3's
Creativity Center
If...children have trouble manipulating the hand lens, **then...**encourage them to use both hands.

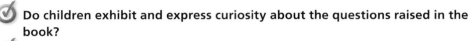

Focus Question
How can I learn by observing?
¿Qué puedo aprender observando las cosas?

 Learning Goals

Emergent Literacy: Reading
• Child identifies the letter that stands for a given sound.

• Child asks and answers questions about books read aloud (such as, "Who?" "What?" "Where?").

Vocabulary

answer	responder	compare	comparar
detective	detective	information	información
scale	balanza	tools	instrumentos

Differentiated Instruction

✋ **Extra Support**
Read Aloud
If...children have difficulty understanding what certain tools are used for, **then...**demonstrate by having children use the tools as you describe the information each tool can help you gain.

⭐ **Enrichment**
Learn About Letters and Sounds
Challenge children to page through books to find words with the letter *i*.

Accommodations for 3's
Read Aloud
If...children have difficulty understanding the concepts of *heavy* and *light*, **then...**work with them individually with various objects to reinforce the concept.

Literacy Time

large group · 15 minutes

📖 Read Aloud

✓ Do children exhibit and express curiosity about the questions raised in the book?

✓ Can children ask questions that show an understanding of the story?

Build Background Display *Let's Investigate/Soy Detective.* Ask children what they remember about the job of a detective. Browse through the book, and talk about some of the tools detectives can use to find information. Remind children that they can be detectives too. Discuss how detectives observe.

● Ask: *How can you find out about something small, like a bug or a leaf? ¿Qué pueden hacer para saber más sobre algo muy pequeño, como un insecto o una hoja?*

Listen for Understanding Remind children that tools help you find answers to questions. Encourage children to name tools they can find in their classroom. Before you begin reading, say: *As I read, think about a question you might have about one of the tools in the story. Cuando me escuchen leer, piensen en una pregunta sobre uno de los instrumentos que se mencionan en el cuento.* Read the book, and direct attention to the different tools mentioned.

Respond to the Story Remind children that they can be detectives and use tools to answer their own questions and find information. Tell children you are interested in ladybugs. Ask: *How can I find out about ladybugs? ¿Qué puedo hacer para saber más acerca de las catarinas?* Encourage children to offer different responses.

● Prepare pairs of items to compare and weigh on a balance scale. Have children predict which object will be lighter and which will be heavier.

ELL Children may not understand how tools are used or what information they can gain from various tools. Reinforce understanding by modeling using real-life tools as you review the words in the book.

Learn About Letters and Sounds

✓ Can children identify the letters *Ii* and the short sound /i/?

Learn About *Ii* Display the *Ii* page of the *ABC Big Book*. Point to the igloo.

● Ask: *What do you see? ¿Qué ven?* Repeat *igloo*, elongating the /i/ sound that begins it. Continue with *iguana*. Then say the following words one at a time: *duck, key, iguana, sun, turtle, important, map*. Have children clap when they hear a word that begins with /i/.

● Say the /i/ sound, and have children repeat it several times. Then point to the uppercase *I*, name it, and say its short sound. Have children repeat several times. Slowly trace uppercase *I*, showing how it is formed. Using the ABC Picture Card *Ii*, have volunteers repeat the process. Repeat with lowercase *i*.

● Recite the alphabet together as you point to the *Alphabet Wall Cards*.

Let's Investigate
Soy Detective

ABC Big Book

Math Time

Observe and Investigate

Can children sort objects?

Shhh...Watch Carefully Tell children they are going to be detectives again. They are going to guess a sorting rule. Discuss sorting before children begin.

- Say: *I am going to sort these shapes.* *Voy a ordenar estas figuras.* Sort Shape Set shapes into piles based on a rule, such as circles versus squares, or four-sided versus three-sided shapes. Put at least two shapes in each pile.

- Hold a shape over one pile, then the other. Say: *Which pile does this shape belong in? ¿En qué pila debo colocar esta figura?* Have each child talk with a partner about where the shape should go. Call on a volunteer to tell you what to do.

- After all the shapes are sorted, ask children to guess your rule. Say: *What is my rule? ¿Cuál es mi regla?* Repeat with other shapes.

TIP Help children differentiate shapes by counting the number of sides as you point to them.

 large group 15 minutes

☥☥☥ Social and Emotional Development

Making Good Choices

Can children communicate to initiate and carry out scenarios?

Can children plan and follow through on a plan?

Working Together Review yesterday's discussion about problem solving and the scenario that took place in the *Making Good Choices Flip Chart*. Tell children you are going to use the Dog Puppets to help you review.

- Hold up the first puppet, and have it say: *The children in the picture are having a problem. What is the problem? Los niños de la ilustración tienen un problema. ¿Cuál es el problema?* Hold up the second puppet, and have it say: *One group has all the blocks! What will the children do? ¡Un grupo tiene todos los bloques! ¿Qué harán los niños?* Encourage discussion from children.

- Use the first puppet to explain that talking about things with others can help solve problems but sometimes it can lead to new ideas too. Say: *The children should talk about the problem they are having with the blocks. They might be able to solve the problem and come up with a new plan so they work with the blocks together! Los niños deberían hablar sobre el problema. Pueden hacer un nuevo plan y así todos podrán trabajar juntos con los bloques.*

Building Blocks

Online Math Activity

Introduce Memory Geometry 2: Turned Shapes, in which children match turned shapes and click yes or no to ensure comprehension.

Making Good Choices Flip Chart, p. 17

Learning Goals

Social and Emotional Development
- Child demonstrates initiative in independent activities; makes independent choices.

Mathematics
- Child sorts objects and explains how the sorting was done.

Vocabulary

carefully	atentamente	circle	círculo
problem	problema	solve	resolver
watch	observar		

Differentiated Instruction

✋ Extra Support
Making Good Choices
If...children have difficulty communicating when they are having a problem, **then...**help them by facilitating their discussion with the classmate.

⭐ Enrichment
Making Good Choices
Challenge children to formulate a plan and a goal with a peer. Allow time for them to carry out their plan and reach their goal.

Accommodations for 3's
Observe and Investigate
If...children struggle with the shapes, **then...**work with them individually to reinforce each shape.

Learning Goals

Social and Emotional Development
• Child is aware of self in terms of abilities, characteristics and preferences, and respects personal boundaries.

Mathematics
• Child recognizes, names, describes, matches, compares, sorts common two-dimensional shapes (such as circle, square, rectangle, triangle, rhombus).
• Child understands and uses words that describe position/location in space (such as under, over, beside, between, on, in, near, far away).

Vocabulary

find	encontrar	step	pisar
triangle	triángulo		

Differentiated Instruction

 Extra Support

Math Time
If...children struggle finding the shapes, **then...** use location words such as *in front of* and *behind* to help them.

 Enrichment

Math Time
Challenge the children to use location words to describe where their shape is in relation to other shapes.

Accommodations for 3's

Math Time
If...children seem reluctant to find and step on the shapes, **then...**have them work with a partner.

 Special Needs

Cognitive Challenges
While learning to name shapes may not be possible for all children, learning to identify things that are similar and different is an important concept. Select two very different shapes to target, for example, the circle and the triangle. Work with these two shapes throughout the week.

Math Time

  large group 15 minutes

Personal Safety Skills Model safe and appropriate ways to play the game while respecting others' space and avoiding bumping into others.

 Can children name common shapes? Can children use location words?

Step on that Shape! Invite children to find a shape and step on it.

● Make several large shapes on the floor using masking or colored tape. (Use larger versions of shapes found in the foam Shape Set.) Make sure the shapes are clearly visible and distributed randomly.

● Have a group of five children play the game. Say: *I am looking for a rectangle. Where is the rectangle? Is it beside the triangle? Is it behind the rhombus? Find that shape! Estoy buscando un rectángulo. ¿Dónde está el rectángulo? ¿Está junto al triángulo? ¿Está detrás del cuadrado? ¡Encuentren esa figura!*

● Give children time to locate the shape on the floor. Say: *Step on that shape! ¡Pisen la figura!*

● Ask children to explain why the shape they stepped on was correct. Say: *How do you know that is a rectangle? ¿Cómo saben que es un rectángulo?*

● Repeat the activity until all groups have stepped on shapes.

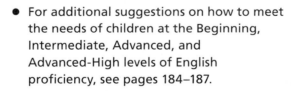 Provide support by asking yes/no questions about the characteristics of each shape. *(Is this shape round? Does this shape have three sides?)* Point to the features of the shapes as you ask questions.

● For additional suggestions on how to meet the needs of children at the Beginning, Intermediate, Advanced, and Advanced-High levels of English proficiency, see pages 184–187.

Center Time

Center Rotation Center Time includes teacher-guided activities and independent activities. Refer to the **Learning Centers** on pages 24–25 for independent activity ideas.

small group · 30 minutes

Math and Science Center

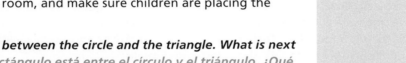

✓ **Encourage children to create patterns with shapes.**

Materials foam Shape Sets or Pattern Blocks

Shape Patterns Give each child a set of shapes. Tell children they are going to arrange the shapes according to the description you give. Have them place the circle in the center of their desk. Say: ***The square is above the circle. Where is the square?*** *El cuadrado está arriba del círculo. ¿Dónde está el cuadrado?*

- Circulate around the room, and make sure children are placing the objects correctly.

- Say: ***The rectangle is between the circle and the triangle. What is next to the triangle?*** *El rectángulo está entre el círculo y el triángulo. ¿Qué hay junto al triángulo?*

- After children place various objects, have them pick up all objects and play the game again.

Center Tip

If...children have difficulty placing objects, **then...**play an example round to demonstrate the meanings of the location words.

✓ Learning Goals

Language and Communication
- Child follows two- and three-step oral directions.

Emergent Literacy: Writing
- Child experiments with and uses some writing conventions when writing or dictating.

Mathematics
- Child recognizes, names, describes, matches, compares, sorts common two-dimensional shapes (such as circle, square, rectangle, triangle, rhombus).
- Child understands and uses words that describe position/location in space (such as under, over, beside, between, on, in, near, far away).

Writing

Recap the day. On chart paper or an interactive whiteboard, record a short description of how children helped each other, asking children to dictate sentences.

Purposeful Play

✓ **Observe children following oral directions and using location words.**

Children choose an open center for free playtime. Encourage children to play a form of Follow the Leader or Simon Says in which one child instructs others where to stand in relation to a specific place using location words.

Let's Say Good-Bye

large group · 15 minutes

 Read Aloud Reread "Going on Safari"/"Ir de safari" for your afternoon Read Aloud. Ask children if they would like to go on safari and what tools they would take with them on a safari.

 Home Connection Refer to the Home Connections activities listed in the Resources and Materials chart on page 21. Remind children to tell their families how they can sort shapes. Sing the "Good-Bye Song"/"Hora de ir a casa" as children prepare to leave.

Let's Start the Day

Focus Question

How can I learn by observing?

¿Qué puedo aprender observando las cosas?

 Learning Goals

Language and Communication
• Child begins and ends conversations appropriately.
• Child uses newly learned vocabulary daily in multiple contexts.

Emergent Literacy: Reading
• Child blends onset and rime to form a word with pictoral support.

Vocabulary

food	comida	mouth	boca
nose	nariz	smell	olor
taste	sabor		

Differentiated Instruction

 Extra Support

Oral Language and Vocabulary
If...children have difficulty describing tastes or smells, **then...**ask about specific foods, and give suggestions such as: *How does a lemon taste? Is it sweet or sour? ¿Qué sabor tiene el limón? ¿Es dulce o ácido?*

Enrichment

Phonological Awareness
Challenge pairs of children to suggest and segment some weather-related words: *snow, rain, sun, wind*.

Accommodations for 3's

Phonological Awareness
If...children are not ready to blend and segment sounds, **then...**work just on beginning sounds. Say: *Listen to this word.* **B-b-b-bed.** *What is the first sound you hear?* Emphasize the initial sound for children.

 Opening Routines and Transition Tips
For **Opening Routines** and **Transition Tips** turn to pages 178–181 and visit DLMExpressOnline.com for more ideas.

 Read **"A Spring Walk"**/**"Una caminata en primavera"** from the *Teacher's Treasure Book*, page 187, for your morning Read Aloud.

Language Time

 large group 15 minutes

Social and Emotional Development Encourage children to discuss favorite foods. Have children explain to peers how their favorite smells and tastes.

Oral Language and Vocabulary

✔ **Can children use newly learned vocabulary to describe how foods smell and taste?**

Good Tastes and Smells Discuss things that taste and smell good. Ask children to describe the smells they like. Ask: *What things smell sour? What things taste sweet? ¿Qué cosas tienen olor ácido? ¿Qué cosas tienen sabor dulce?* Encourage children to use other descriptive words to talk about tastes and smells.

● Display *Oral Language Development Card 32.* Point to a sweet-smelling food. Ask: *How does this smell? What do you use to smell? ¿Qué olor tiene esto? ¿Qué parte del cuerpo usan para oler?*

● Point to a different food, and ask what it tastes like. Say: *What do you use to taste? ¿Qué parte del cuerpo usan para sentir os sabores?*

ELL Reinforce vocabulary by playing a game with children. Tell them you will ask them a question and they have to answer *nose* or *mouth*, saying the word aloud and pointing to the nose or the mouth. Ask: *What do you taste food with? What do you use to smell? What do you use to eat?*

Phonological Awareness

✔ **Can children blend onset and rime with pictorial support to make the words *bed* and *dog*?**

Blend Onset and Rime Display *Rhymes and Chants Flip Chart,* page 17. Read the rhyme aloud.

● Point to the picture of the girl. Say: *We blended sounds to make the word* girl. *Now let's look at what is in her room. What do you see? Combinamos sonidos para formar la palabra* girl. *Ahora, veamos qué hay en el cuarto de esta niña. ¿Qué ven?* Allow children to give answers. Elicit the words *bed* and *dog*.

● Ask: *Can you listen to the sounds in this word? /b/ -ed. When we blend the sounds together, we can make the word* bed. *¿Pueden escuchar los sonidos en esta palabra? /b/ -ed. Cuando combinamos los sonidos, formamos la palabra bed.* Repeat the instruction with the word *dog*

Oral Language Development Card 32

I'm a Detective

I'm a detective.
What do I see?
I see a snowflake
In front of me.

So soft and white,
It floats like a feather
And falls to the ground
In cold winter weather.

Detectives write down
What is seen and is felt.
But I must look quickly,
Because snowflakes melt!

Rhymes and Chants Flip Chart, p. 17

Center Time

► **Center Rotation** Center Time includes teacher-guided activities and independent activities. Refer to the **Learning Centers** on pages 24–25 for independent activity ideas.

 small group 60–90 minutes

Writer's Center | Center Tip

✓ **Can children use sensory language to describe properties of foods?**

Materials *Photo Library* CD-ROM, photos of a variety of familiar foods, paper, crayons, chart paper or interactive whiteboard

Foods We Like Children will use sensory language to write about favorite foods.

● Display photos of a variety of foods.

● Ask children to think of sensory words about food, such as *sweet, sour, salty, creamy.* Write the words on the board or chart paper.

● Have children write a sentence about their favorite food, using at least one of the sensory words. Accept all levels of writing. Then children can create a drawing to go with the sentence.

● Compile children's work in a class "Favorite Foods" book.

Center Tip

If...children cannot write their descriptions, **then...** have them dictate their sentences to an adult.

ABC Center | Center Tip

✓ **Can children form one-syllable words?**

Materials *Rhymes and Chants Flip Chart*

Beginning Sounds Display the *Rhymes and Chants Flip Chart, page 17.* Tell children they will name things that begin with the same sound as *soft* and *see.*

● Ask: **What do you do with your eyes?** (see) *¿Qué hacen con sus ojos? (ver)*

● Ask: **What does the detective see?** (a snowflake) *¿Qué ve el detective? (un copo de nieve)* Then ask: **How does a snowflake feel when you touch it?** (soft) *¿Cómo se siente tocar un copo de nieve? (suave)*

● Have children work in pairs to identify the onset sound of *soft* and *see.* Say: **Each word begins with /s/.** Have children think of and say three more words that begin with that sound. Instruct them to blend the onset and rime as they say each word. **/s/ -ee, see; /s/ -oft, soft.**

Center Tip

If...children have difficulty repeating the sound, **then...** model for them how to isolate the onset, and repeat only that sound a few times before blending the onset and rime.

 Learning Goals

Language and Communication
● Child uses newly learned vocabulary daily in multiple contexts.

Emergent Literacy: Reading
● Child blends onset and rime to form a word with pictoral support.

Differentiated Instruction

 Extra Support
Writer's Center
If...children cannot identify sweet or sour, **then...**give them examples of foods with those tastes and smells, and act out the facial expressions people make when experiencing each kind of food.

 Enrichment
Writer's Center
Challenge children to use other descriptive words to describe the tastes and smells of the food items.

 Special Needs
Vision Loss
Use some real foods for the child to examine, rather than photos, so the child can better understand and express sensory words.

Focus Question

How can I learn by observing?

¿Qué puedo aprender observando las cosas?

Learning Goals

Emergent Literacy: Reading

• Child produces the most common sound for a given letter.

• Child asks and answers questions about books read aloud (such as, "Who?" "What?" "Where?").

Vocabulary

castle	castillo	forest	bosque
ocean	océano	slosh	echar
soggy	húmedo	soil	tierra
tunneled	túnel	wiggle	menearse
worm	gusano		

Differentiated Instruction

 Extra Support

Read Aloud

If...children have difficulty understanding the effects of the different environments that Wally encounters, **then...**use a sponge or a paper towel to demonstrate the difference between dry and soggy.

 Enrichment

Read Aloud

Ask children to draw pictures of worms. Provide nature books that show close-ups of worms.

Accommodations for 3's

Read Aloud

If...children can't tell what makes Wally make-believe, **then...**ask specific questions such as *Do real worms talk? ¿Hablan los gusanos reales?*

Circle Time

Literacy Time

 **Read Aloud**

☑ **Do children exhibit and express curiosity about the story?**

Build Background Tell children they will hear a story about a worm named Wally. Ask them to tell what they know about worms. Explain that worms live in the ground, or soil.

● Have children listen to find out if the worm is a real worm or make-believe.

Listen for Enjoyment Read "Wally Worm's World"/"El mundo del gusano Wally" from the *Teacher's Treasure Book*, page 212 aloud, adding movement and varying your voice.

● Point out words that describe sounds, such as *Thump!* and *Slosh!* Say: **If you don't know what a word means, notice what happens in the story when the sound occurs.** *Si no saben qué significan estas palabras, observen qué sucede en el cuento cuando aparecen esos sonidos.* Explain this will help children understand the sound.

Respond to the Story Talk about the adventures Wally Worm has. Ask children to think of a question they have about Wally. Discuss each question.

● Choose events in the story for children to act out as you ask questions: **How did Wally get around the rock he bumped into? What did Wally do when he peeked out from the sand castle?** *¿Cómo da vuelta Wally a la roca con la que tropezó? ¿Qué hace Wally después de mirar hacia abajo desde el castillo de arena?*

ELL Help children formulate questions about the story by prompting them with a question, emphasizing *who, what, where* words. For example, ask: **Who is the story about? What do you want to know about Wally?** Elicit responses, and help children rephrase responses into questions.

Learn About Letters and Sounds

☑ **Can children identify the letters *Nn* and the sound /n/?**

Learn About *Nn* Display the *Nn* page of *ABC Big Book,* and point to the nose. Ask: **What do you see?** *¿Qué ven?* Repeat **nose**, elongating the /n/ sound that begins it. Continue with *napkin* and *necklace*. Then say the following words one at a time: **worm, nest, hat, nail, lion, moon, nose.** Have children clap when they hear a word that begins with /n/.

● Say the /n/ sound, and have children repeat it several times. Then point to the uppercase *N*, name it, and say its sound. Have children repeat several times. Slowly trace uppercase *N*, demonstrating how it is formed. Using the ABC Picture Card *Nn*, have volunteers repeat the process. Repeat with lowercase *n*. Conclude by reciting the alphabet together as you point to the corresponding *Alphabet Wall Cards.*

Teacher's Treasure Book, p. 212

ABC Big Book

large group 15 minutes

Math Time

Observe and Investigate

✓ **Can children identify shapes?**

Step on that Shape! Working with a small group of children, invite children to find a shape and step on it. Make several large shapes on the floor using masking or colored tape. (Or use larger versions of shapes found in the foam Shape Set.)

● Say: *I am looking for a triangle. Find that shape. Step on that shape! Estoy buscando un triángulo. Encuentren la figura. ¡Pisen la figura!* When children find the shape, ask: *Where is the shape? What is the shape next to? What is the shape in front of? ¿Cuál es la figura? ¿Cuál es la figura que está al lado? ¿Y la que está adelante?*

ELL Provide visual support by giving a shape show before you start.

Building Blocks

Online Math Activity
Children can complete Mystery Pictures 2 and Memory Geometry 2 during computer time or Center Time.

large group 15 minutes

🧑‍🤝‍🧑 Social and Emotional Development

Making Good Choices

✓ **Can children communicate a problem?**

✓ **Can children initiate asking for help in solving a problem?**

Asking for Help Discuss with children that sometimes they may not be able to solve a problem on their own. Display the *Making Good Choices Flip Chart,* page 17. Tell children the Dog Puppets will help them understand how to ask for help.

● Puppet 1: *Look at the children playing dress-up. One child is showing the others what to do. Mira a los niños jugando a disfrazarse. Una niña está mostrando a los demás lo que deben hacer.*

● Puppet 2: *What if the other children don't want her to show them? ¿Y si los demás niños no quieren que ella les muestre lo que deben hacer?*

● Puppet 1: *You might want her to show you how to do things. But if it makes you mad, you could ask an adult to help. Who else could you ask? Tal vez quieran que la niña les muestre cómo hacer algo. Pero, si les molesta, pueden pedir ayuda a un adulto. ¿A quién más podrías pedirle ayuda?*

● Puppet 2: *I could ask the other children to help. Maybe we could all figure out how to do things together. Podría pedir ayuda a los demás niños. Tal vez todos podamos descubrir juntos cómo hacer las cosas.*

Discuss the different ways a child can get help in the classroom. Explain that everyone needs help at times. Encourage children to go to teachers, adults, or friends if they cannot work out issues with classmates.

Making Good Choices Flip Chart, p. 17

✓ Learning Goals

Social and Emotional Development
● Child demonstrates initiative in independent activities; makes independent choices.
● Child initiates play scenarios with peers that share a common plan and goal.

Mathematics
● Child recognizes, names, describes, matches, compares, sorts common two-dimensional shapes (such as circle, square, rectangle, triangle, rhombus).
● Child understands and uses words that describe position/location in space (such as under, over, beside, between, on, in, near, far away).

Vocabulary

find	encontrar	help	ayudar
problem	problema	solve	resolver
step	pisar	triangle	triángulo

Differentiated Instruction

✋ **Extra Support**
Making Good Choices
If...children have difficulty following the puppet discussions, **then...**allow them to use one of the puppets as you tell them what to say and they repeat it.

⭐ **Enrichment**
Observe and Investigate
Ask children to explain why the shape they stepped on is the correct shape.

Accommodations for 3's
Making Good Choices
If...some children are good at helping others, **then...**pair them with children who need help.

Social Studies Time

 large group 20 minutes

Language and Communication Skills Model a respectful, positive, welcoming attitude toward traditions and characteristics that are different from your own.

Oral Language and Academic Vocabulary

 Can children compare their families' languages and customs with those of other children in the classroom?

Discuss differences in families. Encourage children to offer ideas about what is special about their family. Ask children what languages they hear or speak at home.

- On chart paper or an interactive whiteboard, make a chart listing the names of children under the languages. Point out children who hear the *same* languages in their homes and others who hear *different* languages.

Understand and Participate Remind children that Wally Worm left his home in the forest. He learned the forest was where he liked to live. Explain that people decide where they live. They often choose to live in places their family and friends live because they have similar traditions and ways of life.

Ask: ***What is special about your family and where you live?*** *¿Qué les parece especial de su familia y el lugar donde viven?* Prompt discussion with the following ideas:

- languages, or special words used at home; elicit different words for parents, siblings, or relatives

- foods that are special to a family; elicit information about celebrations at which special foods are served

- clothing worn on special occasions; elicit information about occasions when special clothing is worn

- Emphasize with children that everyone's family is special.

TIP Plan a "Families Are Special Day" when children can bring in to share with the class a special food, a costume, a photo, a handicraft, or some other item representing family or culture.

ELL Begin by asking children to think of the names they use for *mother, father, grandmother,* and so on. Have them say the word in their language and then in English. Say: ***The words mean the same thing, but they sound different. Everyone has a special language they use at home.***

- For additional suggestions on how to meet the needs of children at the Beginning, Intermediate, Advanced, and Advanced-High levels of English proficiency, see pages 184–187.

Learning Goals

Social Studies
- Child identifies similarities and differences in families.
- Child respects/appreciates the differing interests, skills, abilities, cultures, languages, and family structures of people.

Vocabulary

different	diferente	family	familia
language	idioma	same	misma

Differentiated Instruction

 Extra Support

Oral Language and Academic Vocabulary
If...children do not understand about family customs, **then...**lead a discussion about various customs, eliciting from children information about the customs they are familiar with.

Enrichment

Oral Language and Academic Vocabulary
Invite a community member or staff member whose family celebrates a specific holiday or who speaks a second language to talk to the class.

Accommodations for 3's

Oral Language and Academic Vocabulary
If...children cannot verbally describe a family custom, **then...**ask them to draw a picture of a special occasion in their family, and discuss the meaning of the drawing with them.

Center Time

> **Center Rotation** Center Time includes teacher-guided activities and independent activities. Refer to the **Learning Centers** on pages 24–25 for independent activity ideas.

 small group · 30 minutes

Refer to the **Learning Centers** on pages 24–25 for independent activity ideas.

Creativity Center

Center Tip

✓ Can children compare unique foods of their family with those of other families?

✓ Can child follow two-step directions?

Materials paper plates, crayons, markers

Our Families' Foods Give children "think time" to remember a favorite food made by someone at home. Have children share ideas. Guide children to conclude that some dishes are alike and some are different.

- Ask children to draw a favorite dish on a paper plate.

- Encourage children to add descriptive words on the plate.

- Then have children describe the drawing to a friend, explaining why this is their favorite dish and how it tastes. Place the drawings on a bulletin board or wall for display.

If...children have difficulty describing or drawing a favorite food, **then...**have a few cutout items from a grocery store flyer or magazine for them to paste on the plate.

Learning Goals

Social and Emotional Development
- Child initiates play scenarios with peers that share a common plan and goal.

Language and Communication
- Child follows two- and three-step oral directions.

Emergent Literacy: Writing
- Child uses scribbles, shapes, pictures, symbols, and letters to represent language.

Shared Writing

Recap the day. Ask children to mention a new food they learned about in the center activity. Chart a few responses. Encourage children to try writing the foods they like best. If they can't write the whole word, have them focus on the first letter and then try writing each subsequent letter individually.

Purposeful Play

✓ Do children initiate play scenarios with common plans?

Children choose an open center area for free playtime. Encourage children to use their paper plates to "serve" a meal in the dramatic play center. Observe how children describe their foods and family customs.

Let's Say Good-Bye

 large group · 15 minutes

 Read Aloud Reread "A Spring Walk"/"Una caminata en primavera" for your afternoon Read Aloud. Ask children what they have seen on walks.

 Home Connection Refer to the Home Connections activities listed in the Resources and Materials chart on page 21. Remind children to discuss their traditions with their families. Sing the "Good-Bye Song"/"Hora de ir a casa" as children prepare to leave.

Let's Start the Day

Focus Question

How can I learn by observing?

¿Qué puedo aprender observando las cosas?

 Opening Routines and Transition Tips
For **Opening Routines** and **Transition Tips** turn to pages 178–181 and visit DLMExpressOnline.com for more ideas.

Read **"Anansi and the Pot of Wisdom"/***"Anansi y la olla de la sabiduría"* from the *Teacher's Treasure Book,* page 312, for your morning Read Aloud.

✔ Learning Goals

Language and Communication
• Child begins and ends conversations appropriately.
• Child uses newly learned vocabulary daily in multiple contexts.

Emergent Literacy: Reading
• Child blends onset and rime to form a word with pictoral support.

Vocabulary

ears	oídos	eyes	ojos
mouth	boca	nose	nariz
see	ver	senses	sentidos
smell	olor	taste	sabor

Differentiated Instruction

 Extra Support
Phonological Awareness
If...children have difficulty blending onset and rime, **then...**ask: *Who can see trees in the picture? I'll start the word, and you finish it.* Say /tr/. Children say -ees.

 Enrichment
Oral Language and Vocabulary
Challenge children to name different descriptive words for each sense. Ask: *What are some different smells? sounds? What are some different ways things feel? ¿Cómo pueden ser los diferentes olores?¿Y los sonidos? ¿De qué manera se sienten diferentes algunas cosas al tocarlas?*

Language Time

large group 15 minutes

✗✗✗ Social and Emotional Development Encourage children to demonstrate positive behaviors toward classmates and friends.

Oral Language and Vocabulary

✔ **Can children use newly learned vocabulary to talk about senses?**

The Senses Remind children that we use our senses to observe the world. Say: *Use your senses to observe your surroundings. Usen los sentidos para observar lo que hay a nuestro alrededor.*

● Encourage children to use one sense at a time and talk about the sense. Say: *Close your eyes, and use your nose to smell. What do you smell? Cierren los ojos y usen la nariz para oler. ¿Qué huelen?*

● Have them do the same with their senses of hearing and touch.

● Then have them focus on their sense of sight. Ask: *What do you see? ¿Qué ven?*

ELL Play a game with children to review the senses. Point to your nose, and say: *What do you do with this?* Point to your ears, and say: *What do you do with these?*

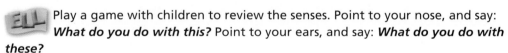

Oral Language Development Card 40

Phonological Awareness

✔ **Can children blend onset and rime with pictorial support?**

Blend Onset and Rime Use the puppets to introduce a game. Use the images on the *Oral Language Development Cards* to find simple words for the children to blend. Use the puppets to hold the cards and direct children in the blending.

● Have the first puppet hold up *Oral Language Development Card 40*. The puppet says: *Look at the truck. It is driving on the road. Miren el camión que está en la ruta.* Point to the road. *Listen to the sounds in this word: /r/ -oad. When we blend the sounds together, we can make the word* road. *Escuchen los sonidos en esta palabra: /r/ -oad. Si combinamos los sonidos, podemos formar la palabra road.*

● Use the second puppet to demonstrate how to blend the onset and rime in the word *road*.

● Use the puppets to practice other one-syllable words pictured on the card.

Center Time

Center Rotation Center Time includes teacher-guided activities and independent activities. Refer to the **Learning Centers** on pages 24–25 for independent activity ideas.

small group | 60–90 minutes

Pretend and Learn Center

 Can children use new vocabulary words to describe items?

Materials small paper bag; various items that have scent, texture, sound (bar of soap, small rock, crayon, cotton ball, bell, block)

What Is It? Display items, and explain children will pretend to be detectives solving a puzzle. They will use their senses of smell, touch, and hearing to guess which item has been placed in the bag. Have children work in pairs. One child, the detective, closes her eyes while the other chooses an item and places it in the bag.

- Model closing your eyes and reaching into the bag. Describe the item. Say: *It feels soft and fluffy. Se siente suave y esponjoso.* Smell into the bag, and say: *It doesn't have a smell. No tiene olor.* Shake the bag: *It makes a very soft sound when I shake the bag. I think it is the cotton ball! Hace un ruido muy suave cuando agito la bolsa. ¡Creo que es algodón!* Help children as needed by asking questions to guide them to use multiple senses. Have pairs switch roles when an item is identified.

Center Tip

If...children cannot name an item, **then...**have them describe it and ask their partner for help.

Construction Center

 Can children form one-syllable words with pictorial support?

 Can children work with peers to initiate pretend play scenarios?

Materials Blocks, boxes, pillows, books, Photo Library CD-ROM or other images of one-syllable items children can build (car, bus, dog, road).

Building Onset and Rime In pairs or small groups, have one child choose an item or an image and the other(s) say what it is. Children will then work together to build the item as they "build" the word.

- Model choosing an item. Say: *It is a car.* Car *begins with* /c/. Car *ends with* -ar. *Éste es un car. Car empieza con /c/. Car termina con -ar.* Blend the sounds, and say: /c/ -ar, /c/ -ar. **Car!** Show "building" a car from blocks as you repeat: /c/ -ar, /c/ -ar, **car.**

Center Tip

If...children have difficulty separating the sounds, **then...** have one child say the onset and the other say the rime.

Learning Goals

Social and Emotional Development
- Child initiates play scenarios with peers that share a common plan and goal.

Language and Communication
- Child uses newly learned vocabulary daily in multiple contexts.

Emergent Literacy: Reading
- Child blends onset and rime to form a word with pictoral support.

Differentiated Instruction

Extra Support
Pretend and Learn Center
If...children are afraid of closing their eyes, **then...**instead have them look at the ceiling.

Enrichment
Construction Center
Challenge children to create a story about the item they are building. Instruct them to blend one-syllable words in their story.

Accommodations for 3's
Construction Center
If...children have difficulty blending onset and rime to make a word **then...**have them say the full word a few times, and go back to identify the onset and rime with them.

Special Needs
Speech/Language Delays
If the child can't come up with words to describe what he or she feels in the bag, ask some prompting questions, such as: *Is it hard? Is it round? Is it made of fur? ¿Es duro? ¿Es redondo? ¿Está hecho de piel?*

Focus Question

How can I learn by observing?

¿Qué puedo aprender observando las cosas?

Learning Goals

Emergent Literacy: Reading

- Child names most upper- and lowercase letters of the alphabet.
- Child identifies the letter that stands for a given sound.
- Child produces the most common sound for a given letter.
- Child describes, relates to, and uses details and information from books read aloud.
- Child asks and answers questions about books read aloud (such as, "Who?" "What?" "Where?").

Vocabulary

cottage	cabaña	darting	lanzar
nectar	néctar	shortcut	atajo
smacked	abofetear	tangled	enredado
yelped	gritó		

Differentiated Instruction

Extra Support

Read Aloud

If...children have difficulty understanding vocabulary in the story, **then...**repeat specific sentences, and help children use context to determine meaning.

Enrichment

Read Aloud

Have children role-play the dialogue between Little Red Riding Hood and the wolf.

Accommodations for 3's

Read Aloud

If...children have difficulty with action words such as *skipped, darting,* or *yelped,* **then...**act out the word(s), and have children mimic you.

Literacy Time

large group — 15 minutes

📖 Read Aloud

✓ **Do children understand which parts of the story could be real and which could not?**

Build Background Tell children they will hear a story about a little girl who visits her grandmother. Display the flannel board characters. Tell children the girl wears a red cape with a hood, so she is called Little Red Riding Hood.

- Have children listen to find out which parts of the story could be real and which are make-believe.

Listen for Understanding Read "Little Red Riding Hood"/"Caperucita Roja" from the *Teacher's Tresure Book,* page 162, adding movement and varying your voice throughout to create the drama.

- When Little Red Riding Hood comments on the appearance of the wolf ("What big eyes you have"), invite children to recite the dialogue with you.

- Ask children to identify the first person who appears in the story. Then ask: *What is Little Red Riding Hood doing in the forest? Is the wolf real or make-believe? How do you know? ¿Qué hace Caperucita Roja en el bosque? ¿Es el lobo real o imaginario? ¿Cómo lo saben?*

Respond to the Story Talk about the adventures of Little Red Riding Hood. Ask: *Have you heard this story before? Was the story the same or different? If it was different, what was different about it? Why do you think Little Red Riding Hood didn't recognize the wolf? ¿Han oído este cuento antes? ¿Era igual o diferente? Si era diferente, ¿en qué era diferente? ¿Por qué creen que Caperucita Roja no reconoció al lobo?*

- Say that this story contains a lesson. Ask: *What is the lesson? ¿Cuál es la enseñanza?*

 Ask if there is a version of this story in the children's language of origin. If so, have them talk about the version they know.

Learn About Letters and Sounds

✓ **Can children identify the letters *Kk* and the sound /k/?**

Learn About the Letter *Kk* Display the *Kk* page of the *ABC Big Book,* and point to the kite. Ask: *What do you see? ¿Qué ven?* Repeat *kite,* stressing the /k/ sound. Continue with *key* and *king.* Then say: *circle, kangaroo, ladder, koala, van, pig, kite.* Have children clap when they hear a word that begins with /k/.

- Say the /k/ sound, and have children repeat it several times. Then point to the uppercase *K,* name it, and say its sound. Have children repeat several times. Slowly trace uppercase *K,* demonstrating how it is formed. Using the ABC Picture Card *Kk,* have volunteers repeat the process. Repeat the process with lowercase *k.*

- Conclude by reciting the alphabet together as you point to the corresponding *Alphabet Wall Cards.*

Teacher's Treasure Book, p. 162

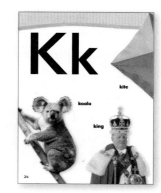

ABC Big Book, Letter Kk

large group · 15 minutes

Math Time

Observe and Investigate

 Can children sort objects?

Shhh...Watch Carefully Tell children they are still detectives. Now they are going to guess a sorting rule. Discuss sorting before children begin.

- Note: This lesson repeats the activity introduced on Day 2. Vary the game slightly, or increase the difficulty as children grasp the concepts.

- Say: *Watch carefully. I am going to sort these shapes. Miren atentamente. Voy a clasificar estas figuras.* Sort Shape Set shapes into piles based on a rule, such as circles versus squares, or four-sided shapes versus three-sided shapes. Put at least two shapes in each pile in front of you.

- Hold another shape over one pile and then the other. Say: *Which pile does this shape belong in? ¿A qué pila corresponde esta figura?* Have each child turn to a neighbor and talk about where the shape should go. Call on a volunteer to tell you what to do.

- After all the shapes are sorted, ask children to guess your rule. Ask: *What is my rule? ¿Cuál es mi regla?* Repeat with other shapes.

ELL Provide support by asking yes/no questions about the characteristics of each shape. *(Is this shape round? Does this shape have three sides?)* Point to the shapes as you ask questions.

large group · 15 minutes

Social and Emotional Development

Making Good Choices

 Can children recognize and communicate a problem?

 Can children initiate the need to ask for help in solving a problem?

Act It Out Tell children that they will use the puppets to act out a problem they have seen happen in the classroom.

- Say: *Let's name some problems that have happened in our class. Mencionemos algunos problemas que hayamos tenido en el salón de clases.* List the responses. Have children choose one scenario. Ask: *How did your friends solve the problem? How else could they have worked out the problem? ¿Cómo resolvieron sus amigos el problema? ¿Qué otra cosa podrían haber hecho para resolverlo?*

- Invite two children to use the puppets to act out the scenario. Ask: *Did the puppets work it out? Did they ask for help from someone? ¿Resolvieron los títeres el problema por sí solos? ¿Pidieron ayuda a alguien?* Continue with another scenario. Emphasize that everyone needs to ask for help sometimes. Discuss a time you asked for help to solve a problem.

Online Math Activity

Children can complete Mystery Pictures 2 and Memory Geometry 2 during computer time or Center Time.

 **Learning Goals**

Social and Emotional Development
- Child demonstrates initiative in independent activities; makes independent choices.
- Child initiates play scenarios with peers that share a common plan and goal.
- Child demonstrates appropriate conflict-resolution strategies, requesting help when needed.

Mathematics
- Child sorts objects and explains how the sorting was done.

Vocabulary

act out	representar	carefully	atentamente
help	ayudar	problem	problema
watch	mirar	work	trabajar

Differentiated Instruction

Extra Support
Math Time
If...children struggle to guess the sorting rule, **then...**use simpler sorting rules and more examples of shapes that fit the rule.

Enrichment
Social and Emotional Development
Offer praise to children who ask for help when they need it or who offer to help others when appropriate.

Accommodations for 3's
Math Time
If...children need reinforcement with the shapes, **then...**partner them with an older child to practice.

Social and Emotional Development
• Child is aware of self in terms of abilities, characteristics and preferences, and respects personal boundaries.

Mathematics
• Child recognizes, names, describes, matches, compares, sorts common two-dimensional shapes (such as circle, square, rectangle, triangle, rhombus).

• Child understands and uses words that describe position/location in space (such as under, over, beside, between, on, in, near, far away).

Vocabulary

detective	*detective*	find	*encontrar*
observe	*observar*		

Differentiated Instruction

Extra Support
Math Time
If...children struggle, **then...**place fewer Shape Set shapes, and refer repeatedly to them.

Enrichment
Math Time
Consider using other, more difficult, shapes such as isosceles triangles or shapes that are in different orientations.

Accommodations for 3's
Math Time
If...children have difficulty finding shapes, **then...**guide them around the room, asking yes/no questions about the shapes of objects.

Special Needs
Delayed Motor Development
Try assigning a peer buddy to partner with the child to explore the room and look for shapes.

large group   15 minutes

Math Time

Social Emotional Skills Model for children how to go around the room calmly looking for the appropriate shapes while respecting the space of others.

 Can children correctly identify shapes?

 Do children demonstrate understanding of location words?

I Spy Invite children to play another game of "detective." Tell them they are going to find shapes in the classroom. Discuss how detectives observe their environment.

● Before children arrive, place various Shape Set shapes throughout the classroom.

● Say: ***I am a detective. I spy a shape. It has three sides. It is next to a [object].*** *Soy detective. Veo una figura. Tiene tres lados. Está junto a [objeto].* Help children by giving them clues about the location of the shape. Allow children time to think about the meanings of the location words (*next, below, behind*, and so on) and then to look around the room to find the shape.

● When a child guesses the object correctly, say: ***Yes! That is the shape I spied. What is the name of the shape?*** *¡Sí! Esa es la figura que vi. ¿Cuál es el nombre de la figura?* Allow children time to give the name of the shape.

● Display *Math and Science Flip Chart*, page 30. Say: ***Which shape on the chart matches the shape I spied?*** *¿Qué figura del rotafolio coincide con la figura que vi?* Guide children to point to the shape on the chart.

● Ask the child who gave the correct answer to whisper another shape for the class to guess and find.

● As a variation, point to a shape on the *Math and Science Flip Chart* first, and then have children find the shape in the classroom. Say: ***I spy this shape. It is in the classroom. Can you find it?*** *Veo esta figura. Está en el salón de clases. ¿Pueden encontrarla?*

● Repeat with other shapes from the Shape Set.

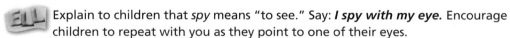 Explain to children that *spy* means "to see." Say: ***I spy with my eye.*** Encourage children to repeat with you as they point to one of their eyes.

● For additional suggestions on how to meet the needs of children at the Beginning, Intermediate, Advanced, and Advanced-High levels of English proficiency, see pages 184–187.

Math and Science Flip Chart, p. 30

Center Time

▶ **Center Rotation** Center Time includes teacher-guided activities and independent activities. Refer to the **Learning Centers** on pages 24–25 for independent activity ideas.

   small group 30 minutes

Math and Science Center | Center Tip

 **Can children match shapes to tracings of shapes?**

Materials tracings of shapes, shape sets

Match the Shape Give children tracings of shapes and foam Shape Sets. Ask children to match the foam shape to the traced shape.

- Make several shape sets, and trace each shape from the set onto a large sheet of paper.

- Guide children to match the shapes to the tracings. Give them a shape set, and say: *Can you match the shapes to the traced shape? ¿Pueden hacer coincidir las figuras con los contornos?*

Center Tip

If...children have difficulty matching the traced shape, **then...**demonstrate by placing a foam shape over a tracing, and talk about how it matches or does not match.

Purposeful Play

 Observe children matching shapes.

Children choose an open center for free playtime. Encourage children to trace shapes and then draw pictures over the tracings or color in the traced shapes.

Let's Say Good-Bye

  large group 15 minutes

Read Aloud Reread "Anansi and the Pot of Wisdom"/"Anansi y la olla de la sabiduría" for your afternoon Read Aloud. Have children listen for the /n/ sound.

Home Connection Refer to the Home Connections activities listed in the Resources and Materials chart on page 21. Remind children to look for shapes as they travel home. Sing the "Good-Bye Song"/"Hora de ir a casa" as children prepare to leave.

✓ Learning Goals

Emergent Literacy: Writing
• Child writes some letters or reasonable approximations of letters upon request.

Mathematics
• Child recognizes, names, describes, matches, compares, sorts common two-dimensional shapes (such as circle, square, rectangle, triangle, rhombus).

Writing

Recap the day by reviewing different shapes found in the classroom. Ask: *What shape is a window? What shape is the door? ¿Qué figura es la ventana? ¿Qué figura es la puerta?* Have children dictate or complete the following sentence frame: *The _____ has a _____ shape. El/la _____ tiene forma de _____.* Write shape names on chart paper or an interactive whiteboard for children to copy as needed.

Let's Start the Day

Focus Question

How can I learn by observing?

¿Qué puedo aprender observando las cosas?

Learning Goals

Language and Communication
• Child begins and ends conversations appropriately.
• Child uses newly learned vocabulary daily in multiple contexts.

Emergent Literacy: Reading
• Child blends onset and rime to form a word with pictoral support.

Vocabulary

cold	frío	detective	detective
feel	sentir	observe	investigar
see	ver	snowflake	copo de nieve
soft	suave		

Differentiated Instruction

 Extra Support

Phonological Awareness
If...children have difficulty blending sounds, **then...**work with them to say the onset and rime slowly, and then repeat more quickly until the sounds are blended: /c/...-old; /c/ -old, /c/ -old, *cold.*

 Enrichment

Oral Language and Vocabulary
Challenge pairs of children to create their own chant about how snowflakes look and feel.

Accommodations for **3's**

Phonological Awareness
If...three-year-olds have difficulty separating onset and rime, **then...**say the two parts, and have children repeat with you.

 Opening Routines and Transition Tips
For **Opening Routines** and **Transition Tips** turn to pages 178–181 and visit DLMExpressOnline.com for more ideas.

Read **"Going on a Whale Watch"**/*"Vamos a mirar ballenas"* from the *Teacher's Treasure Book*, page 202, for your morning Read Aloud.

Language Time

large group / 15 minutes

Social and Emotional Development Listen to children's conversations to determine if they are asking and answering questions to satisfy their own or others' curiosity.

Oral Language and Vocabulary

Can children use new vocabulary to describe a snowflake?

Snowflakes Remind children that they have learned to use all five senses to observe things. Ask: **What are your five senses?** *¿Cuáles son los cinco sentidos?* Help children recall all five senses, and then have them repeat the senses aloud after you.

● Review the *Rhymes and Chant Flip Chart*, page 17, with children. Ask: **Which words describe how a snowflake looks?** *¿Qué palabras describen el aspecto de un copo de nieve?*

● Remind children that there are many ways to describe how something feels. One can describe the temperature of something, the texture, the weight, and so on. Ask: **Which words describe how a snowflake feels?** *¿Qué palabras describen cómo se siente al tacto copo de nieve?*

ELL Help children understand the chant better by explaining difficult parts. For example, explain that the phrase *It floats like a feather* is a comparison describing the weight of the snowflake.

Phonological Awareness

Can children blend onset and rime to make words?

Blend Onset and Rime Review the *Rhymes and Chants Flip Chart*, page 17, again. Have children repeat the chant with you. Talk about the illustration. Then model how to blend the word *cold* with its onset /c/ and rime *-old*. Have children try it. Follow with more words from the chart: *soft, fall, felt, me, look.*

Teacher's Treasure Book, p. 202

I'm a Detective

I'm a detective.
What do I see?
I see a snowflake
In front of me.

So soft and white,
It floats like a feather
And falls to the ground
In cold winter weather.

Detectives write down
What is seen and is felt.
But I must look quickly,
Because snowflakes melt!

Rhymes and Chants Flip Chart, p. 17

Center Time

► **Center Rotation** Center Time includes teacher-guided activities and independent activities. Refer to the **Learning Centers** on pages 24–25 for independent activity ideas.

small group 60–90 minutes

Construction Center

 Do children express pride in learning about letter names?

 Can children use new vocabulary to describe something?

✓ Are children able to perform tasks needing small-muscle control?

Materials scissors, white paper folded into quarters, crayons, yarn

My Snowflake Tell children they will make a snowflake, write some descriptive words about it, and put their initials on it.

● Model making cuts on the folded paper. Say: *Cut small shapes out of the folded paper. Be sure to cut some shapes along the edges. Corten pequeñas figuras del papel doblado. Asegúrense de cortar algunas figuras por los bordes.* Unfold and display your snowflake. Help children cut out and write on the snowflake three words that describe a real snowflake.

● Have children put their initials on their snowflakes. Praise children's efforts as they learn and write their initials. Put a piece of yarn through each snowflake. Hang snowflakes around the classroom.

Center Tip

If...children cannot describe the snowflake, **then...** provide examples of descriptive words or ask questions about the snowflake; for example: *Is it hot? ¿Es caliente el copo de nieve?*

Pretend and Learn Center

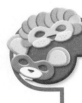

✓ Can children supply a rime to form a word when given an onset?

Materials dress-up clothes and props

Act Out Onset and Rime Display the *Rhymes and Chants Flip Chart*. Review the words. Tell children they are going to act out a word you give them. Explain that they say only the beginning of a word as they act out the word. Classmates will then guess the full word.

● Model acting out the word *fall.* Say: /f/, /f/, /f/. Pretend to fall on the floor. Guide children to supply the rime and finish the word.

● Whisper a word to one child at a time. Allow time for the child to act it out. Continue with words not in the chart.

Center Tip

If...children have difficulty taking turns in the Center, **then...**set a timer. When the timer goes off, it's time for others to share the activity.

Learning Goals

Social and Emotional Development
• Child identifies self by categories (such as gender, age, family member, cultural group).

Language and Communication
• Child uses newly learned vocabulary daily in multiple contexts.

Emergent Literacy: Reading
• Child blends onset and rime to form a word with pictoral support.

Physical Development
• Child develops small-muscle strength and control.

Differentiated Instruction

👋 Extra Support

Construction Center

If...children have difficulty constructing snowflakes, **then...**help them fold the paper, and then guide them to make the appropriate cuts.

⭐ Enrichment

Construction Center

Challenge children with good small-motor coordination to make additional snowflakes of various types.

Accommodations for 3's

Pretend and Learn Center

If...children are not confident enough to perform for the group in the Pretend and Learn Center, **then...**have them work one-on-one with a partner.

💜 Special Needs

Cognitive Challenges

Encourage the child to attempt an activity, even if it is difficult. If the child cannot fully participate, let her/him partially participate.

Focus Question

How can I learn by observing?

¿Qué puedo aprender observando las cosas?

Learning Goals

Emergent Literacy: Reading

• Child produces the most common sound for a given letter.

• Child describes, relates to, and uses details and information from books read aloud.

• Child asks and answers questions about books read aloud (such as, "Who?" "What?" "Where?").

Vocabulary

answer	respuesta	compare	comparar
curious	curioso	tools	instrumentos

Differentiated Instruction

 Extra Support

Read Aloud

If...children have difficulty matching the appropriate tool to the situation, **then...**ask leading questions, such as *If I want to cut a piece of paper to fit in an envelope, what tool can I use to measure before I cut? Si quiero cortar un trozo de papel para colocarlo en un sobre, ¿qué instrumento debo usar para medirlo antes de cortar?*

 Enrichment

Read Aloud

Encourage children to brainstorm and share other places they have seen tools used, such as in a kitchen or in a garage or workshop.

Accommodations for 3's

Read Aloud

Reread pages 22 and 23 of *Let's Investigate*. Have children compare two or three classroom items of varying sizes. Encourage them to use vocabulary such as *bigger, longer, small, tiny, huge.*

Literacy Time

large group / 15 minutes

📖 Read Aloud

✔️ **Do children exhibit and express curiosity about ideas raised in the book?**

Build Background Review with children that detectives and people who are curious look for answers to questions. Ask them to remember what tools detectives might use to find answers to questions like the following: ***How many spots does a ladybug have? How long is a footprint? ¿Cuántas manchas tiene una catarina? ¿Cuán pesada es una bolsa de manzanas? ¿Cuán larga es una huella?***

Review the tools children have used in the classroom. Ask them to think about ways similar tools are used in their everyday lives; for example, a scale is used at a grocery store to weigh fruits and vegetables.

Listen for Enjoyment Display *Let's Investigate*/Soy Detective. Tell children to think of questions they might have about the book as you reread it. As you point to each photo, ask children to identify the tools being used.

Respond to the Story Help answer questions that arose while you were reading.

● Explain that information gathering happens all around us. Ask children to think about when they visit the doctor. Tell children that a doctor is like a detective who needs to find information. Ask: ***What does the doctor use to measure how much you have grown? To check that your eyes are healthy? ¿Qué usa el médico para medir cuánto han crecido? ¿Y para revisar si sus ojos están saludables?***

● Ask children what other tools a doctor uses to find information.

ELL Children may not understand common comparisons used in the book. Help reinforce their understanding by using real-life examples. For instance, have a child hold a connecting cube in one hand and a full paint bottle in the other to demonstrate *heavier* and *lighter*; place a big book next to a small reader to demonstrate *big* and *small*; and so on.

TIP Label tools children are using in the classroom; for example, *scale, hand lens, ruler, connecting cubes.*

Learn About Letters and Sounds

✔️ **Can children identify the letters *Bb, Ii, Nn, Kk* and their sounds?**

Learn About *Bb, Ii, Nn, Kk* Using the *ABC Big Book,* review the letters children learned this week. Then ask children to name the letters that stand for the beginning sounds of these words: *bed, igloo, nest,* and *key.*

● Using the *ABC Picture Cards*, repeat each letter sound and show the card.

● Conclude by reciting the alphabet together as you point to the corresponding *Alphabet Wall Cards*. Then have children sing "The ABC Song."

Let's Investigate
Soy detective

ABC Big Book

large group 15 minutes

Math Time

Observe and Investigate

Can children determine which number is greater?

Compare Game Invite children to play the Compare Game. Tell children that they will have to know which number is greater. Divide children into pairs. Give each pair two or more sets of Counting Cards. Have children mix the cards and deal them evenly facedown.

- Say: ***Flip your card at the same time as your partner. Whose card is greater?*** *Den vuelta la tarjeta al mismo tiempo que su compañero. ¿Quién tiene la tarjeta con el número mayor?*
- Guide the child with the greater card to say "Mine!" Say: ***The person with the greater card gets both cards.*** *La persona con la tarjeta mayor se queda con las dos tarjetas.* If the cards are equal, guide children to say at the same time "No one!" Say: ***If no one's card is greater, flip over a new card with your partner. The next winner takes all the flipped cards.*** *Si nadie tiene la tarjeta mayor, den vuelta otra tarjeta. El siguiente ganador se queda todas las tarjetas dadas vuelta.* The game is over when all cards have been played, and the winner is the player with the most cards.

Building Blocks

Online Math Activity

Children can complete Mystery Pictures 2 and Memory Geometry 2 during computer time or Center Time.

large group 15 minutes

Social and Emotional Development

Making Good Choices

Do children show initiative in independent situations?

Can children interact and communicate with peers?

Talking with Peers Display the *Making Good Choices Flip Chart,* page 17. Review ways children can communicate ideas and resolve problems with one another.

- Point to the children in the block area. Ask: ***What might the child be saying as she taps the other child to get her attention? Do you think this is a better way to solve the problem than the girl who is angry? Why or why not?*** *¿Qué estará diciendo la niña que llama la atención del otro niño? ¿Creen que es una forma mejor de resolver diferencias que enojarse, como la otra niña? ¿Por qué?*
- Point to the children playing dress-up. Ask: ***Do you ever show your friends how you want to play something? What do you do if they don't want you to tell them how to do it?*** *¿Ustedes explican a sus amigos cómo quieren jugar? ¿Qué hacen si ellos no quieren que les digan qué hacer?*

Have children look around the room at their classmates. Say: ***Every one of you can be a helper. What would you do if your friend asked you to help him/her work out a problem with another classmate?*** *Todos pueden ayudar. ¿Qué harían si un amigo les pide ayuda para resolver un problema con otro compañero?* Discuss responses, and praise good ideas. Encourage all children to respond.

Making Good Choices Flip Chart, p. 17

Learning Goals

Social and Emotional Development

- Child demonstrates initiative in independent activities; makes independent choices.
- Child initiates play scenarios with peers that share a common plan and goal.

Mathematics

- Child tells how many are in a group of up to 5 objects without counting.

Vocabulary

cards	tarjetas	compare	comparar
greater	mayor	help	ayudar
problem	diferencia	solve	resolver

Differentiated Instruction

Extra Support

Observe and Investigate

If...children are having difficulty with the Counting Cards, **then...**use cards with numbers 1 to 3 only.

Enrichment

Observe and Investigate

Challenge children by having players count dot pairs instead of cards.

Accommodations for 3's

Making Good Choices

If...children are unsure of when to ask for help, **then...**act out situations in which you have trouble, and ask a child for help.

Special Needs

Hearing Impairment

Make sure the child is able to hear the rules of the Compare Game and understands them.

Focus Question

How can I learn by observing?

¿Qué puedo aprender observando las cosas?

 Learning Goals

Mathematics

• Child recognizes, names, describes, matches, compares, sorts common two-dimensional shapes (such as circle, square, rectangle, triangle, rhombus).

• Child sorts objects and explains how the sorting was done.

Fine Arts

• Child uses and experiments with a variety of art materials and tools in various art activities.

Vocabulary

circle	círculo	rectangle	rectángulo
side	lado	square	cuadrado
triangle	triángulo		

Differentiated Instruction

 Extra Support

Observe and Investigate

If...children have difficulty determining the number of sides each shape has, **then...**show them an example, and have them count the sides aloud with you.

 Enrichment

Observe and Investigate

Challenge children to create a drawing using only shapes.

Accommodations for 3's

Oral Language and Academic Vocabulary

If...children have difficulty describing the characteristics of shapes, **then...**help them by giving them specific vocabulary, such as *sides, long, short,* and so on.

Art Time

Oral Language and Academic Vocabulary

✓ **Can children name and describe the characteristics of common shapes?**

Ask children to name different shapes they have learned in this unit.

● Discuss the characteristics of each shape. Ask: ***How many sides does a square have? A rectangle? A triangle? What is a circle like?*** *¿Cuántos lados tiene un cuadrado? ¿Un rectángulo? ¿Un triángulo? ¿Qué aspecto tiene un círculo?* Encourage children to describe other shapes.

● Ask children to name common items that have these shapes.

Observe and Investigate

✓ **Do children use a variety of art materials for exploration?**

✓ **Can children sort objects and describe how the items are the same and how they are different?**

Ask children to talk about shapes in art. Have available various books of paintings and/or photographs that include squares, circles, triangles, and rectangles. Display some of the books for the children. Ask: ***Can you find anything in this picture that looks like a circle?*** *¿Pueden encontrar algo en esta imagen que parezca un círculo?*

● Challenge children to tell you why these shapes are circles.

● Follow the same process with other drawings/photographs and shapes.

● Then point out two objects that are different shapes. Ask: ***Are these shapes the same or different?*** *¿Son estas figuras iguales o diferentes?* Guide children to tell you what shape each object is.

 Give children cutouts of a circle, a square, a rectangle, and a triangle. Encourage children to hold up the correct cutout as you call out the name of each shape. Then have children repeat the name of the shape aloud as they hold up the cutouts.

● For additional suggestions on how to meet the needs of children at the Beginning, Intermediate, Advanced, and Advanced-High levels of English proficiency, see pages 184–187.

Center Time

▶ **Center Rotation** Center Time includes teacher-guided activities and independent activities. Refer to the **Learning Centers** on pages 24–25 for independent activity ideas.

small group 30 minutes

Library and Listening Center

✓ **Can children observe the properties of common shapes and sort them?**

Materials books of shapes, pictures of shapes, various objects of different shapes, hand lens

Look for Shapes Have children look through books and pictures to choose a favorite shape. Tell children to find objects similar to that shape around the classroom. If possible, take groups outside to look for more shapes. Encourage children to complete this sentence frame as they find an object: *A <coin> is a <circle> shape. Un/una <moneda> tiene forma de <círculo>.*

● Allow children to use the hand lens to look around for objects.

● Have children combine their shapes into piles.

Center Tip

If...children have difficulty finding objects, **then...**ask questions to help them, such as *What shape is a book?* *¿Qué forma tiene un libro?*

Learning Goals

Social and Emotional Development
• Child demonstrates initiative in independent activities; makes independent choices.

Emergent Literacy: Writing
• Child writes some letters or reasonable approximations of letters upon request.

Mathematics
• Child recognizes, names, describes, matches, compares, sorts common two-dimensional shapes (such as circle, square, rectangle, triangle, rhombus).
• Child sorts objects and explains how the sorting was done.

Science
• Child uses senses to observe, classify, investigate, and collect data.

Social Studies
• Child participates in voting for group decision-making.

Purposeful Play

✓ **Can children persist in attempting to solve a problem?**

Encourage children to work with partners to search for more objects that are similar to shapes. Challenge children to explain how the objects are the same as those shapes and different from other shapes.

Writing

Recap the week's activities. Help children describe a favorite activity. After polling the children, write a sentence about the most-often mentioned activity as children watch. Have children copy the sentence or any letters they are able to write, draw a picture, and take their work home to share with their family.

Let's Say Good-Bye

large group 15 minutes

 Read Aloud Reread "Going on a Whale Watch"/"Vamos a mirar ballenas" for your afternoon Read Aloud. As you read, have children listen for the sounds the names of members of their family begin with.

 Home Connection Refer to the Home Connections activities listed in the Resources and Materials chart on page 21. Remind children to act like detectives as they look for shapes around their house. Sing the "Good-Bye Song"/"Hora de ir a casa" as children prepare to leave.

Week 2

Focus Question

How can I use tools to investigate?

¿Qué instrumentos puedo usar para investigar?

This week children will learn to use simple tools as they study common objects. They will role-play asking for directions and hear a story about a little boy who cooks with his mother. Children will predict which of two items is heavier, and they will use a balance scale to check their predictions.

✓ Learning Goals

Social and Emotional Development	1	2	3	4	5
Child is aware of self in terms of abilities, characteristics and preferences, and respects personal boundaries.					✓
Child demonstrates initiative in independent activities; makes independent choices.				✓	✓
Child shows eagerness, curiosity, and confidence while learning new concepts and trying new things.	✓				
Child demonstrates positive social behaviors, as modeled by the teacher.					✓
Child initiates play scenarios with peers that share a common plan and goal.	✓	✓	✓		✓
Child understands that others have specific attributes and characteristics.			✓		

Language and Communication	1	2	3	4	5
Child demonstrates an understanding of oral language by responding appropriately.	✓		✓		
Child follows two- and three-step oral directions.			✓		✓
Child names and describes actual or pictured people, places, things, actions, attributes, and events.	✓		✓	✓	✓
Child exhibits an understanding of instructional terms used in the classroom.	✓				
Child uses newly learned vocabulary daily in multiple contexts.			✓	✓	
Child builds English listening and speaking vocabulary for common objects and phrases. (ELL)			✓		

Emergent Literacy: Reading	1	2	3	4	5
Child enjoys and chooses reading-related activities.			✓	✓	✓
Child blends onset and rime to form a word with pictoral support.	✓	✓	✓	✓	✓
Child names most upper- and lowercase letters of the alphabet.			✓	✓	
Child identifies the letter that stands for a given sound.	✓	✓		✓	✓
Child produces the most common sound for a given letter.			✓		✓
Child retells or reenacts poems and stories in sequence.					✓
Child describes, relates to, and uses details and information from books read aloud.			✓	✓	✓
Child asks and answers questions about books read aloud (such as, "Who?" "What?" "Where?").			✓	✓	✓

Emergent Literacy: Writing	1	2	3	4	5
Child participates in free drawing and writing activities to deliver information.		✓	✓	✓	
Child experiments with and uses some writing conventions when writing or dictating.				✓	

Mathematics	1	2	3	4	5
Child understands that objects, or parts thereof, can be counted.		✓			
Child demonstrates that, when counting, the last number indicates how many objects were counted.		✓			
Child recognizes and names numerals 0 through 9.		✓			
Child understands and uses words that describe position/location in space (such as under, over, beside, between, on, in, near, far away).			✓		
Child explores capacity; recognizes how much can be placed in a container.	✓		✓	✓	✓
Child compares the length, height, weight, volume (capacity), area of people or objects.	✓	✓		✓	✓

Science	1	2	3	4	5
Child uses senses to observe, classify, investigate, and collect data.	✓				
Child uses basic measuring tools to learn about objects.	✓				
Child follows basic health and safety rules.					✓

Social Studies	1	2	3	4	5
Child identifies common areas and features of home, school, and community.			✓		

Fine Arts	1	2	3	4	5
Child uses and experiments with a variety of art materials and tools in various art activities.		✓			
Child expresses ideas, emotions, and moods through individual and collaborative dramatic play.		✓			

Physical Development	1	2	3	4	5
Child coordinates body movements in a variety of locomotive activities (such as walking, jumping, running, hopping, skipping, climbing).					✓
Child engages in a sequence of movements to perform a task.					✓
Child develops small-muscle strength and control.	✓			✓	

Technology	1	2	3	4	5
Child knows some ways that technology affects people's lives.	✓				

Materials and Resources

DAY 1	DAY 2	DAY 3	DAY 4	DAY 5
Program Materials				
• Teacher's Treasure Book • Oral Language Development Card 33 • Rhymes and Chants Flip Chart • Book: *I Like Making Tamales* • ABC Big Book • ABC Picture Cards • Alphabet Wall Cards • Building Blocks Online Math Activities • Math and Science Flip Chart • Making Good Choices Flip Chart • Primary Balance Scale • Connecting Cubes • Home Connections Resource Guide	• Teacher's Treasure Book • Book: *I Like Making Tamales* • Dog Puppets • ABC Picture Cards • Alphabet Wall Cards • Building Blocks Online Math Activities • Making Good Choices Flip Chart • Primary Balance Scale • Math and Science Flip Chart	• Teacher's Treasure Book • Oral Language Development Card 34 • Rhymes and Chants Flip Chart • Concept Big Book 2: *Let's Investigate* • ABC Big Book • Making Good Choices Flip Chart • Dog Puppets	• Teacher's Treasure Book • Oral Language Development Card 33 • Rhymes and Chants Flip Chart • Dog Puppets • Book: *I Like Making Tamales* • Primary Balance Scale • Building Blocks Online Math Activities • Two-Color Counters • Home Connections Resource Guide	• Teacher's Treasure Book • Rhymes and Chants Flip Chart • Book: *I Like Making Tamales* • ABC Big Book • Two-Color Counters • Making Good Choices Flip Chart • ABC Picture Cards
Other Materials				
• potting soil • fiber/plastic trays • craft sticks, index cards, tape • crayons, markers • varied seed packets • watering can • picture cards of one-syllable words • objects to weigh and measure • containers for pouring/measuring • water table • sand, scoop	• kitchen props (bowls, spoons, pretend food, etc.) • paper, crayons, markers, scissors • magazines with food photographs • 2 sets building blocks, different sizes • small objects to weigh • glue sticks	• small cup, masking tape • containers of many different sizes • small objects (pennies, marbles) • images of 10 people of varying characteristics (tall/short; old/young; male/female; with/without hats; and so on) • poster board • sand or other pourable material • containers for pouring/measuring • blindfold • maps, book, lunch bag, backpack	• paper, crayons, markers, pencils • aluminum foil • play clay or cotton • diagrams of how to fold tamales • colored paper plates • objects of different weights • box with lid • containers of 2, 4, 8 cup volumes • 1-cup measuring cup • water, sand • eight different-sized containers • sand or other pourable material	• small toys for dipping in paint • paints, paper • containers of many different sizes and shapes • water or sand • lively music • picture cards of moving objects • box
Home Connection				
Encourage children to explain to their families what they learned about comparing the weights of objects. Send home the following materials: • Weekly Parent Letter, Home Connections Resource Guide, pp. 39 - 40	Invite children to act out for their family how a balance scale works, using their arms and body.	Remind children to take home their maps and explain them to their families.	Encourage children to play Ten Questions at home with their families. Send home the following materials: • Storybook 10, Home Connections Resource Guide, pp. 117–120	Remind children to talk with their families about the measuring activity and what they learned from it.

Assessment

As you observe children throughout the week, you may fill out an Anecdotal Observational Record Form to document an individual's progress toward a goal or signs indicating the need for developmental or medical evaluation. You may also choose to select work for each child's portfolio. The Anecdotal Observational Record Form and Weekly Assessment rubrics are available in the assessment section of DLMExpressOnline.com.

More Literature Suggestions

• **You Can Use a Magnifying Glass** by Wiley Blevins
• **Weight** by Henry Arthur Pluckrose
• **Inch by Inch** by Leo Leonni
• **Counting on Frank** by Rod Clement
• **Mi mano es una regla** por Kim Seong-Eun

Daily Planner

		DAY 1	**DAY 2**
Let's Start the Day **Language Time**	large group	**Opening Routines** p. 64 **Morning Read Aloud** p. 64 **Oral Language and Vocabulary** p. 64 Exploring Gardens **Phonological Awareness** p. 64 Review Blending Sounds	**Opening Routines** p. 70 **Morning Read Aloud** p. 70 **Oral Language and Vocabulary** p. 70 What Does Kiko Do? **Phonological Awareness** p. 70 Blend Onset and Rime
Center Time	small group	**Focus On:** **Construction Center** p. 65 **ABC Center** p. 65	**Focus On:** **Pretend and Learn Center** p. 71 **Creativity Center** p. 71
Circle Time **Literacy Time**	large group	**Read Aloud** *I Like Making Tamales*/*Me gusta hacer tamales* p. 66 **Learn About Letters and Sounds:** **Learn About *Bb* and *Ii*** p. 66	**Read Aloud** *I Like Making Tamales* p. 72 **Learn About Letters and Sounds:** **Learn About the Letters *Bb* and *Ii*** p. 72
Math Time	large group	**Compare Weights** p. 67	**Mr. Mixup** p. 73
Social and Emotional Development	large group	**Find Out What You Don't Know** p. 67	**Understanding Making Plans** p. 73
Content Connection	large group	**Science:** **Oral Language and Academic Vocabulary** p. 68 **Observe and Investigate** p. 68	**Math:** **Weigh Blocks** p. 74
Center Time	small group	**Focus On:** **Math and Science Center** p. 69 **Purposeful Play** p. 69	**Focus On:** **Math and Science Center** p. 75 **Purposeful Play** p. 75
Let's Say Good-Bye	large group	**Read Aloud** p. 69 **Writing** p. 69 **Home Connection** p. 69	**Read Aloud** p. 75 **Writing** p. 75 **Home Connection** p. 75

DAY 3

Opening Routines p. 76
Morning Read Aloud p. 76
Oral Language and Vocabulary
p. 76 Full or Empty
Phonological Awareness p. 76
Review Combining Onset
and Rime

Focus On:
ABC Center p. 77
Library and Listening Center p. 77

Read Aloud
Let's Investigate/
Soy detective p. 78
**Learn About Letters and
Sounds: Learn About
Letters Bb and Ii** p. 78

Which Holds More? p. 79

Generating Ideas p. 79

Social Studies:
Oral Language and Academic Vocabulary
p. 80 Talking About Where We Are
Understand and Participate
p. 80 Making a Map

Focus On:
Pretend and Learn Center p. 81
Purposeful Play p. 81

Read Aloud p. 81
Free Writing p. 81
Home Connection p. 81

DAY 4

Opening Routines p. 82
Morning Read Aloud p. 82
Oral Language and Vocabulary
p. 82 Describing Environments
Phonological Awareness
p. 82 Review Combining Sounds

Focus On:
Writer's Center p. 83
Construction Center p. 83

Read Aloud "The Crow and the Pitcher"/
"El cuervo y el cántaro"
p. 84
Learn About Letters and Sounds: Bb and Ii
p. 84

Compare Weights p. 85

Show Curiosity p. 85

Math:
How Much Does It Hold? p. 86

Focus On:
Math and Science Center p. 87
Purposeful Play p. 87

Read Aloud p. 87
Writing p. 87
Home Connection p. 87

DAY 5

Opening Routines p. 88
Morning Read Aloud p. 88
Oral Language and Vocabulary
p. 88 Leaving Tracks
Phonological Awareness
p. 88 Review Onset and Rime

Focus On:
Library and Listening Center p. 89
Creativity Center p. 89

Read Aloud
*I Like Making Tamales/Me gusta hacer
tamales* p. 90
**Learn About Letters and
Sounds: The Letters
Bb and Ii** p. 90

Which Holds More? p. 91

Initiative and Persistence p. 91

Science:
Seesaw Scale p. 92

Focus On:
Pretend and Learn Center p. 93
Purposeful Play p. 93

Read Aloud p. 93
Writing p. 93
Home Connection p. 93

Week 2

My Detective's Tools

Learning Centers

Math and Science Center

Volume
Children fill containers to determine volume, p. 69

Compare Weights
Children use a scale to compare weights of objects, p. 75

Compare Capacities
Children experiment to see how much a container can hold, p. 87

Cube Box
Provide a small square box. Children fill the box with connecting cubes and count how many fit in the box.

Observe Objects
Supply a hand lens and various common objects, such as fabric, shells, feathers, and so on. Children use the hand lens to observe and describe objects.

ABC Center

Combine Sounds
Children use pictures to combine onset and rime, p. 65

Recognizing Letters
Children play hopscotch using letters, p. 77

Lining Up Letters
Each child chooses three letters. One child places the letters in alphabetical order. Each subsequent child inserts his/her letters into the sequence, with the goal of lining up the alphabet.

Letter Soup
Lay out children's name tags on the table. Put alphabet letter tiles in a bag. Children draw one tile and try to identify all their classmates whose names begin with that letter. Then they gather all the name tags that begin with that letter and put them in a pile with the tile on top.

Creativity Center

Make a Cookbook
Children put together favorite recipes into a book, p. 71

Make Tracks
Children use paint to make mysterious tracks, p. 89

Hot Box, Cold Box
Children make a Hot Box or a Cold Box by gluing pictures of things that are hot or cold on the outside of a box. Throughout the week, children fill their boxes with pictures of hot or cold items.

Close Up
Children use hand lenses to examine a leaf. Then they draw the leaf with crayon, bearing down hard. Children paint over the page with thin paint and watch the leaf come through!

Map It Out
Pairs make a map of the classroom, including doors and windows. Encourage simple language that shows understanding of direction and location. (next to, behind, and so on.)

Library and Listening Center

Look Closely Game
Children use clues to identify people, p. 77

Act Out the Chant
Children use a chant to act out various roles, p. 89

Sound Effects
Children listen to a story and decide which sound effects should accompany the events. Then, as they listen again, they supply the appropriate sounds.

Fabulous Food
Children read another book in which food is an important part of the story, such as *Bee-Bim Bop!* by Linda Sue Park. Then they compare that book to *I Like Making Tamales*.

Listen to Big Book
Children listen in pairs to *I Like Making Tamales* and discuss things in the illustrations that help them understand the story.

Construction Center

Making Seedling Trays
Children plant seeds, p. 65

Making Tamales
Children make tamales out of corn husks and clay, p. 83

Footprints to the Castle
Children build a castle. Others trace their footprints on heavy paper and tape the tracings to the floor to indicate paths. Footprints on one path have a dot on them; this path leads to the castle. Children use hand lenses to observe the footprints and find the path to the castle.

Build a Map
Children use building materials to build a map of the school. They build the school and areas around the school, including roads, parking lot, playground.

Test the Bridge
Children build a poster board bridge. They experiment placing various items on the bridge to test predictions about whether the bridge will collapse.

Writer's Center

Describing Plans
Children draw pictures of detectives, p. 83

Special Objects
Provide rocks, seeds, shells, etc. Children choose one object, draw it, describe what is special about it, and label its special characteristics.

Where Is It?
Children draw a picture of a book under a table and an apple on top of the table. They write to complete the following sentence frames:
The apple is _____ the table.
The book is _____ the table.

Folktale Lessons
Discuss lessons from folktales. Ask children to think of a lesson and make up a story to teach that lesson. Have them draw and label pictures of the characters in the setting.

Finding Home
Children think about someone who is lost and how the person gets home safely, and they illustrate the story.

Pretend and Learn Center

Make a Family Meal
Children pretend to make and eat a meal, p. 71

Asking for Directions
Children role-play asking for directions, p. 81

What Is It?
Children act out and identify moving objects, p. 93

To The Market
Ask children to pretend to be in a market. Have them compare fruits and vegetables they are thinking of buying, using a scale for weighing.

Giving Advice
Provide baking utensils, bowls, spoons, aprons, etc. Children plan how to make a cake together to celebrate Fun Friday at school. Then they act out the process of making the cake.

Let's Start the Day

Focus Question

How can I use tools to investigate?

¿Qué instrumentos puedo usar para investigar?

Learning Goals

Social and Emotional Development
• Child initiates play scenarios with peers that share a common plan and goal.

Language and Communication
• Child exhibits an understanding of instructional terms used in the classroom.

Emergent Literacy: Reading
• Child blends onset and rime to form a word with pictoral support.

Vocabulary

flowers	flores	garden	jardín
hand lens	lupa	hold	sujetar
investigate	investigar	tool	instrumento

Differentiated Instruction

Extra Support

Phonological Awareness
If...children have difficulty combining sounds, **then...**model for children the onset and rime in a few familiar one-syllable words. End by repeating the blended words together.

Enrichment

Oral Language and Vocabulary
Challenge children to draw a picture of a garden and label the things in the garden.

Accommodations for 3's

Phonological Awareness
If...three-year-olds have difficulty understanding how the speaker in the rhyme figured out what made the tracks, **then...**talk about what happens when someone walks in mud or water and the kind of trail they leave.

▶ Opening Routines and Transition Tips

For **Opening Routines** and **Transition Tips** turn to pages 178–181 and visit **DLMExpressOnline.com** for more ideas.

Read **"Going on a Trail Ride"/"Vamos a un paseo por el camino"** from the *Teacher's Treasure Book,* page 191, for your morning Read Aloud.

large group | 15 minutes

Language Time

Social and Emotional Development Ask children if they have ever pretended to be detectives. Ask volunteers to describe what they did.

Oral Language and Vocabulary

✓ Do children understand terms used in classroom instruction?

Exploring Gardens Talk about gardens. Ask: *Do you know what a garden is? ¿Saben qué es un jardín?* Point out that there are many kinds of gardens. Ask: *Can you name some things that grow in gardens? Have you ever helped in a garden? What did you do? ¿Qué plantas crecen en los jardines y huertas? ¿Alguna vez han ayudado en un jardín? ¿Qué hicieron?*

● Display *Oral Language Development Card 33*. Point to the illustration, and explain that the picture shows children exploring a garden. Then follow the suggestions on the back of the card.

Oral Language Development Card 33

Phonological Awareness

✓ Can children blend onset and rime in one-syllable words?

Review Blending Sounds Display the *Rhymes and Chants Flip Chart*, page 18. Read the rhyme aloud. Allow students to ask questions, and clarify unfamiliar words or ideas from the rhyme. Say: *I will say a word. Listen to the sounds, say the word, and point to the picture of the word on the chart. Voy a decir una palabra. Escuchen los sonidos, digan la palabra y señalen la ilustración correspondiente en el rotafolio.* /tr/ (pause) -acks /tr/ (pause) -acks. Help children blend the sounds and find the tracks in the picture.

Repeat with other words pictured on the chart, such as *shed, fence,* and *bed*.

ELL Use the illustrations in the *Rhymes and Chants Flip Chart* to provide visual support for new words such as *tracks, cucumber,* and *shed*.

● For additional suggestions on how to meet the needs of children at the Beginning, Intermediate, Advanced, and Advanced-High levels of English proficiency, see pages 184–187.

Rhymes and Chants Flip Chart, p. 18

Center Time

▶ **Center Rotation** Center Time includes teacher-guided activities and independent activities. Refer to the **Learning Centers** on pages 62–63 for independent activity ideas.

 small group 60–90 minutes

Construction Center

✓ **Can children use a variety of words to label things?**

✓ **Do children show the ability to perform tasks that require small-muscle control?**

Materials potting soil, fiber or plastic trays (2–3 inches deep), craft sticks, crayons/markers, varied packets of seeds, index cards, tape

Making Seedling Trays Invite children to grow their own plants. Remind them that plants need light, soil, and water in order to grow.

● Display a variety of seed packets for children to examine. Allow children to choose one or two packets of seeds. Give each child a tray. Help the children fill the trays with potting soil.

● Ask: *How will we remember what kind of seeds we're planting? ¿Cómo recordaremos qué semillas estamos sembrando?* Show children how to make labels by drawing a picture on half an index card, taping it to a craft stick, and inserting the stick into the soil.

● Determine how deep to plant the seeds. Mark a craft stick with the measurement, and model using the stick to make a trough in the soil at the right depth. Demonstrate how to place the seeds.

● Ask: *What do we need to do next? ¿Qué debemos hacer a continuación?* (Water the plants, and put them in light.) Remind children to clean up as necessary.

Center Tip
If...children have difficulty making labels, **then...**allow them to tape the seed packets to craft sticks.

ABC Center

✓ **Observe to see if children can blend onset and rime.**

Materials *Photo Library* CD-ROM, picture cards of familiar one-syllable words such as *book, desk, car, dog.*

Combine Sounds Invite pairs to combine onset and rime.

● Children should look at a card and decide what the word is: *book.*

● One child should say the onset /b/ while the other completes the rime -*ook*. Children should then combine the word together.

Center Tip
If...children have difficulty blending the sounds, **then...** model the activity with a child before Center Time.

✓ Learning Goals

Language and Communication
• Child names and describes actual or pictured people, places, things, actions, attributes, and events.

Emergent Literacy: Reading
• Child blends onset and rime to form a word with pictoral support.

Physical Development
• Child develops small-muscle strength and control.

Differentiated Instruction

 Extra Support
Construction Center
If...children have difficulty planting seeds at the proper depth, **then...**help them make the indentations for the seeds.

 Enrichment
Construction Center
Challenge children to label their plants by copying the name of the plant from the seed packet.

Accommodations for 3's
Construction Center
If...three-year-olds have difficulty drawing a flower or a vegetable, **then...**allow them to make a scribble instead, using a crayon corresponding to the plant's color.

 Special Needs
Hearing Impairment
Use the Sequence Cards set "Seed to Flower" to cue the child about the activity. Make sure the child understands that a seed is planted, grows, and then becomes a plant such as a flower, a tree, and so on. Present this sequence prior to Center Time each day this week.

large group 15 minutes

 Learning Goals

Language and Communication
• Child demonstrates an understanding of oral language by responding appropriately.

Emergent Literacy: Reading
• Child names most upper- and lowercase letters of the alphabet.

Vocabulary

broth	caldo	corn husk	hojas de maíz
package	amasar	tamale	tamal

 Differentiated Instruction

 Extra Support

Read Aloud

If...children have difficulty figuring out the process for making tamales, **then...**review the illustrations, asking questions about each step involved.

 Enrichment

Read Aloud

Have children retell the story in their own words.

Accommodations for 3's

Read Aloud

If...three-year-olds don't understand how Kiko makes corn husks into packages, **then...**use a piece of paper to demonstrate.

♥ Special Needs

Vision Loss

Give the child an actual corn husk and corn meal to feel and smell as you read the book *I Like Making Tamales/ Me gusta hacer tamales.*

Literacy Time

 Read Aloud

✓ **Can children answer questions about the story?**

Build Background Tell children you will be reading the book *I Like Making Tamales.*

● Ask: *Have you ever helped cook in the kitchen? Who was with you? What did you make? What do you enjoy about cooking? ¿Alguna vez ayudaron a cocinar en la cocina? ¿Quién estaba con ustedes? ¿Qué prepararon? ¿Qué es lo que disfrutan de cocinar?*

Listen for Enjoyment Display *I Like Making Tamales/Me gusta hacer tamales,* and read the title. Ask children to tell what they know about cooking. Have anyone who has eaten or made tamales explain what they are.

● Read the story, pausing to give children time to view the illustrations.

● Discuss ways people can learn new things. Ask children to expain how they learn. Point out that a good way to learn is by working side by side with someone who can show you what to do.

● Have children tell about a time they learned something new from a family member. Say: *Sometimes we can learn from our brothers or sisters. Sometimes we learn from grown-ups, such as a parent or grandparent. Who is teaching Kiko to make tamales? A veces podemos aprender de nuestros hermanos o hermanas. A veces aprendemos de los adultos, como los padres o los abuelos. ¿Quién le enseña a Kiko a preparar tamales?*

Respond to the Story Discuss the story. Ask children why it is sometimes easier to learn something if you watch someone else make it first or at the same time. Use pictures to explain the meaning of *broth, dough, flour,* and *corn husks.*

ELL Talk about the words *heavy* and *light.* Ask children to name things that are heavy and things that are light. Point out that the pot Kiko picks up is heavy. Talk about other objects that can be heavy or light, such as a table or a corn husk.

Learn About Letters and Sounds

✓ **Can children identify the letters and sounds for *Bb* and *ii*?**

Learn About *Bb* and *Ii* Display the *Bb* page of the *ABC Big Book,* and point to the ball. Ask: *What do you see? ¿Qué ven?* Repeat *ball,* emphasizing the /b/ sound that begins it. Continue with *bee.* Then say the following words one at a time: *bed, book, bear.* Have children repeat each word. Add the names of any children whose names begin with *Bb.*

● Then point to uppercase *B,* name it, and say its sound. Have children repeat several times. Slowly trace uppercase *B,* demonstrating how it is formed. Using the *ABC Picture Card Bb,* have volunteers repeat the process. Repeat with lowercase *b.*

● Repeat the activity with the letter *Ii.*

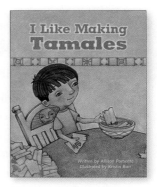

I Like Making Tamales
Me gusta hacer tamales

ABC Big Book

Math Time

large group 15 minutes

Observe and Investigate

✓ **Can children recognize and compare the weights of people and objects?**

Compare Weights Tell children they are going to compare weights of objects. Discuss that some people and things are heavier than others and some people and things are lighter than others. Ask: *Which is lighter, a baby or a grown-up? Which is heavier, a box of crayons or a box of markers? Sometimes it's not clear just by looking which person or object weighs more than another. We use tools to show us what is lighter and what is heavier.* *¿Qué es más liviano: un bebé o un adulto? ¿Qué es más pesado: una caja de crayones o una caja de marcadores? A veces no sabemos si un si una persona o un objeto pesa más que otro con sólo mirarlo. Usamos instrumentos para descubrirlo.*

● Introduce a balance scale to children. Say: *This is a balance scale. It is a tool used to compare the weights of two objects. When I put one object on one side and another on the other side, the side with the heavier object will move down and the side with the lighter object will move up. If two objects weigh the same, they will be at the same level. Let me show you.* *Esto es una balanza de platillos. Es un instrumento que se usa para comparar los pesos de dos objetos. Cuando pongo un objeto de cada lado, el platillo con el objeto más pesado baja y el otro sube. Si los dos objetos pesan lo mismo, la balanza queda en equilibrio. Déjenme mostrarles.*

● Demonstrate how the scale works with objects of varying weights. Say: *What do you think will happen if I put these objects on the scale? Which is heavier? Which side will go down?* *¿Qué creen que sucederá si coloco estos objetos en la balanza? ¿Cuál es más pesado? ¿Qué platillo bajará?* Have children pretend they are scales and "tip" from one side to the other. Give children objects of different weights to hold and experiment with.

✗✗✗ Social and Emotional Development

large group 15 minutes

Making Good Choices

✓ **Do children interact with peers to initiate scenarios with a common goal?**

Find Out What You Don't Know Discuss ways people gather information.

● Ask children to think of ways they see people working together to get information. Make a list on the board with their responses. Display the *Making Good Choices Flip Chart*, page 18. Help children act out ideas from the chart about how to answer questions and work together.

● Ask: *What are some ways you could use technology to gather information?* *¿De qué maneras podemos usar la tecnología para reunir información?* Remind children that tools such as computers and phones can also help them gather information.

Making Good Choices Flip Chart, p. 18

Building Blocks

Online Math Activity

Introduce Comparisons, in which children use and apply direct comparison. They click on the object that is longer, wider, taller, or the like than another object. Each child should complete the activity this week.

✓ **Learning Goals**

Social and Emotional Development
• Child initiates play scenarios with peers that share a common plan and goal.

Mathematics
• Child compares the length, height, weight, volume (capacity), area of people or objects.

Technology
• Child knows some ways that technology affects people's lives.

Vocabulary

heavy	pesado	detective	detective
scale	balanza	weight	peso

Differentiated Instruction

✋ **Extra Support**

Observe and Investigate

If...children associate the scale going up with a heavier weight, **then...**demonstrate, using a real scale, that when one side of the scale goes up, it means the object on that side is lighter than the object on the other side.

⭐ **Enrichment**

Observe and Investigate

Challenge children by having them predict weights of objects that are large but light and small but heavy.

Accommodations for 3's

Observe and Investigate

If...children have difficulty pretending to be scales, **then...**provide individual support.

Science Time

 large group · 20 minutes

Social and Emotional Skills If children seem distracted, use questions and invite individuals to participate to help children regain focus.

Oral Language and Academic Vocabulary

✓ **Can children use a balance scale to identify which of two objects is heavier?**

Balancing Point to the objects on the balance scale in the *Math and Science Flip Chart*, page 31. Point to the balance in the picture. Say: ***This a a balance scale. A balance scale tells you what is heavier and what is lighter.*** *Esto es una balanza. Una balanza se usa para ver qué objetos son más pesados y cuáles son más livianos.*

● Show children a heavy object and a light object. Have a volunteer place one object on each side of the balance. Ask: ***Which object is lower, or closer to the table? What do you think that means?*** *¿Qué objeto está más abajo, o más cerca de la mesa? ¿Qué creen que significa eso?* Guide children to see which object is heavier.

● Ask: ***Which object is higher, or farther from the table? What do you think that means?*** *¿Qué objeto está más arriba, o más lejos de la mesa? ¿Qué creen que significa eso?* Guide children to see that which object is lighter.

● Show children two other objects, and have them recognize which object is heavier. Have a volunteer place one object on one side of the balance and the other object on the other side. Continue with other objects, using a variety to help children discover that bigger objects are not always heavier.

Observe and Investigate

✓ **Can children investigate characterisics of objects?**

Compare Length and Weight Provide children with several objects of varying length and weight, a balance scale, and Connecting Cubes. Say: ***You can measure and compare the same objects in more than one way.*** *Pueden medir y comparar los mismos objetos de distintas maneras.*

● Show children how to use linked Connecting Cubes to measure the length of an object. Ask: ***Which objects are longer, and which are shorter?*** *¿Qué objetos son más largos? ¿Cuáles son más cortos?*

● Reinforce how to use the balance scale to compare two objects. Ask: ***Which objects are heavier? Which are lighter?*** *¿Qué objeto es más pesado? ¿Cuál es más liviano?*

ELL Explain that measurement uses a lot of comparison words. Say: ***The comparison words are opposites.*** Say a term, such as *long*, and invite children to say its opposite. Use hand gestures to illustrate each term. Then have children say the two terms one after the other and mimic your gestures.

Math and Science Flip Chart, p. 31

Center Time

Center Rotation Center Time includes teacher-guided activities and independent activities. Refer to the **Learning Centers** on pages 62–63 for independent activity ideas.

 small group   30 minutes

Math and Science Center

 Observe children as they compare capacities of containers.

Materials various containers, water or sand, table, a scoop

Tell children they will observe how much will fit inside various containers.

- Allow children to experiment with filling different containers, pouring the contents of one container into another. Explain that if the amount in one container can be poured into another container with room left over, the second container holds more than the first container.

- Have children choose which container they think holds the most. Have them check whether the contents of another container could fit into that container.

Center Tip

If...children spill as they go from one container to the next, **then...**encourage them to go slowly and take their time. You can also place a mat under the materials.

 Learning Goals

Mathematics
- Child explores capacity; recognizes how much can be placed in a container.

Science
- Child uses senses to observe, classify, investigate, and collect data.
- Child uses basic measuring tools to learn about objects.

 Writing

Tell children: *Imagine you have a hand lens and you are looking up close at something in a garden. Draw a picture of what you see. Write about your picture.* Compile student work into a class book; display the book in the classroom library.

Purposeful Play

 Encourage children to explore the measurement of various classroom objects.

Children choose an open center for free playtime. Encourage children to choose a variety of classroom objects and compare the length, weight, and capacity of the items.

Let's Say Good-Bye

large group 15 minutes

 Read Aloud Revisit the story "Going on a Trail Ride"/"Vamos a un paseo por el camino" for your afternoon Read Aloud. Remind children that part of being friendly is being quiet at story time so that everyone is able to listen and hear the story.

 Home Connection Refer to the Home Connections activities listed in the Resources and Materials chart on page 59. Remind children to tell family members about comparing light and heavy things. Sing the "Good-Bye Song"/"Hora de ir a casa" as children prepare to leave.

Let's Start the Day

Focus Question

How can I use tools to investigate?
¿Qué instrumentos puedo usar para investigar?

Learning Goals

Social and Emotional Development
• Child initiates play scenarios with peers that share a common plan and goal.

Emergent Literacy: Reading
• Child blends onset and rime to form a word with pictoral support.

Vocabulary

broth	caldo	corn husk	hoja de maíz
dough	amasar	flour	harina
heavy	pesado	measure	medida
tamales	tamales		

Differentiated Instruction

 Extra Support

Oral Language and Vocabulary
If...children have difficulty pantomiming something Kiko does, **then...**model the action, and invite children to imitate what you are doing.

Enrichment

Phonological Awareness
Challenge children to point to objects in the classroom and combine onset and rime on their own as they name the object.

▶ **Opening Routines and Transition Tips**
For **Opening Routines** and **Transition Tips** turn to pages 178–181 and visit **DLMExpressOnline.com** for more ideas.

📖 Read **"The Donut Machine"/**"La máquina de hacer rosquillas" from the *Teacher's Treasure Book, page 182,* for your morning Read Aloud.

Language Time

large group   15 minutes

Social and Emotional Development Encourage children to initiate play scenarios with others.

Oral Language and Vocabulary

✓ **Can children use the vocabulary from the book?**

What Does Kiko Do? Take a picture walk through the book *I Like Making Tamales/Me gusta hacer tamales.* As you review the pages, ask children to note the actions Kiko does. Have children take turns acting out one of Kiko's actions for the class. Say to the class: **Explain what Kiko is doing.** *Expliquen qué está haciendo Kiko.*

● Ask: **How does Kiko's mama make sure she has the right amount of flour? What tool does she use to measure the flour? What measuring tools have you used in the kitchen?** *¿Cómo sabe la mamá de Kiko que tiene la cantidad necesaria de harina? ¿Qué instrumento usa para medir la harina? ¿Qué instrumentos para medir han usado ustedes en la cocina?*

ELL Have children practice the two sentences Kiko repeats: *"What can I do?"* and *"See what I can do!"* Check that they understand the meanings of the sentences.

Phonological Awareness

✓ **Can children blend onset and rime?**

Blend Onset and Rime Display the Dog Puppets. Have the puppets help the children practice blending onset and rime.

● Point to a one-syllable object in the classroom, and model blending onset and rime. For example, point to the door. Have the first puppet say: /d/ and the second puppet say -*oor.* Have the whole class practice blending the onset and rime.

● Next, have a child take the place of the first puppet. Point to another object, and ask the child to say the onset; then have the second puppet say the rime. Have the class combine onset and rime and say the word.

● Then ask another child to take the place of the second puppet as you point to a different object in the classroom. Have the first puppet say the onset and the child say the rime. Have the class combine the onset and rime and say the word. Continue practicing and changing roles until all children have had a chance to participate.

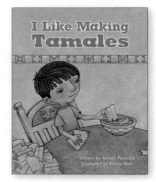

I Like Making Tamales
Me gusta hacer tamales

Center Time

▶ **Center Rotation** Center Time includes teacher-guided activities and independent activities. Refer to the **Learning Centers** on pages 62–63 for independent activity ideas.

`small group` `60–90 minutes`

Pretend and Learn Center

| Center Tip |

☑ Observe children as they role-play a scenario.

☑ Track childen's re-creation of experiences through dramatic play.

Materials children's kitchen props such as bowls, spoons, pretend food, and a kitchen stove/sink/refrigerator, if available

Make a Family Meal Have children play in small groups to plan, prepare, and eat a family meal. To get children started, ask: **How did Kiko help cook in the story?** *En este cuento, ¿cómo ayuda Kiko a cocinar?* Then have children act out some of the details from the story.

- Ask children to work together to plan a meal to eat as a family. Children can portray different family members and take various roles in the kitchen.

- Children should pretend with kitchen props and play food.

Center Tip

If...children have difficulty deciding what foods to pretend to prepare, **then...**provide pictures of various meals that are familiar to the children.

Creativity Center

Center Tip

☑ Can children use a variety of art materials to explore?

Materials crayons, markers, paper, magazine pictures of a variety of foods and ingredients, glue sticks, safety scissors

Make a Cookbook Explain that children will write a recipe for a dish they eat at home. Model the activity by drawing the steps of preparing a simple meal, portraying yourself as you choose and mix ingredients, cook or bake, and assemble a dish.

- Encourage children to be creative and to decorate their recipe pages with drawings and cutouts of a combination of food items and cooking tools. Ask children to label their recipes as possible.

- Have children talk about their recipes. Note when they use full sentences. Assemble the recipes into a class cookbook. Discuss healthful food choices and the need to eat a variety of foods.

Center Tip

If...children have trouble figuring out the steps in their recipes, **then...**have them talk through the recipe and steps with an adult.

Learning Goals

Social and Emotional Development
- Child initiates play scenarios with peers that share a common plan and goal.

Fine Arts
- Child uses and experiments with a variety of art materials and tools in various art activities.
- Child expresses ideas, emotions, and moods through individual and collaborative dramatic play.

Differentiated Instruction

✋ **Extra Support**

Pretend and Learn Center
If...children have difficulty thinking of steps for making and enjoying a meal, **then...**give them a scenario to act out, illustrated on a piece of paper.

⭐ **Enrichment**

Creativity Center
Challenge children to label ingredients and tools in their recipes.

Accommodations for 3's

Creativity Center
If...three-year-olds have difficulty with the glue stick **then...**have them choose pictures and arrange them on the page. Ask an older child to help by gluing the pictures into place.

Focus Question

How can I use tools to investigate?

¿Qué instrumentos puedo usar para investigar?

✓ Learning Goals

Emergent Literacy: Reading

• Child identifies the letter that stands for a given sound.

• Child asks and answers questions about books read aloud (such as, "Who?" "What?" "Where?").

Vocabulary

broth	caldo	corn husk	hoja de maíz
dough	amasar	flour	harina
heavy	pesado	measure	medida
tamales	tamales		

Differentiated Instruction

✋ Extra Support

Read Aloud

If...children have trouble understanding the vocabulary words, **then...**use the words in another context to see if they can determine the meaning.

⭐ Enrichment

Learn About Letters and Sounds
Have children think of additional words that begin with the letters *B* and *I*.

Accommodations for 3's

Read Aloud

If...three-year-olds have difficulty understanding vocabulary words, **then...**review the story, and use illustrations to support the vocaulary.

Literacy Time

large group · 15 minutes

📖 Read Aloud

✓ **Can children distinguish between questions and statements?**

Build Background Tell children that you are going to reread *I Like Making Tamales*/ *Me gusta hacer tamales* aloud to them. Ask what they remember from yesterday. Explain that the flour used in tamales is made from corn.

Listen for Understanding Tell children that as you read the story, they should listen for a question Kiko asks several times. Invite them to join in when Kiko asks, "What can I do?" As you read the story, pause each time before Kiko asks his question, so children have an auditory cue.

Respond to the Story Ask: *Why do you think Kiko asks what he can do? Does he repeat any other phrases? How does Kiko know which corn husks are big enough for tamales? What questions do you have about the story? ¿Por qué piensan que Kiko pregunta qué puede hacer? ¿Cómo sabe Kiko qué tamaño deben tener las hojas de maíz para que los tamales salgan bien?*

ELL Point out the inverted question marks in the Spanish version of the story. Help a Spanish-speaking child explain them to the class.

Learn About Letters and Sounds

✓ **Can children recognize the sounds for the letters *B* and *I*?**

Learn About the Letters *Bb* and *Ii* Use the *Alphabet Wall Cards* for *ball* and *igloo* to review the letters *Bb* and *Ii*.

● Give partners four sheets of paper and a marker. As needed, help teams write a large uppercase *B* and *I* on paper. Give teams the picture cards for words beginning with /b/ and /ĭ/. Tell them to take turns choosing a card, naming the picture, and placing it on the letter that makes the first sound.

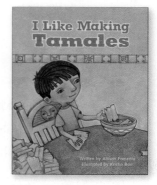

I Like Making Tamales
Me gusta hacer tamales

Alphabet Wall Cards

large group 15 minutes

Math Time

Observe and Investigate

☑ **Can children count up to 10 items?**

☑ **Can children recognize one-digit numerals, 0 - 9?**

Mr. Mixup Tell children that Mr. Mixup is always making mistakes. Invite them to help Mr. Mixup correct his mistakes.

- Say: *Mr. Mixup always makes mistakes!* *¡El Sr. Confundido siempre comete errores! Necesita nuestra ayuda.* Have children listen to Mr. Mixup's counting. Say: *Listen as Mr. Mixup counts. If he makes a mistake, say STOP!* *Escuchen cómo cuenta el Sr. Confundido. Si comete un error, digan ¡DETÉNGASE!*

- As Mr. Mixup, say: *Hello, I am Mr. Mixup. Let me count for you! 1, 2, 3, 4, 6, 5...* *"Hola, soy el Sr. Confundido. ¡Voy a contar! 1, 2, 3, 4, 6, 5..."* Continue until children yell *Stop!* If children don't notice the mistake, ask them if 6 comes before 5. Say: *Wait. Does 6 come before or after 5?* *Esperen un momento. ¿El 6 viene antes o después del 5?* Continue with another sequence. Say: *Oops. I made a mistake. Let me try counting again. 1, 3, 4, 5.* *¡Ay! Cometí un error. Voy a contar otra vez. 1, 3, 4, 5.* Allow children time to catch the mistake.

- Repeat with other examples of Mr. Mixup making mistakes when counting objects. For example, he might skip an object or count the same object twice. If children get good at catching mistakes with numbers 1–5, extend the activity using number 6–10 and greater.

 Provide support by reviewing the term *mistake*. Explain that a mistake is something that is not correct and should be fixed.

✖✖✖ Social and Emotional Development

Making Good Choices

☑ **Can children discuss the idea of making a plan?**

Understanding Making Plans Display the *Making Good Choices Flip Chart,* page 18, and remind children of the previous day's discussion.

- Point to the children in the photo. Ask: *What is each child doing? Why do you think each person is doing something different?* *¿Qué hace cada niño? ¿Por qué piensan que cada uno hace algo distinto?* Guide children to realize that before this scene, the children had to plan who would do what. Say: *Did the children all agree what to do? Do you think they had a leader?* *¿Están todos los niños de acuerdo? ¿Creen que los niños eligieron un líder?* Ask: *When is it helpful to have a plan? Why?* *¿Cuándo es útil tener un plan? ¿Por qué?* Have children discuss plans they make with friends before playing a game or drawing a picture.

Building Blocks

Online Math Activity

Introduce Deep Sea Compare, in which children use indirect comparison to compare the lengths of two different fish using coral. Each child should complete the activity this week.

Making Good Choices Flip Chart, p. 18

✓ Learning Goals

Social and Emotional Development
- Child initiates play scenarios with peers that share a common plan and goal.

Mathematics
- Child demonstrates that, when counting, the last number indicates how many objects were counted.
- Child recognizes and names numerals 0 through 9.

Vocabulary

correct	correcto
mistake	error

help	ayudar

Differentiated Instruction

 Extra Support

Observe and Investigate

If...children have trouble correcting Mr. Mixup, **then...**clearly exaggerate the mistakes by using numbers less than 5.

 Enrichment

Observe and Investigate

Challenge children by making Mr. Mixup's mistakes less obvious and by using greater numbers.

Accommodations for 3's

Making Good Choices

If...children have difficulty describing a plan, **then...**provide simple examples of activities that need a plan, such as playing a game or lining up for recess.

Focus Question
How can I use tools to investigate?
¿Qué instrumentos puedo usar para investigar?

Learning Goals

Mathematics
• Child understands that objects, or parts thereof, can be counted.
• Child compares the length, height, weight, volume (capacity), area of people or objects.

Vocabulary

| balance | balanza | compare | comparar |
| side | lado | weights | pesos |

 Differentiated Instruction

 Extra Support

Math Time
If...children have difficulty determining equivalent groupings of blocks, **then...**count with them as you add each block.

Enrichment

Math Time
Challenge children to find group multiples for up to four square, or larger, blocks.

Accommodations for 3's

Math Time
If...children struggle as they weigh blocks, **then...**have them hold the blocks in their hands to compare weights.

Special Needs

Behavioral Social/Emotional
Learning measurement is important, so encourage the child to participate in the activities. Compare the weights of other objects, besides blocks, to engage and hold the interest of all children.

Math Time

  large group 20 minutes

☑ **Can children recognize and compare the weights of objects and people?**

☑ **Do children understand that objects can be counted?**

Weigh Blocks Children compare weights of blocks using a balance scale.

● Review the concept of weight. Ask: *Who weighs more, a child or a grown-up? Do some grown-ups weigh more than others? ¿Quién es más pesado: un niño o un adulto? ¿Son algunos adultos más pesados que otros?* Lead children in a respectful discussion about the comparative weights of people.

● Display a balance scale. Ask: *Do you remember this tool? ¿Recuerdan este instrumento?* Allow children to answer. Reinforce that the scale is a tool for comparing weights of objects.

● Display the *Math and Science Flip Chart,* page 32. Say: *Look at the balance scale. Which side is higher? Which side is lower? Which side has something that is heavier? Miren esta balanza de platillos. ¿Qué lado está más alto? ¿Qué lado está más bajo? ¿Qué platillo tiene algo más pesado?* Guide children to understand that the sand weighs more.

● Provide two sets of blocks. The blocks in one set should be smaller than the blocks in the other. Guide children to figure out a method to determine how many smaller blocks equal the weight of one larger block.

● Say: *Let's weigh these blocks. Look at the smaller blocks. How could you figure out how many smaller blocks weigh the same as one larger block? Pesemos estos bloques. Miren los bloques más pequeños. ¿Qué harían para descubrir cuántos bloques más pequeños pesan lo mismo que un bloque más grande?* Children should say they would place one large block on one side of the scale and add smaller blocks on the other side until the scale is balanced.

● Say: *Let's place one large block on the scale. Count with me as I place the smaller blocks on the other side one by one. One, two, three. . . . Coloquemos un bloque grande en la balanza. Cuenten conmigo mientras coloco los bloques más pequeños en el otro platillo, uno por uno. Uno, dos, tres...* Place smaller blocks until the scale balances.

● Say: *Good. These smaller blocks together weigh about the same as one large block. Bien. Estos bloques más pequeños, juntos, pesan lo mismo que un bloque grande.* Make sure children see the equivalency.

● Repeat with other types of blocks. Allow children time to count as they place blocks and then to understand how many smaller blocks are needed to make the scale balance (or come close to balancing).

Comparing Weights
Comparar peso

Math and Science Flip Chart, p. 32

Center Time

▶ **Center Rotation** Center Time includes teacher-guided activities and independent activities. Refer to the **Learning Centers** on pages 62–63 for independent activity ideas.

 small group 30 minutes

Math and Science Center

Center Tip

If...children struggle to compare weights of objects, **then**...talk them through the comparing process as they place objects on the scale.

☑ **Children use a balance scale to explore and compare weights of classroom objects.**

Materials balance scale, various small classroom objects

Compare Weights Provide various classroom objects that are small enough that children can place them on the balance scale to compare.

● Ask: *Do any of these objects weigh the same? How will the balance look if they are? Are some heavier than others? What will the balance scale look like then?* ¿*Pesan lo mismo algunos de estos objetos? ¿Hay algunos más pesados? ¿Qué pasará con la balanza de platillos?* Have children select two objects to compare.

● Encourage discussion to describe what happens to the scale and what shows which object is heavier and which is lighter.

Learning Goals

Emergent Literacy: Writing
• Child participates in free drawing and writing activities to deliver information.

Mathematics
• Child compares the length, height, weight, volume (capacity), area of people or objects.

Writing

Review the story *I LIke Making Tamales.* Mention that Kiko asks, "What can I do?" Say: *People ask questions for different reasons. When do you ask questions?* *Las personas hacen preguntas por distintas razones. ¿Cuándo hacen preguntas ustedes?* Have children draw a picture of themselves asking someone a question. Draw a question mark on the board. Have children first trace it with a finger on the desk and then add it to their drawing as they label their pictures independently. Display the finished work in the classroom.

Purposeful Play

☑ **Observe children comparing weights of people and objects.**

Children choose an open center for free playtime. Encourage cooperation by suggesting children work together and talk about the weights of people and objects.

Let's Say Good-Bye

 large group 15 minutes

 Read Aloud Revisit the story "The Donut Machine"/"*La máquina de hacer rosquillas*" from *Teacher's Treasure Book* for your afternoon Read Aloud. Remind children to listen for the sound the letter *B* makes.

 Home Connection Refer to the Home Connections activities listed in the Resources and Materials chart on page 59. Remind children to talk to family members about how much people and objects weigh. Sing the "Good-Bye Song" as children prepare to leave.

Focus Question
How can I use tools to investigate?
¿Qué instrumentos puedo usar para investigar?

Learning Goals

Language and Communication
• Child names and describes actual or pictured people, places, things, actions, attributes, and events.
• Child uses newly learned vocabulary daily in multiple contexts.
• Child builds English listening and speaking vocabulary for common objects and phrases. (ELL)

Emergent Literacy: Reading
• Child blends onset and rime to form a word with pictoral support.

Mathematics
• Child explores capacity; recognizes how much can be placed in a container.

Vocabulary

container	recipiente	empty	vacío
full	lleno	guess	adivinar
measure	medir		

Differentiated Instruction

 Extra Support
Oral Language and Vocabulary
If...children have difficulty understanding the concept of full, **then...**fill the container to different increments and say: *It's not full yet. It's still not full. Now it is full.* *Todavía no está lleno. Aún no está lleno. Ahora sí está lleno.*

Enrichment
Phonological Awareness
Challenge children to think of more words that rhyme with *do*.

Let's Start the Day

Opening Routines and Transition Tips
For **Opening Routines** and **Transition Tips** turn to pages 178–181 and visit **DLMExpressOnline.com** for more ideas.

Read **"How Two Brothers Solved a Problem"/**"De cómo dos hermanos aprendieron a resolver un problema" from the *Teacher's Treasure Book*, page 308, for your morning Read Aloud.

Language Time

large group 15 minutes

Social and Emotional Development Encourage children to ask questions when they don't know something.

Oral Language and Vocabulary

✓ **Can children use pictures to obtain meaning?**

Full or Empty Ask children to name measuring tools they have used. Have them tell what objects they measured.

● Display *Oral Language Development Card 34*. Describe what the children are doing. Then follow the suggestions on the back of the card.

● Ask: *After you eat a big favorite meal, is your tummy empty or full? After you eat, is your plate empty or full of food? When you take a bath, do you want the tub to be empty, full. or in between?* *Después de comer mucho, ¿tienen la panza vacía o llena? ¿Su plato está vacío o lleno? Cuando se bañan, ¿quieren que la tina esté vacía, con agua hasta la mitad o llena?*

● In the classroom, display a large, empty jar; a container full of small objects such as pennies, toy figurines, or marbles; and a small cup. Ask children to guess how many times they would need to fill the cup with the small objects and then empty it into the jar in order to fill the jar. Write out a chart showing each child's guess, and put the chart on the bulletin board. Later in the day, children will experiment with measuring to refine their guesses.

 Review the meanings of words such as *empty, full,* and *guess*.

Phonological Awareness

✓ **Can children substitute different onsets to change a word?**

Review Combining Onset and Rime Display *Rhymes and Chants Flip Chart*, page 18. Reread the rhyme. Then reread just these two lines: *But I'm a detective. I know what to do.* *Y, como soy detective, me puse a buscar las pistas.* Ask children to sound out the word *do* (/d/ + /oo/). Have them say just the initial sound and then just the rime. Finally, have them blend the sounds together and repeat the word. Give them more initial sounds, and for each one, have them repeat the sound, add the rime, and say the word as a whole. Rhyming words may include *too, moo, boo, goo,* and *Sue*.

Oral Language Development Card 34

Tracks
Way out in our garden
behind the shed,
Some tracks appeared
In the cucumber bed.
"Who made them?" I wondered.
I hadn't a clue.
But I'm a detective.
I know what to do.
I measured the tracks.
My thumb was my guide.
I measured the circles
And each little side.
And then I asked Mom
what had happened that day.
The tracks were a rabbit's...
and he hopped away!

Rhymes and Chants Flip Chart, p. 18

Center Time

▶ **Center Rotation** Center Time includes teacher-guided activities and independent activities. Refer to the **Learning Centers** on pages 62–63 for independent activity ideas.

small group 60–90 minutes

ABC Center

☑ **Notice children's ability to recognize letter shapes.**

Materials masking tape

Recognizing Letters Create a hopscotch-style board by laying out masking tape on the floor. Make at least 10 squares, plus a "home" square. Use the masking tape to label the squares with letters studied to date, such as *A, S, M, D, B, I, N, K, P, F,* and *E.*

• Explain the rules of hopscotch, but say that instead of numbers, children will be hopping on letters. Tell children you will change the game by calling out a letter. That letter then becomes "hot." Children may not hop on the hot letter or put their marker on it until you change it back. Warn that you can make a letter hot any time, so children will need to think and move quickly to be sure they don't step on a hot square.

• Continue until everyone has a chance to play.

Center Tip

If...children seem concerned about recognizing the letters, **then...**review all letters before you begin.

Library and Listening Center

☑ **Observe if children demonstrate understanding of characteristics.**

Materials magazine or clip art pictures of no more than ten people with different physical characteristics: male/female; tall/short; old/young; with/without hats; and so on. Mount the pictures on poster board, and number the pictures from 1 to 10.

Look Closely Game Tell children you will think of one of the people on the poster. You will give the children clues, and they will use the clues to identify the correct person. Say, for example: *I am thinking of a person who is tall and young. Look closely. Who am I thinking of? Estoy pensando en una persona joven y alta. Miren con atención. ¿En quién estoy pensando?* Children should respond with the correct number.

• Display the poster prior to starting the game. Allow time for children to study the poster and note characteristics of each person.

Center Tip

If...children have difficulty seeing the details of the pictures from their seats, **then...**have them take turns coming up in small groups to play the Look Closely Game with you.

 Learning Goals

Social and Emotional Development
• Child understands that others have specific attributes and characteristics.

Language and Communication
• Child demonstrates an understanding of oral language by responding appropriately.

Emergent Literacy: Reading
• Child names most upper- and lowercase letters of the alphabet.

Differentiated Instruction

 Extra Support

Library and Listening Center
If...children have difficulty figuring out your clues, **then...**talk about each person, helping children think of the different characteristics of each.

Enrichment

Library and Listening Center
Challenge children to write a sentence about one of the people on the poster.

Accommodations for 3's

Library and Listening Center
If...three-year-olds have trouble understanding the clues, **then...**walk them through the process of elimination. Have them discuss what they know about one or two people.

Circle Time

Learning Goals

Emergent Literacy: Reading

• Child enjoys and chooses reading-related activities.

• Child produces the most common sound for a given letter.

• Child describes, relates to, and uses details and information from books read aloud.

• Child asks and answers questions about books read aloud (such as, "Who?" "What?" "Where?").

Vocabulary

answers	respuestas	compare	comparar
detective	detective	float	flotar
observe	observar	rough	áspero
scale	balanza	smooth	suave
tools	instrumentos		

Differentiated Instruction

 Extra Support

Read Aloud

If...children have difficulty understanding what a detective does, **then...**target photos in *Let's Investigate,* and say: *A detective, like this child, looks at things very closely.*

⭐ **Enrichment**

Learn About Letters and Sounds

Challenge children to make a *Bb* and *Ii* book for the class. Have them find and draw as many things as they can that begin with these letters.

Accommodations for 3's

Read Aloud

If...children have difficulty remembering elements of the story, **then...**read and discuss the story in sections.

Literacy Time

📖 Read Aloud

 Do children engage in pre-reading and reading-related activities?

Build Background Tell children that you will be reading the book about being a detective.

● Ask: ***Do you remember what a detective is? What does a detective do?*** *¿Recuerdan qué es un detective? ¿Qué hace un detective?*

Listen for Understanding Display *Let's Investigate/Soy Detective,* and read the title.

● Read the story, pausing to give children time to view the photos.

● Discuss ways detectives can solve cases. Ask: ***How do detectives get information? What tools do they use to investigate?*** *¿Cómo obtienen información los detectives? ¿Qué instrumentos usan para investigar?*

Respond to the Story Discuss the story. Talk about what characteristics a good detective might need. Ask: ***Why does a detective need to ask questions?*** *¿Por qué debe hacer preguntas un detective?*

 Review the word *compare*. Model comparing the characteristics of classroom objects, and then ask volunteers to compare objects they choose.

Learn About Letters and Sounds

 Can children sort words that begin with *Bb* or *Ii*?

Learn About Letters *Bb* and *Ii* Write the letters *Bb* and *Ii* on large sheets of chart paper. Place the paper in front of the class.

● Review the letters and sounds. Say: ***The sound of the letter B is /b/.*** *El sonido de la letra B es /b/.* Hold up the *Bb* page of the *ABC Big Book*. Point to the ball and say: **/b/ /b/ ball *starts with the letter* Bb.** */b/ /b/ ball empieza con la letra Bb.* Repeat using the letter *Ii*.

● Hold up other *Bb* and *Ii* pictures. Say: ***Who can tell me what letter the word /i/ /i/ ice begins with?*** *¿Quién puede decirme con qué letra empieza la palabra /i/ /i/ ice?* Continue with other *Bb* and *Ii* pictures.

● Name the word, and ask what sound the word begins with. Include other letter sounds children are confident in naming.

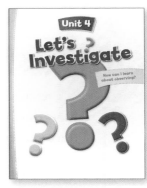

Let's Investigate
Soy detective

ABC Big Book

Math Time

Observe and Investigate

☑ **Can children recognize how much a container holds?**

Which Holds More? Tell children they are going to compare containers to figure out which holds more.

- Prepare up to eight containers of varying widths and heights. Have available material that can be poured, such as sand. Show two of the containers. Say: **Look at these containers. Which holds more? How can we check?** *Miren estos recipientes. ¿Cuál creen que contiene más? ¿Cómo lo saben?*

- Fill the smaller container and pour the contents into the larger container. Say: **I poured everything from this container into the other container, and there is still room for more. The other container holds more than this container.** *Puse todo el contenido de este recipiente en otro recipiente, y ahora hay más espacio. El nuevo recipiente contiene más que el primero.* Point out the large jar the children made guesses about earlier. Using the cup, pour two scoops of the small objects into the large jar. Say: **I have just put two scoops into the large jar. Is the jar full yet, or can it hold more?** *Acabo de poner dos cucharadas en el recipiente grande. ¿Está lleno el recipiente grande o puede contener más?* Continue pouring scoops and keeping track of the total until the large jar is full. Write the total number of cups on the prediction chart you made earlier.

✕✕✕ Social and Emotional Development

Making Good Choices

☑ **Can children brainstorm ideas and make a plan using a word web?**

Generating Ideas Display the *Making Good Choices Flip Chart,* page 18, and the Dog Puppets. Say: **Today you and the puppets will plan by making a word web.** *Hoy, ustedes y los títeres planificarán el trabajo de detectives creando una red de palabras.*

- Draw a circle in the middle of the board. Write "DETECTIVE" in the circle, and say the word. Explain that yesterday someone left a big purple ball in the puppets' yard. The puppets want to identify who left the ball so they can return it. Say: **Let's brainstorm tools and strategies we can use to solve the mystery.** *Hagamos una lluvia de ideas para buscar instrumentos y estrategias que nos ayuden a resolver el misterio.*

- Have children and the puppets call out tools and strategies, such as "Put up signs around the neigborhood." Write reminder words and phrases on lines extending from the circle. When the word web is completed, discuss how it can be used for planning. Elicit responses from children about how everyone worked together to make a plan.

Making Good Choices Flip Chart, p. 18

☑ Learning Goals

Social and Emotional Development
- Child initiates play scenarios with peers that share a common plan and goal.

Mathematics
- Child explores capacity; recognizes how much can be placed in a container.

Vocabulary

compare	comparar	container	recipiente
more	más	holds	contiene
question	pregunta		
investigation	investigación		

Differentiated Instruction

👋 **Extra Support**
Observe and Investigate
If...children have difficulty comparing the amounts in the containers, **then...**make the difference in amounts more noticeable.

⭐ **Enrichment**
Observe and Investigate
Challenge children by using containers that are similar in size.

Accommodations for 3's
Making Good Choices
If...children have difficulty thinking of ideas to suggest, **then...** ask a leading question, such as: **Should the puppets ask their neighbors to help?** *¿Deberían los títeres pedir ayuda a sus vecinos?*

💜 **Special Needs**
Cognitive Challenges
Participating in the creation of a word web is a good way to build vocabulary. Ask the child specific questions to help her/him find words for the web.

Focus Question
How can I use tools to investigate?
¿Qué instrumentos puedo usar para investigar?

Learning Goals

Language and Communication
• Child names and describes actual or pictured people, places, things, actions, attributes, and events.

Mathematics
• Child understands and uses words that describe position/location in space (such as under, over, beside, between, on, in, near, far away).

Social Studies
• Child identifies common areas and features of home, school, and community.

Vocabulary

amazing	asombroso	collage	collage
community	comunidad	library	biblioteca
feature	característica		

Differentiated Instruction

Extra Support
Understand and Participate
If...children have difficulty copying the map key, **then...**ask them to draw just the symbols, and you can fill in their equivalents.

Enrichment
Understand and Participate
Challenge children to make up their own map symbols and create a corresponding key.

Accommodations for 3's
Understand and Participate
If...children have difficulty understanding what a map key is, **then...**show them the universal symbols for women and men. Have them explain the meanings. Help them realize that a map symbol works the same way.

Social Studies Time

large group 20 minutes

Language and Communication Skills Model using words and pictures to describe where something is.

Oral Language and Academic Vocabulary

☑ **Can children use words to talk about locations?**

Talking About Where We Are Tell children that paying attention to what's around us is a skill that is useful not only for detectives but for everyone. Say: *When you want to go to the playground, how do you know where it is? If we notice where a place is and remember the location, we can find the place again.* Cuando quieren ir al patio, ¿cómo saben dónde está? Si observamos dónde queda un lugar y recordamos su ubicación, podemos volver a encontrarlo.

● Ask children to carefully look around the classroom and notice where everything is. Say: *Pretend you have a camera, and take a picture of the room.* Imaginen que tienen una cámara y sacan una foto del salón. Ask for a volunteer who has a good picture in his or her mind. Say: *We're going to blindfold [name] and see what he/she remembers. We're also going to help by giving directions, such as* left, right, straight, *and* turn. Vamos a vendarle los ojos a [nombre del voluntario] y ver qué recuerda. Lo ayudaremos con indicaciones, como vé hacia la izquierda/derecha, sigue derecho y dobla.

● Blindfold the volunteer, and ask him/her to walk to another location in the room, such as your desk. Say: *Go slowly. Stop if you're unsure, and we will help you.* Camina lentamente. Si no estás seguro, detente y te ayudaremos.

● If the volunteer gets off course, have the other children give instructions, such as: *Turn right; take a step to the left.* Dobla a la derecha; da un paso a la izquierda. Allow a few more volunteers to repeat the process.

● Discuss what happened. Help children realize that if the volunteer has a good mental picture and the class gives clear directions, it is easier for the volunteer to get to the target location.

Understand and Participate

☑ **Can children use words and pictures to indicate locations?**

Making a Map Ask children what they know about maps. Explain that mapmakers often use symbols, or simple mini-pictures of things. Discuss why symbols might work better than words for maps. Ask children to call out items they see in the classroom, while you list them on an interactive white board or chart paper. Next to each item, have a volunteer draw a simple symbol to represent it.

● Distribute paper and pencils. Help children draw a simple map of the classroom. Talk about each item on the list, and have children place the symbol for the item on their maps.

Center Time

Center Rotation Center Time includes teacher-guided activities and independent activities. Refer to the **Learning Centers** on pages 62–63 for independent activity ideas.

small group · 30 minutes

Refer to the **Learning Centers** on pages 62–63 for independent activity ideas.

Learning Goals

Language and Communication
• Child names and describes actual or pictured people, places, things, actions, attributes, and events.

Emergent Literacy: Writing
• Child participates in free drawing and writing activities to deliver information.

Social Studies
• Child identifies common areas and features of home, school, and community.

Pretend and Learn Center

Center Tip

If...children don't understand the concept of right and left, **then...**have them gesture or mime instead.

✓ **Encourage children to demonstrate a sense of direction.**

Materials a book, a lunch bag or a backpack

Asking for Directions Review that when we don't know a location, we ask questions and use tools to find our way.

- Pair children. Have one child be a visitor to the school and have the other provide directions.

- Have the first child role-play being new to the school. He/she asks how to find locations, such as the hallway, the playground, front door, and so on. Have children use props when appropriate.

- Have the second child act as a guide. The guide should welcome the new child to the school and offer to help the new child find his or her classroom and other important places. Encourage the second child to be as specific as possible by gesturing, describing landmarks, or drawing a map.

Free Writing

Review the activities of the day with children. Ask them to draw a picture of something they might find at every playground. Have them label their drawing. Accept all levels of writing.

Purposeful Play

✓ **Observe children's use of vocabulary as they describe places.**

Children choose an open center for free playtime. Suggest that children work with partners to make a map of the school and its surroundings.

Let's Say Good-Bye

large group · 15 minutes

 **Read Aloud** Revisit the story "How Two Brothers Solved a Problem"/"De como dos hermanos aprendieron a reslover un problema" from *Teacher's Treasure Book,* for afternoon Read Aloud. Remind children to think of different ways to solve a problem.

 Home Connection Refer to the Home Connections activities in the Resources and Materials chart on page 59. Tell children to discuss role-plays at home. Sing the "Good-Bye Song" as students prepare to leave.

Focus Question

How can I use tools to investigate?

¿Qué instrumentos puedo usar para investigar?

 Learning Goals

Language and Communication
• Child names and describes actual or pictured people, places, things, actions, attributes, and events.

Emergent Literacy: Reading
• Child blends onset and rime to form a word with pictoral support.

Vocabulary

detective	*detective*	garden	*jardín*
measure	*medir*	tracks	*huellas*

Differentiated Instruction

 Extra Support
Phonological Awareness
If...children have difficulty, **then...**you can provide all the onset sounds while the children provide rime as a group. Then switch roles.

Enrichment
Oral Language and Vocabulary
Challenge children to draw their favorite place and to scribble or write labels on their drawing.

Accommodations for 3's
Oral Language and Vocabulary
If...three-year-olds have difficulty describing a place, **then...**work with them to elicit some sensory words they could use in a description.

Let's Start the Day

 Opening Routines and Transition Tips
For **Opening Routines** and **Transition Tips** turn to pages 178–181 and visit DLMExpressOnline.com for more ideas.

 Read **"Keiko's Good Thinking"/**"Keiko resuelve un problema" from the *Teacher's Treasure Book,* page 169, for your morning Read Aloud.

Language Time

large group — 15 minutes

Social and Emotional Development Encourage children to express curiosity about topics that interest them.

Oral Language and Vocabulary

✓ **Can children use descriptive words to discuss a place?**

Describing Environments Talk about places. Ask: *Do you have a favorite place? ¿Tienen un lugar preferido?* Point out that there are many kinds of places. Ask: *How would you describe that place? What can you see there? What activities happen there? How do you feel when you are there? ¿Cómo describirían ese lugar? ¿Qué pueden ver allí? ¿Qué actividades se desarrollan allí? ¿Cómo se sienten cuando están allí?* Encourage children to use descriptive language to communicate information about their favorite place.

• Display *Oral Language Development Card 33.* Point to the illustration, and ask children to describe the place in the picture. Then follow the suggestions on the back of the card.

Phonological Awareness

✓ **Can children substitute onset to make new rhyming words?**

Review Combining Sounds Say the word *crow.* Ask volunteers to say words that rhyme with *crow,* and write their suggestions on the board. Display a puppet. Explain that you are going to play a sound game with the puppet. Have a child say the initial sound from the list, and then have the puppet say the rest of the word. Have the class repeat the whole word.

ELL Use the *Rhymes and Chants Flip Chart,* page 18, to revisit the words *garden* and *shed.* Explain what the words mean. Use the illustration as an aid. Ask children to say the names for these items in their first languages.

Oral Language Development Card 33

Rhymes and Chants Flip Chart, p. 18

Center Time

▶ **Center Rotation** Center Time includes teacher-guided activities and independent activities. Refer to the **Learning Centers** on pages 62–63 for independent activity ideas.

 small group 60–90 minutes

 Learning Goals

Language and Communication
• Child names and describes actual or pictured people, places, things, actions, attributes, and events.

Emergent Literacy: Writing
• Child participates in free drawing and writing activities to deliver information.

Physical Development
• Child develops small-muscle strength and control.

Writer's Center

Center Tip

 Observe children's understanding of the words *investigate* and *mystery* as they draw and label their pictures.

Materials white paper, crayons or markers, pencils

Describing Plans Ask if children have ever heard the words *mystery* or *mysterious*. Discuss what they think *mystery* means. Say that detectives often try to solve mysteries.

● Have children draw a picture showing a detective or group of detectives trying to solve a mystery. When they finish, ask them to label their pictures.

● Provide time to discuss finished drawings. Ask: **What tools are the detectives using? What mystery do you think the detective is investigating?** *¿Qué instrumentos usan los detectives? ¿Qué misterio creen que está investigando el detective?*

If...children need more space for drawing, **then...**suggest they use the other side of the paper.

Differentiated Instruction

 Extra Support
Construction Center
If...children have difficulty labeling their plates, **then...**tell them to write the first letter, and you will write the rest.

Enrichment
Writer's Center
Challenge children to write a sentence describing what the picture is about.

Accommodations for 3's
Construction Center
If...three-year-olds have difficulty folding tamales, **then...**ask an older child to demonstrate the technique for them.

Special Needs
Cognitive Challenges
Encourage the child to participate, even if you can't recognize what s/he is drawing. Ask the child to tell you about the picture. Have the child dictate a descriptive sentence.

Construction Center

Center Tip

 Observe as children follow directions, demonstrate small-muscle control, and write their names.

Materials pieces of aluminum foil, play clay or cotton, directions showing how to fold tamales, colorful paper plates

Making Tamales Open *I Like Making Tamales*/*Me gusta hacer tamales*, and display it at the front of the classroom. Remind children that this is a story about a boy who helps his mother make tamales.

● Tell children they are going to make pretend tamales. Have children describe the directions that show how to make a tamale.

● Show children how to put a lump of clay or some cotton onto the wrapper and fold the wrapper the way Kiko learned.

● Have children label a plate with their name and then place their "tamale" on their plate. Set up a display of the finished tamales.

If...children have trouble following directions, **then...** model the activity several times using sequence words such as *first*, *next*, and *last*.

Focus Question

How can I use tools to investigate?

¿Qué instrumentos puedo usar para investigar?

✓ Learning Goals

Emergent Literacy: Reading

• Child enjoys and chooses reading-related activities.

• Child names most upper- and lowercase letters of the alphabet.

• Child identifies the letter that stands for a given sound.

• Child describes, relates to, and uses details and information from books read aloud.

• Child asks and answers questions about books read aloud (such as, "Who?" "What?" "Where?").

Vocabulary

crow	cuervo	halfway	mitad
handle	asa	pitcher	cántaro
reach	llegar	thirsty	sediento

Differentiated Instruction

Extra Support

Read Aloud

If...children have difficulty understanding how Crow raised the water level, **then...**review the process, demonstrating with a cup of water and some pebbles.

Enrichment

Read Aloud

Challenge children to think of another way Crow might have solved his problem.

Accommodations for 3's

Learn About Letters and Sounds

If...children cannot name objects on the *ABC Big Book* page, **then...**model each word for them as you point to the picture and emphasize the *Bb* and *Ii* sounds.

Literacy Time

large group · 15 minutes

📖 Read Aloud

✓ Can children use information from the story to describe and relate?

✓ Can children ask appropriate questions about the story?

Build Background Tell children that you will read a story about a thirsty crow with a problem. Ask what children know about crows. Explain that crows are smart birds and that crows like small, shiny things.

Listen for Enjoyment Display the flannel-board characters of "The Crow and the Pitcher,"/"El cuervo y el cántaro", page 317, and read the story title. Read the story aloud, using the flannel-board characters to act out the events. As you read, pause to discuss story elements. Ask: *Who is the story about? What problem does he have?* *¿Acerca de quién trata este cuento? ¿Qué problema tiene?*

Respond to the Story Talk about how people solve problems. Elicit ideas about being willing to keep trying, asking for help, asking questions, and learning from others.

● Ask: *How did the crow solve his problem? Did he have any good ideas? ¿Cómo resolvió el cuervo su problema? ¿Tuvo alguna buena idea?* Ask children if they have any questions about the story.

ELL Be sure children understand the language. Display pictures, use gestures, and explain any unfamiliar words. Explain what it means to give up.

● For additional suggestions on how to meet the needs of children at the Beginning, Intermediate, Advanced, and Advanced-High levels of English proficiency, see pages 184–187.

Learn About Letters and Sounds

✓ Can children make sounds for the letters *B* and *I*?

Review the Letters *Bb* and *Ii* Review the the letters and sounds of *Bb* and *Ii* using the *ABC Big Book*. Display the *Bb* page. Ask children to point to the pictures, name them, and make the sound for the letter *Bb*. Repeat the activity for the letter *Ii*.

ABC Big Book

Math Time

Online Math Activity

Children can complete Comparisons and Deep Sea Compare during computer time or Center Time.

Observe and Investigate

 Can children compare the weights of objects and people?

Compare Weights Tell children they are going to compare weights of objects. Discuss that some things are heavier and some things are lighter.

- Review the balance scale with children. Say: *When I put one object on one side and another on the other side, the heavier side will go down, and the lighter side will go up, or they will be at the same level if they weigh the same. Let me show you.* *Cuando pongo un objeto de un lado y un objeto del otro lado, el platillo del objeto más pesado baja y el del más liviano sube. Si los objetos tienen el mismo peso, la balanza queda equilibrada. Voy a mostrarles lo que ocurre.*

- Demonstrate how the scale works with objects of varying weights. Ask: *What do you think will happen if I put these objects on the scale? Which side will go down? Which is heavier?* *¿Qué piensan que sucederá si pongo estos objetos en la balanza? ¿Qué lado bajará? ¿Qué objeto es más pesado?*

- Have children pretend they are scales and "tip" from one side to the other. Give them objects of different weights to hold in their hands, and help them "tip" accordingly.

- Ask children who have much younger or older siblings to compare weights of people in their families. For example, ask: *Who weighs more, you or or your baby brother? Who weighs more, you or your mother?* *¿Quién pesa más: ustedes o su hermanito pequeño? ¿Quién pesa más: ustedes o su mamá?*

✝✝✝ Social and Emotional Development

Making Good Choices

 Can children ask questions to gain information?

Show Curiosity Before class starts, place a small classroom object inside a box; close the box. Explain that you are going to play a game called Ten Questions. The children will ask questions about what is in the box, but you will answer only *yes* or *no*. Children get ten questions to figure out what is in the box. Give an example of *a yes/no* question, such as "Is it heavy?" "¿Es pesado?" Discuss with children that they need to take turns and be good listeners when others ask questions. Keep a tally of the questions. If children can't guess after ten questions, give some hints.

 Review descriptive words that relate to color, weight, size, and so on.

Social and Emotional Development
- Child demonstrates initiative in independent activities; makes independent choices.

Mathematics
- Child compares the length, height, weight, volume (capacity), area of people or objects.

Vocabulary

light	liviano	scale	balanza
weight	peso		

Differentiated Instruction

✋ Extra Support
Observe and Investigate
If...children confuse the scale going up with a heavier weight, **then...**review that the scale going up means the object is lighter.

⭐ Enrichment
Observe and Investigate
Challenge children by having them predict weights of objects that are large but light and small but heavy.

Accommodations for 3's
Observe and Investigate
If...children have difficulty pretending to be scales, **then...**provide individual support.

Focus Question
How can I use tools to investigate?
¿Qué instrumentos puedo usar para investigar?

Math Time

  large group · 20 minutes

✓ **Can children recognize the capacities of containers?**

How Much Does It Hold? Invite children to explore the capacities of various containers. Discuss the term *capacity* with children. Tell them this word means how much a container holds.

● Cut three half-gallon containers to hold two, four, and eight cups of pourable material. Make the containers different colors so children can more easily differentiate them.

● Have available a one-cup measuring cup, the three containers, and water or sand. Show the materials to children. Say: **Look at these containers. We are going to find out how much each holds. One holds two cups, one holds four cups, and one holds eight cups.** *Miren estos recipientes. Vamos a descubrir cuánto contiene cada uno. Uno contiene dos tazas, otro contiene cuatro tazas y el otro contiene ocho tazas.*

● Ask: **Which container do you think holds eight cups?** *¿Qué recipiente creen que contiene ocho tazas?* Allow children time to answer. **Why do you think this container holds eight cups?** *¿Por qué piensan que este recipiente contiene ocho tazas?* Guide children to see that the largest container would hold the most cups.

● Slowly fill the container that holds two cups with sand or water. As you pour the material into the container by cup, count the cups. Ask: **Does this container hold more or less than the largest container?** *¿Este recipiente contiene más o menos que el recipiente más grande?*

● Then point to the container that holds four cups. Say: **How many more cups than the last container does this hold?** *¿Cuántas tazas más que el último recipiente contiene éste?* Allow children time to answer. Guide children to see it holds two more cups. Say: **Yes, it holds two more cups. Let's fill this container. It holds four cups.** *Sí, contiene dos tazas más. Llenémoslo. Contiene cuatro tazas.*

● Slowly fill the eight-cup container, asking children to count cups as you pour.

● Empty the containers and allow children to refill the containers and pour from one container to another to compare which holds more and which holds less. Children can use the measuring cup to check.

Center Time

> **Center Rotation** Center Time includes teacher-guided activities and independent activities. Refer to the **Learning Centers** on pages 62–63 for independent activity ideas.

 small group | 30 minutes

Refer to the **Learning Centers** on pages 62–63 for independent activity ideas.

Learning Goals

Emergent Literacy: Writing
• Child experiments with and uses some writing conventions when writing or dictating.

Mathematics
• Child explores capacity; recognizes how much can be placed in a container.

Math and Science Center

	Center Tip
☑ **Observe children experimenting with the capacities of containers and measuring techniques.** **Materials** eight or fewer containers of various widths and heights; safe material that can be poured **Compare Capacities** Provide containers and material that can be poured. Ask children to compare the capacities of the containers. • Ask: *Which of these containers holds the most? Which holds the least? Find out how much each holds. ¿Cuál de estos recipientes contiene más? ¿Cuál contiene menos? Descubran cuánto contiene cada uno.* Discuss ideas with children. • Guide children to fill the containers.	**If...**children have difficulty filling containers, **then...**provide individual support.

Writing

Have each child dictate a sentence discussing what they learned about containers and measuring. As you print each child's sentence, point out concepts of print, such as capitalization of the first word in the sentence, spacing between words, and end punctuation. Then read the sentence back to the child, tracking the print as you read. Send the sentences home with the children to share with their families.

Purposeful Play

☑ **Observe children appropriately measuring and manipulating containers.**

Children choose an open center for free playtime. Encourage children to discuss ideas together about how to find out which container holds more.

Let's Say Good-Bye

 large group | 15 minutes

 Read Aloud Revisit the story "Keiko's Good Thinking"/"Keiko resuelve un problema" from *Teacher's Treasure Book* for your afternoon Read Aloud. Remind children to listen for the sounds the letters Bb and Ii make.

 Home Connection Refer to the Home Connections activities listed in the Resources and Materials chart on page 59. Remind children to tell family members about containers and measuring. Sing the "Good-Bye Song" as children prepare to leave.

DAY 5

Let's Start the Day

Focus Question

How can I use tools to investigate?

¿Qué instrumentos puedo usar para investigar?

 Learning Goals

Language and Communication
• Child names and describes actual or pictured people, places, things, actions, attributes, and events.

Emergent Literacy: Reading
• Child blends onset and rime to form a word with pictoral support.

Vocabulary

feet	pies	shoes	zapatos
track	huella		

Differentiated Instruction

 Extra Support
Phonological Awareness
If...children have difficulty supplying onset and rime, **then...**supply one part of the sound for the child, and help the child combine the onset and the rime.

Enrichment
Phonological Awareness
Challenge children to choose other images from the flip chart and combine onset and rime.

Accommodations for 3's
Oral Language and Vocabulary
If...three-year-olds have difficulty figuring out why tracks differ, **then...**help them compare the sizes of various children's feet and the patterns on the bottom of different shoes.

 Opening Routines and Transition Tips
For **Opening Routines** and **Transition Tips** turn to pages 178–181 and visit DLMExpressOnline.com for more ideas.

Read **"The Little Spaceman"/"El pequeño hombre del espacio"** from the *Teacher's Treasure Book,* page 304, for your morning Read Aloud.

Language Time

large group — 15 minutes

Social and Emotional Development Encourage children to share their ideas about different ways people can solve problems.

Oral Language and Vocabulary

✓ **Can children use words to describe differences?**

Leaving Tracks Discuss how we know that an animal has been in the area if we don't actually see the animal. Display *Rhymes and Chants Flip Chart,* page 18. Recite the rhyme slowly. Point out the tracks. Ask: *How do we know these tracks were not left by a dog or a cat? What kinds of tracks do humans leave? How is the track left by your bare feet different from the track left by your shoes?* ¿Cómo sabe el niño que no son huellas de perro o gato? ¿Qué clases de huellas dejan los seres humanos? ¿En qué se diferencia la huella que deja su pie descalzo de la huella que dejan sus zapatos? Talk about what makes it easier to see tracks, such as snow, mud, or water.

ELL Use your hand and fingers to reinforce the concept of tracks. Dip your fingers in water, and press them on a piece of construction paper. Say: *This is the track left by my fingers. What is this? This is a _____.* Repeat the activity with your whole hand.

Phonological Awareness

✓ **Can children combine onset and rime with pictorial support?**

Review Onset and Rime Continue to display the *Rhymes and Chants Flip Chart,* page 18. Ask children to stand in a circle. Point to images in the illustration, such as a track, the fence, the shed, a leaf, and the dirt. Ask one child at a time to combine the onset and rime for an image. As each child finishes, he or she sits down. When all the children are seated, repeat the activity, and ask each child to stand to combine the onset and rime.

Rhymes and Chants Flip Chart, p. 18

Center Time

Center Rotation Center Time includes teacher-guided activities and independent activities. Refer to the **Learning Centers** on pages 62–63 for independent activity ideas.

 small group 60–90 minutes

Library and Listening Center

	Center Tip
Observe children as they act out scenes from a poem.	**If...**children need more support, **then...**have them choose which role they wish to play first.

Materials audio of *Rhymes and Chants Flip Chart*

Act out the Chant Play the audio reading of the *Rhymes and Chants Flip Chart,* page 18. Ask children to listen carefully.

- Ask children to listen to the chant again and act out what they hear.
- They can pretend to walk around in the garden, pick cucumbers, and see the tracks.
- Children can also pretend to be the rabbit who left the tracks in the garden before the chant begins.
- Children should play the chant multiple times and try out different roles.

Creativity Center

	Center Tip
Notice children's use of vocabulary when comparing characteristics of tracks.	**If...**children have difficulty choosing a toy, **then...**limit the choices in the center to one or two things.

Materials paints, paper, toy cars, small balls, other toys that have wheels or interesting textures

Make Tracks Children will use paint to make mysterious tracks.

- Each child chooses a toy to dip into the paint. Then the child runs the toy over the paper to make a track.
- Children put as many toys on their page as they like and then compare the different marks and textures of the tracks.
- When children have finished their tracks painting, they can ask a friend to match the tracks to the toy that was used.

Learning Goals

Social and Emotional Development
- Child initiates play scenarios with peers that share a common plan and goal.

Language and Communication
- Child names and describes actual or pictured people, places, things, actions, attributes, and events.

Emergent Literacy: Reading
- Child retells or reenacts poems and stories in sequence.

Differentiated Instruction

 Extra Support
Library and Listening Center
If...children have difficulty knowing what to act out, **then...**ask them leading questions, such as *What does the detective do with the tracks?*

Enrichment
Creativity Center
Challenge children to label the tracks on their paper.

Accommodations for 3's
Creativity Center
If...three-year-olds have difficulty manipulating the toys, **then...**provide individual support.

Special Needs
Delayed Motor Development
Remember to use objects that can be easily picked up by the child. For children with severe motor problems, this would be a good "peer buddy" activity.

Learning Goals

Emergent Literacy: Reading

• Child enjoys and chooses reading-related activities.

• Child blends onset and rime to form a word with pictoral support.

• Child identifies the letter that stands for a given sound.

• Child produces the most common sound for a given letter.

• Child describes, relates to, and uses details and information from books read aloud.

• Child asks and answers questions about books read aloud (such as, "Who?" "What?" "Where?").

Vocabulary

balance	balanza	bigger	grande
corn husk	hoja de maíz	measure	medir
smaller	pequeña	tamale	tamal

Differentiated Instruction

Extra Support

Learn About Letters and Sounds

If...children have difficulty finding objects that begin with one of the target letters, **then...**ask them to name something they know that begins with one of the letters.

Enrichment

Read Aloud

Challenge children to retell the story in their own words.

Accommodations for 3's

Read Aloud

If...three-year-olds have difficulty remembering the enitre story, **then...**retell the story, inviting them to share the parts they remember.

Literacy Time

📖 Read Aloud

✓ **Can children identify the characters, the setting, and some events in the story?**

Build Background Display *I Like Making Tamales*. Ask children to share what they remember about the story.

● Ask: ***Who are the people in the story? What do they like to do?*** *¿Quiénes son los personajes? ¿Qué les gusta hacer?*

Listen for Understanding Display *I Like Making Tamales/Me gusta hacer tamales,* and read the title. Read the story aloud. As you read, pause to discuss story elements.

● Tell children that where a story happens is often important to the story. Explain that *to take place* means "to happen." Ask: ***Where does this story take place? How do you know?*** *¿Dónde tiene lugar este cuento? ¿Cómo saben?*

● Say: ***Kiko and his mama work together to make tamales. What task does each one do? How do you think they feel at the end?***

Respond and Connect Discuss the story. Ask: ***How is this experience like one you have had? How is it different?*** *¿En qué se parece esta experiencia a alguna que ustedes hayan tenido ? ¿En qué se diferencia?*

ELL Help children understand idiomatic phrases such as *take place* by connecting them to idiomatic phrases in their own language.

● For additional suggestions on how to meet the needs of children at the Beginning, Intermediate, Advanced, and Advanced-High levels of English proficiency, see pages 184–187.

ABC Big Book

Learn About Letters and Sounds

✓ **Can children identify and name objects that begin with *Bb* and *Ii*?**

The Letters *Bb* and *Ii* Review the letter names, upper case and lower case, the sounds they make, and letter formation.

● Display the *ABC Big Book* pages for *Bb*. Practice saying the words pictured with children, first saying the words, then separating the onset and rime.

● Then show children the pages for *Ii*. Have them repeat the words after you.

● Have children look around the classroom and name as many objects as they can that begin with *Bb* or *Ii*.

● Demonstrate proper letter formation.

large group 15 minutes

Math Time

Observe and Investigate

☑ **Can children recognize how much a container holds?**

Which Holds More? Tell children they are going to compare containers to tell which holds more.

- Note: This lesson repeats the activity introduced on Day 3. Vary the container types and sizes and the materials in order to challenge children. Prepare up to eight different containers of various sizes and shapes. Fill the containers with materials that can be poured, such as sand. Say: *Look at these containers. Which holds more? Miren estos recipientes. ¿Cuál contiene más?* As children answer, ask them how they know. Ask: *How do you know which holds more? ¿Cómo saben cuál contiene más?*

- Explain to children that the height of a container is different from its capacity. Say: *Look how tall this container is. Miren la altura de este recipiente.* Show them a container with the same height but a different capacity. *It is as tall as this container. But it holds more (or less) than this container. Es tan alto como este recipiente. Pero contiene más (o menos) que este recipiente.* Demonstrate to children the different capacities by pouring out the contents of each.

  ELL Model comparing by using these phrases: *as tall as _____, as heavy as _____, as much as _____,* while you discuss and compare objects around the classroom.

large group 15 minutes

☆☆☆ Social and Emotional Development

Making Good Choices

☑ **Can children talk about problem solving and persistence?**

Initiative and Persistence Display *Making Good Choices Flip Chart*, page 18. Review ways detectives go about solving a mystery. Say: *Being a detective is not always easy. Sometimes detectives can't figure things out. No siempre es fácil ser un detective. A veces, los detectives no lograr resolver los problemas fácilmente.*

- Ask: *Do you remember how Crow solved his problem and got the water? If Crow had given up right away, what might have happened? Has there ever been a time when you didn't give up? ¿Recuerdan que el cuervo pudo tomar agua después de resolver su problema? Si se hubiera rendido enseguida, ¿qué habría ocurrido?*

- Ask: *If the detectives in the chart can't solve the mystery, should they give up? What would you say to help the detectives? Imaginen que el equipo de detectives del rotafolios no puede resolver el misterio. ¿Creen que deberían rendirse? ¿Qué les dirían para ayudarlos?*

Making Good Choices Flip Chart, p. 18

Learning Goals

Social and Emotional Development
- Child demonstrates initiative in independent activities; makes independent choices.

Mathematics
- Child explores capacity; recognizes how much can be placed in a container.

Vocabulary

| compare | comparar | container | recipiente |
| holds | contiene | more | más |

Differentiated Instruction

 Extra Support
Observe and Investigate
If...children have difficulty comparing the amounts in the containers, **then...**make the difference in amounts noticeable.

 Enrichment
Observe and Investigate
Challenge children by using containers that are similar in size.

Accommodations for 3's
Observe and Investigate
If...children have difficulty with the concept of *more,* **then...**demonstrate with Counting Cubes.

Learning Goals

Social and Emotional Development
• Child is aware of self in terms of abilities, characteristics and preferences, and respects personal boundaries.
• Child demonstrates positive social behaviors, as modeled by the teacher.

Mathematics
• Child measures the length and height of people or objects using standard or non-standard tools.

Science
• Child follows basic health and safety rules.

Physical Development
• Child coordinates body movements in a variety of locomotive activities (such as walking, jumping, running, hopping, skipping, climbing).
• Child engages in a sequence of movements to perform a task.

Vocabulary

compare	comparar	left	izquierda
observe	observar	right	derecha
straight	derecho	turn	girar

Differentiated Instruction

 Extra Support

Observe and Investigate
If...children have difficulty comparing weights, **then...**work with them independently.

Enrichment

Observe and Investigate
Challenge children to describe their dances step by step, using appropriate vocabulary.

Accommodations for 3's

Observe and Investigate
If...children have trouble taking turns, **then...**have the older children sit while the younger children use the equipment. Then have them switch roles.

Music and Movement Time

large group · 15 minutes

Personal Safety Skills Before the activity, review playground rules, reminding students to be careful when they are using the playground equipment.

Observe and Investigate

✓ **Can children use playground equipment to compare weights of people?**

✓ **Can children move to the beat of the music?**

Seesaw Scale Ask children what measurement tool the seesaw, or teeter-totter, resembles. (a balance) Ask children to predict what will happen if a child gets on one side of the seesaw. Have a child get on the seesaw, and discuss the result.

● Ask: *What do you think will happen if I get on the other side of the seesaw? ¿Qué creen que pasará si yo me subo al otro lado del subibaja?* Give students time to respond, and then get on the other side. Ask: *Who is heavier, [child's name] or me? ¿Quién es más pesado: [nombre del niño] o yo?*

● Ask: *What do you think will happen if a child gets on this side? ¿Qué creen que pasará si un niño se sube a este lado del subibaja?* Give students time to respond, and then have a child take your place.

● Play music, and have students move to the beat of the music on the seesaw as other children find ways to move to the beat on the ground or on other playground equipment. Rotate students so each student has a turn on the seesaw "scale."

ELL Review the words *up* and *down.* Ask children to demonstrate their understanding of these terms by acting out each word.

● For additional suggestions on how to meet the needs of children at the Beginning, Intermediate, Advanced, and Advanced-High levels of English proficiency, see pages 184–187.

Center Time

▶ **Center Rotation** Center Time includes teacher-guided activities and independent activities. Refer to the **Learning Centers** on pages 62–63 for independent activity ideas.

Pretend and Learn Center

| | Center Tip |

✓ **Encourage children to observe and think before making guesses.**

Materials picture cards showing different moving objects, such as a rubber ball, a sled, a rowboat, an airplane, and so on; box

What Is It? Invite children to play "What is it?" in pairs. Place picture cards in a box. Have one child choose a card and act out the motion of the object in the picture while the other child tries to guess the object. Then have the children switch roles.

● Say: *Watch carefully. Try to think of how different objects move.*
Miren atentamente. Intenten pensar en cómo se mueven los diferentes objetos.

Center Tip

If...children have difficulty guessing the objects, **then...** have the child who is acting say a few descriptive words to help.

Purposeful Play

✓ **Are children aware of their bodies in space, and do they respect others' space too?**

Children choose an open center for free playtime. Encourage children to control the movement of their bodies in order to respect things and people around them.

Let's Say Good-Bye

 large group 15 minutes

 Read Aloud Read Aloud Revisit the story "The Little Spaceman"/"El pequeño hombre del espacio" from *Teacher's Treasure Book* for your afternoon Read Aloud. Ask children what they learned this week about tracks.

 Home Connection Refer to the Home Connections activities listed in the Resources and Materials chart on page 59. Remind children to show someone at home how they can move like different objects. Sing the "Good-Bye Song" as children prepare to leave.

✓ Learning Goals

Social and Emotional Development
• Child understands that others have specific attributes and characteristics.

Language and Communication
• Child names and describes actual or pictured people, places, things, actions, attributes, and events.

Physical Development
• Child engages in a sequence of movements to perform a task.

• Child identifies and participates in exercises and activities to enhance physical fitness.

✏ Writing

Review the story "The Crow and the Pitcher." Ask children to tell how the story would change if the main character was a rabbit instead of a crow. Ask: *What can a crow do that a rabbit can't?* ¿Qué puede hacer un cuervo que un conejo no puede? Make a chart on an interactive whiteboard or chart paper with the headings *Rabbit* and *Crow*. Under "Crow," write: *A crow can fly.* Un cuervo puede volar. Have children discuss differences as you write them. Then have children draw a picture of the crow and label it with a word or a scribble. Display children's work.

Week 3

Focus Question

How can I compare things?
¿Cómo puedo comparar cosas?

This week children will continue to measure and sort objects. They will build towers from blocks and look at rocks with a hand lens. Children will learn more about how to be good listeners. After they talk about what it might be like to be very big or very small, they will pretend to shrink or grow.

✓ Learning Goals

Social and Emotional Development	DAY				
	1	2	3	4	5
Child uses classroom materials carefully.	✓		✓		✓
Child maintains concentration/attention skills until a task is complete.	✓	✓	✓	✓	✓
Child shows eagerness, curiosity, and confidence while learning new concepts and trying new things.				✓	✓
Child demonstrates appropriate conflict-resolution strategies, requesting help when needed.	✓				

Language and Communication	1	2	3	4	5
Child names and describes actual or pictured people, places, things, actions, attributes, and events.	✓	✓	✓	✓	✓
Child uses newly learned vocabulary daily in multiple contexts.	✓				

Emergent Literacy: Reading	1	2	3	4	5
Child independently engages in pre-reading behaviors and activities (such as, pretending to read, turning one page at a time).		✓			
Child blends onset and rime to form a word with pictoral support.	✓				
Child blends onset and rime to form a word without pictoral support.		✓	✓	✓	✓
Child identifies the letter that stands for a given sound.		✓	✓	✓	
Child describes, relates to, and uses details and information from books read aloud.	✓	✓	✓	✓	✓
Child asks and answers questions about books read aloud (such as, "Who?" "What?" "Where?").				✓	

Emergent Literacy: Writing	1	2	3	4	5
Child participates in free drawing and writing activities to deliver information.					✓
Child writes own name or a reasonable approximation of it.				✓	
Child experiments with and uses some writing conventions when writing or dictating.	✓	✓	✓	✓	

Mathematics	DAY				
	1	2	3	4	5
Child demonstrates that, when counting, the last number indicates how many objects were counted.	✓	✓			
Child measures the length and height of people or objects using standard or non-standard tools.	✓	✓	✓	✓	✓

Science	1	2	3	4	5
Child uses senses to observe, classify, investigate, and collect data.	✓				✓
Child follows basic health and safety rules.		✓			

Social Studies	1	2	3	4	5
Child identifies similarities and differences among people.			✓		

Fine Arts	1	2	3	4	5
Child uses and experiments with a variety of art materials and tools in various art activities.	✓			✓	✓
Child expresses ideas, emotions, and moods through individual and collaborative dramatic play.				✓	✓

Materials and Resources

	DAY 1	DAY 2	DAY 3	DAY 4	DAY 5
Program Materials	• Teacher's Treasure Book • Oral Language Development Card 35 • Rhymes and Chants Flip Chart • Book: *Nature Spy* • ABC Big Book • Connecting Cubes • Building Blocks Online Math Activities • Making Good Choices Flip Chart • Math and Science Flip Chart • Home Connections Resource Guide	• Teacher's Treasure Book • Dog Puppets • Book: *Nature Spy* • Photo Library CD-ROM • ABC Picture Cards • Pattern Blocks • Building Blocks Online Math Activities • Making Good Choices Flip Chart	• Teacher's Treasure Book • Oral Language Development Card 36 • Rhymes and Chants Flip Chart • Jumbo Hand Lenses • Concept Big Book 2 • ABC Picture Cards • Dog Puppets • Making Good Choices Flip Chart • Photo Library CD-ROM	• Teacher's Treasure Book • Flannel Board and Characters for "The Three Little Pigs" • Oral Language Development Card 36 • Dog Puppets • ABC Picture Cards • Connecting Cubes • Math and Science Flip Chart • Home Connections Resource Guide	• Teacher's Treasure Book • Rhymes and Chants Flip Chart • ABC Picture Cards • Book: *Nature Spy* • Connecting Cubes • Making Good Choices Flip Chart
Other Materials	• sponges cut in shapes of fruits and vegetables • paper, paint, small paper plates • flour, salt, sugar, corn meal • small bowls • items for texture painting, such as tree bark, potato, sponge, scrubber • paint, brushes, paper	• objects of different sizes (balls, toys) • drawing paper, crayons • books w/ images of natural objects • aluminum pie plates • play sand • plastic knives, straws, unsharpened pencils • objects for stacking • string, scissors	• dishpan(s), play sand, rocks • small shovels • building blocks • drawing paper, crayons • rocks with different textures • images of many kinds of weather • photographs of children in various climates • photographs of holiday celebrations in many cultures	• craft items (buttons, empty thread spools, safety pins, pipe cleaners, beads, paper plates, craft sticks, egg cartons, tissue boxes) • classroom objects (chairs, backpacks, books) • clothing props (hats, glasses, jackets) • five flat objects (to compare length) • classroom toys	• white paper, crayons, markers • poster board • old magazines with photos • glue sticks, safety scissors • numeral cards • various stuffed animals • classroom toys
Home Connections	Invite children to explain to their families what they learned about describing the textures of materials. Send home the following materials: • Weekly Parent Letter, Home Connections Resource Guide, pp. 41 - 42	Encourage children to take their strings home and find objects at home that are about the same length as their bodies.	Tell children to talk with their families about the various places they saw in the photographs.	Encourage children to order five objects by length with their families. Send home the following materials: • Storybook 11, Home Connections Resource Guide, pp. 121–124	Remind children to tell their families which house they drew from "The Three Little Pigs" and to describe the drawing.

Assessment

As you observe children throughout the week, you may fill out an Anecdotal Observational Record Form to document an individual's progress toward a goal or signs indicating the need for developmental or medical evaluation. You may also choose to select work for each child's portfolio. The Anecdotal Observational Record Form and Weekly Assessment rubrics are available in the assessment section of DLMExpressOnline.com.

More Literature Suggestions

• **What the Moon Saw** by Brian Wildsmith
• **Pattern Fish** by Trudy Harris
• **Animal: My Heart is Like a Zoo** by Michael Hall
• **Biggest, Strongest, Fastest** by Steve Jenkins
• **The Three Bears (Los tres osos)** by Paul Galdone
• **Is It Larger? Is It Smaller?** by Tana Hoban

Week 3

Daily Planner

	DAY 1	DAY 2
Let's Start the Day Language Time *large group*	**Opening Routines** p. 102 **Morning Read Aloud** p. 102 **Oral Language and Vocabulary** p. 102 Fruits and Vegetables **Phonological Awareness** p. 102 Onset and Rime	**Opening Routines** p. 108 **Morning Read Aloud** p. 108 **Oral Language and Vocabulary** p. 108 Noticing Nature **Phonological Awareness** p. 108 Onset and Rime
Center Time *small group*	**Focus On:** **Creativity Center** p. 103 **Writer's Center** p. 103	**Focus On:** **Library and Listening Center** p. 109 **ABC Center** p. 109
Circle Time Literacy Time *large group*	**Read Aloud** *Nature Spy/Espía de la naturaleza* p. 104 **Learn About Letters and Sounds: Learn About the Letters** *Nn* **and** *Kk* p. 104	**Read Aloud** *Nature Spy/Espía de la naturaleza* p. 110 **Learn About Letters and Sounds: Review the Letters** *Kk* **and** *Nn* p. 110
Math Time *large group*	**Mr. Mixup** p. 105	**Knock It Down!** p. 111
Social and Emotional Development *large group*	**Time to Share** p. 105	**Circle Time** p. 111
Content Connection *large group*	**Science:** **Oral Language and Academic Vocabulary** p. 106 **Observe and Investigate** p. 106	**Math:** **As Long As My Arm** p. 112
Center Time *small group*	**Focus On:** **Math and Science Center** p. 107 **Purposeful Play** p. 107	**Focus On:** **Math and Science Center** p. 113 **Purposeful Play** p. 113
Let's Say Good-Bye *large group*	**Read Aloud** p. 107 **Writing** p. 107 **Home Connection** p. 107	**Read Aloud** p. 113 **Shared Writing** p. 113 **Home Connection** p. 113

DAY 3

Opening Routines p. 114
Morning Read Aloud p. 114
Oral Language and Vocabulary
p. 114 All About Size
Phonological Awareness
p. 114 Onset and Rime

Focus On:
Pretend and Learn Center p. 115
Construction Center p. 115

Read Aloud
Let's Investigate/*Soy detective* p. 116
Learn About Letters and Sounds: Learn About the Letters *Kk* and *Nn* p. 116

Observe and Investigate
Line Up by Height p. 117

Listen and Learn
p. 117

Social Studies:
Oral Language and Academic Vocabulary
p. 118
Understand and Participate
p. 118 All Kinds of People

Focus On:
Library and Listening Center p. 119
Purposeful Play p. 119

Read Aloud p. 119
Writing p. 119
Home Connection p. 119

DAY 4

Opening Routines p. 120
Morning Read Aloud p. 120
Oral Language and Vocabulary
p. 120 Making Comparisons
Phonological Awareness
p. 120 Onset and Rime

Focus On:
Creativity Center p. 121
Pretend and Learn Center p. 121

Read Aloud
"The Three Little Pigs"/
"Los tres cerditos"
p. 122
Learn About Letters and Sounds: Learn about the Letters *Nn* and *Kk* p. 122

Missing Step p. 123

Staying Focused p. 123

Math:
Order Lengths p. 124

Focus On:
Math and Science Center p. 125
Purposeful Play p. 125

Read Aloud p. 125
Free Writing p. 125
Home Connection p. 125

DAY 5

Opening Routines p. 126
Morning Read Aloud p. 126
Oral Language and Vocabulary
p. 126 Contrasting
Phonological Awareness
p. 126 Onset and Rime

Focus On :
Writer's Center p. 127
Creativity Center p. 127

Read Aloud
Nature Spy/*Espía de la naturaleza* p. 128
Learn About Letters and Sounds: Learn About the Letters *Nn* and *Kk* p. 128

What's This Step? p. 129

Following Through p. 129

Dramatic Play Time:
Oral Language and Academic Vocabulary
p. 130
Observe and Investigate
p. 130

Focus On:
Pretend and Learn Center p. 131
Purposeful Play p. 131

Read Aloud p. 131
Shared Writing p. 131
Home Connection p. 131

Learning Centers

Math and Science Center

Comparing Textures
Children compare textures they have painted, p. 107

As Long As I Am Tall
Children find objects that are as long as they are tall, p. 113

Compare Lengths
Children compare the lengths of toys, p. 125

String Ruler
Provide three pieces of string or yarn in varying lengths to pairs. Ask children to find one object in the room the same length as each piece of string.

Paper-Clip Measures
Children work in groups to measure a classroom object such as a crayon, using paper clips as the unit of measure. One child measures the item; a partner draws it on a piece of paper and writes how many clips it took to measure the length.

ABC Center

Sand Writing
Children write letters in sand, p. 109

Animal ABC
Have children look through magazines or books for pictures of animals that have names beginning with the same sound; for example, mouse and monkey.

Letter Matchup
Make pairs of cards with a capital letter on one card and the corresponding lowercase letter on another. Distribute cards randomly, and ask children to find the person with the card that matches theirs.

My Initial Icon
Children use the first initial of their name to create an icon design. Show children examples of letter icons. Then have them use their initial to create a design they would like to have made into an icon.

Creativity Center

Food Prints
Children use food to make prints, p. 103

Comparing Big and Small
Children make furniture for story characters, p. 121

Compare and Contrast Collage
Children make a comparison collage, p. 127

Water Forms
Display pictures of water as snow, liquid, steam, and so on. Children compare the forms. Then they create a snowflake by cutting folded tissue paper squares.

Making Tracks
Children flatten a large clump of play clay into a circle about three-quarters of an inch thick. Ask them to press their hand or shoe into the clay. Then have them use connecting cubes to measure the depth, length, and width of their "track."

Library and Listening Center

Nature Discoveries
Children make nature drawings, p. 109

Celebrate Around the World
Children draw celebrations from around the world, p. 119

Hard, Soft, Hot, Cold
Provide nature books and magazines. Pairs browse through the books identifying things that are hard, soft, hot or cold. They use full sentences to describe each item: *A fire is hot.*

Comparing Pigs
Children listen to "The Three Little Pigs" and look at the pictures to compare the three little pigs to one another.

Solving Problems
Children browse books that show how people solve problems by exploring and investigating.

Construction Center

Build It Big!
Children build towers to describe, p. 115

Build the Location
Supply labeled pictures that show an item next to another, behind another, and so on. Children build structures that follow the items in the pictures and say: *This tower is in front of that tower.*

Tall, Taller, Tallest
Provide three picture cards, each with a small, a medium, or a large building on it. Children choose a card and build a tower that represents that image. They compare the images and their buildings.

How Many Blocks?
Children lay out the longest block. They find out how many smaller blocks equal the long block by placing smaller blocks on top of the long block and then count how many.

Writer's Center

What I Like!
Children write about what they like to eat, p. 103

Color Spy
Children write about colors they see around them, p. 127

More Words
Prepare cards comparing two items; label the items using comparison words. Children choose a card and draw two items that match the comparison. They label their drawing by following the letters on the picture cards.

Today's Tasks
On sheets of paper folded into three sections, children draw in each section one task they did in school or at home. Have them dictate or label each task.

Celebrate!
Children draw a picture of something they look forward to at a family celebration (food, music, clothing, and so on.) They dictate or write to describe what they drew.

Pretend and Learn Center

Be A Rock Hunter
Children pretend to hunt for rocks, p. 115

Suddenly Being Big
Children imagine what it's like to be a giant, p. 121

Create a Story
Children use stuffed animals to act out a story, p. 131

Huff and Puff
Children play roles of the wolf and the pigs in "The Three Little Pigs." They act out the story as one child retells it.

Interviewing Nature Spy
Children think of questions to ask the girl in *Nature Spy* before acting out an interview. One child acts as the person asking the questions, and another acts as the Nature Spy girl. The other children are the audience.

Let's Start the Day

Focus Question

**How can I compare things?
¿Cómo puedo comparar cosas?**

✔ Learning Goals

Social and Emotional Development
• Child uses classroom materials carefully.

Language and Communication
• Child names and describes actual or pictured people, places, things, actions, attributes, and events.

Vocabulary

different	diferente	food	alimentos
fruits	frutas	group	grupo
vegetables	vegetales		

Differentiated Instruction

🖐 Extra Support
Phonological Awareness

If...children have difficulty blending sounds, **then...**work with them to say the onset and the rime slowly. Repeat the onset/rime more quickly until the sounds are blended: /s/ . . . -un; /s/. -un, /s/ -un, sun.

⭐ Enrichment
Oral Language and Vocabulary

Challenge children to make a drawing of fruits or vegetables that shows a comparison, such as big/bigger; fat/fatter; long/longer, small/smaller. Have children use what they know about the sounds of letters to label the drawing.

Accommodations for 3's
Phonological Awareness

If...children have difficulty blending onset and rime, **then...**exaggerate the onset in pet, /p/. Point to your lips as you do so. Repeat for the rime, -et. Be sure children watch carefully as you form both onset and rime. Blend the sounds slowly, and guide children to repeat after you.

▶ **Opening Routines and Transition Tips**
For **Opening Routines** and **Transition Tips** turn to pages 178–181 and visit DLMExpressOnline.com for more ideas.

📖 Read **"What's in the Box?"/"¿Qué hay en la caja?"** from the Teacher's Treasure Book, page 253, for your morning Read Aloud.

Language Time

 large group 15 minutes

👥👥👥 **Social and Emotional Development** Encourage children to think of activities as having three parts: getting materials and preparing to work, doing the activity itself, and then completing the activity, which includes cleaning up and putting away materials in an appropriate manner. Discuss activities the class has completed, and encourage children to think about how they might do things differently in the future.

Oral Language and Vocabulary

✔ **Can children name a variety of common fruits and vegetables?**

Fruits and Vegetables Talk about foods children like. Ask: **What is your favorite fruit? What is your favorite vegetable?** ¿Cuál es su fruta favorita? ¿Cuál es su verdura favorita? List children's responses on chart paper. Display Oral Development Language Card 35. Ask: **What is a fruit you see here? What words can we use to talk about this fruit?** ¿Qué fruta ven aquí? ¿Qué palabras podemos escribir para hablar de esa fruta? Repeat for another fruit and several vegetables. Talk about color, shape, and feel of children's favorite fruits. Then follow the suggestions on the back of the card.

ELL Use Oral Language Development Card 35 to review and extend children's vocabulary. For example, point to a fruit and say: **This is a [fruit name].** Ask questions such as: **Have you ever tasted this fruit? How does it taste? Did you enjoy it?** Elicit descriptive words, such as sweet, crunchy, sour, and juicy from children.

Phonological Awareness

✔ **Can children blend word parts to form familiar words?**

Onset and Rime Display Rhymes and Chants Flip Chart, page 19. Say: **Look at this picture. It is very wet outside. It is raining and snowing.** Observen esta ilustración. Está muy húmedo afuera. Llueve y nieva. Track the text as you recite "Let's Compare."

● Say: **Listen: /w/ -et. Let's put the word parts together to make a word: /w/ -et, wet.** Escuchen: /w/ -et. Unamos las partes para formar una palabra: /w/ -et, wet. Say: **Let's blend -et with other beginning sounds to make new words. Say /b/ -et. Now put the parts together: /b/ -et, bet.** Vamos a combinar otros sonidos iniciales para formar nuevas palabras. Digan /b/ -et. Ahora, unan las partes: /b/ -et, bet. Repeat to blend onset and rime for the words get, pet, let, jet, set.

Oral Language Development Card 35

Rhymes and Chants Flip Chart, p. 19

Center Time

Center Rotation Center Time includes teacher-guided activities and independent activities. Refer to the **Learning Centers** on pages 100–101 for independent activity ideas.

 small group 60-90 minutes

Creativity Center

	Center Tip
Can children use art materials for sensory experience and exploration? **Materials** sponges cut into fruit and vegetable shapes, paper, paint (red, yellow, green, orange), small paper plates **Food Prints** Explain to children that they can make fruit and vegetable prints. Put a small amount of each color of paint on paper plates. Model pressing a sponge into the paint and then onto paper. ● Have children use sponges to create designs on their papers. Remind them to use a variety of shapes and colors. ● Help children listen as they work for onset and rime in one-syllable words such as *red* and *big*.	**If**...children have difficulty with their prints running together, **then**... suggest they press the sponge on a paper towel to remove excess paint before making the print.

Writer's Center

	Center Tip
Can children use appropriate writing conventions when writing or giving dictation? **Materials** paper with the sentence frame *I like to eat* _____. **What I Like!** Remind children they have learned about fruits and vegetables. Say: **We will write about fruits and vegetables you like to eat.** *Vamos a escribir sobre las frutas y verduras que les gusta comer.* ● Read aloud the sentence frame. Say: **Draw a picture that shows a fruit or vegetable that you like to eat.** *Hagan un dibujo de una fruta o una verdura que les guste.* ● Ask children to finish the sentence with the fruit or the vegetable they like to eat. Tell children to use scribble writing for sounds they do not know.	**If**...children have difficulty completing the sentence frame, **then**...have them dictate their ideas instead.

Learning Goals

Social and Emotional Development
• Child maintains concentration/attention skills until a task is complete.

Emergent Literacy: Writing
• Child experiments with and uses some writing conventions when writing or dictating.

Fine Arts
• Child uses and experiments with a variety of art materials and tools in various art activities.

Differentiated Instruction

Extra Support
Writer's Center
If...children have difficulty thinking of a fruit or vegetable they like, **then**...have them refer to *Oral Language Development Card 35*, Fruits and Vegetables, for ideas.

Enrichment
Writer's Center
Challenge children to create a book about fruits and vegetables they like. Have them each make three or more pages with drawings and labels. Staple the pages together, and have children share their books with a partner.

Accommodations for 3's
Creativity Center
If...three-year-olds have difficulty handling paints, **then**...cut the fruit and vegetable shapes from colored paper. Have children glue the shapes to drawing paper.

Circle Time

Learning Goals

Language and Communication
• Child uses newly learned vocabulary daily in multiple contexts.

Emergent Literacy: Reading
• Child identifies the letter that stands for a given sound.

• Child describes, relates to, and uses details and information from books read aloud.

Vocabulary

closer	cerca	curious	curiosa
discover	descubrir	nature	naturaleza
outside	afuera	spy	espía

Differentiated Instruction

Extra Support
Read Aloud

If...children have difficulty with the concept of comparatives, **then...**use photographs from *Nature Spy* to increase their understanding. For example, turn to page 11, and ask: **Which leaf seems closer?** *¿Qué hoja parece estar más cerca?* Repeat with the frog on page 16 and the raspberries on page 28.

Enrichment
Read Aloud

Challenge children to use the photos to retell the story to a friend.

Accommodations for 3's
Read Aloud

If...three-year-olds have difficulty attending to the entire book in one sitting, **then...**break the reading up into shorter segments.

Literacy Time

📖 Read Aloud

✓ **Can children use information from a story to compare and contrast?**

Build Background Explain that you will read a book about exploring nature.

• Say: **Nature describes the things in our world that people don't make, such as rocks, plants, and animals.** *En la naturaleza están las cosas de nuestro mundo que no crearon las personas, como las rocas, las plantas o los animales.* Ask: **Where could we go to explore nature?** *¿Dónde podrían ir para explorar la naturaleza?* Explain that many objects of nature are found outside.

Listen for Enjoyment Display *Nature Spy/ Espía de la naturaleza,* and read the title. Explain that a spy is someone who discovers secrets. Point out and read the names of the authors and the photographer. Ask: **What did the authors do to make this book? What did the photographer do?** *¿Qué hicieron los autores para hacer este libro? ¿Qué hizo el fotógrafo?*

• Ask: **Where is the girl going? What do you think she will discover?** *¿Adónde va la niña? ¿Qué creen que descubrirá?*

• Read the book aloud. Pause to have children make comparisons. On pages 14 and 15, ask: **Which picture shows a closer look at the bird's feathers?** *¿En qué fotografía se ven más de cerca las plumas del pájaro?*

Respond to the Story Discuss the story. Review the photographs, and talk about what the girl discovers outside. Say: **The girl was very curious. Did anything in this book make you curious? How could you learn more?** *La niña era muy curiosa. ¿Hay algo de este libro que les dé curiosidad? ¿Cómo pueden aprender más sobre eso?*

ELL Remind children that people do not make the things found in nature. Display and identify pictures of objects found in nature. Say: **This is a (tree). It is part of nature.** Have children repeat the names of the objects.

Learn About Letters and Sounds

✓ **Can children identify the letters Nn and Kk and the sound each makes?**

Learn About the Letters Nn and Kk Display the *Nn* page in the *ABC Big Book.* Say the letter name.

• Point to the picture of the nose. Say: **This is a nose. What sound do you hear at the beginning of nose? What letter makes the /n/ sound?** *¿Qué es esto? ¿Qué sonido escuchan al principio de nose? ¿Qué letra tiene el sonido /n/?.*

• Repeat with the *Kk* page, pointing to the kite to review the /k/ sound.

• Refer to the Letter Formation Chart on page 348 to review the formation strokes. Have children trace each letter in the air or on a tabletop. Ask: **Which letter is formed with straight lines? Which letter has a curved line?** *¿Qué letra se forma con líneas rectas? ¿Qué letra tiene una línea curva?*

Nature Spy
Espía de la naturaleza

ABC Big Book

large group · 15 minutes

Math Time

☑ **Can children correctly compare the heights of objects?**

☑ **Can children count up to ten items?**

Mr. Mixup (Comparing) Tell children Mr. Mixup has come to class today.

- Present two Connecting Cubes towers. Place a cube tower of eight cubes on the floor and a cube tower of four cubes on a chair. Ask Mr. Mixup which cube tower has more cubes. Have Mr. Mixup say: *Well, the cube tower on the chair has more cubes, of course. Bien, la torre que está sobre la silla tiene más cubos, por supuesto.* Ask children to verify whether Mr. Mixup is correct. Say: *Did Mr. Mixup answer my question correctly? Are there more cubes in the tower on the floor or on the tower on the chair? ¿Respondió el Sr. Confundido mi pregunta correctamente? ¿Hay más cubos en la torre sobre el suelo o en la torre que está en la silla?* Count the cubes in both towers together with the class.

- Discuss how even though the top of the tower on the chair is higher above the ground, that tower doesn't have more cubes than the tower on the floor. Say: *Mr. Mixup has made another mistake! Even though this cube tower is higher, it has fewer cubes than the tower on the floor. ¡El Sr. Confundido ha cometido otro error! Aunque esta torre de cubos es más alta, tiene menos cubos que la torre que está sobre el suelo.*

- Repeat with other towers of up to ten cubes and similar scenarios.

large group · 15 minutes

✝✝✝ Social and Emotional Development

Making Good Choices

☑ **Do children listen and participate in classroom discussion?**

Time to Share Say: *It is fun to share things at school. Es divertido compartir cosas en la escuela.* Display the *Making Good Choices Flip Chart,* page 19.

- Discuss the illustration. Say: *These children are having Show and Tell time. They are learning about something and sharing with one another. Estos niños están aprendiendo y compartiendo entre sí.*

- Ask: *What is the boy sharing? Who is listening? Are they all good listeners? ¿Qué está compartiendo el niño? ¿Quién está escuchando? ¿Todos están escuchando correctamente?*

- Encourage children to discuss strategies if others are not listening to them. Ask: *How do you feel if people don't listen when you share? ¿Cómo se sentirían si alguien no escuchara cuando están compartiendo algo?*

ELL Use the illustration to enhance children's vocabulary. Point to the teacher. Say: *This is the teacher. Who is this?* Then point to the shell. Say: *This is a shell. What is this?* Repeat for *girl, boy, book, truck,* and so on.

Making Good Choices Flip Chart, p. 19.

Building Blocks

Online Math Activity

Introduce Build Stairs 3: Find the Missing Step, in which children choose the step that is missing from a staircase. Keep Connecting Cubes by the computer so children can use them to help solve computer problems with hands-on items.

 Learning Goals

Social and Emotional Development
- Child demonstrates appropriate conflict-resolution strategies, requesting help when needed.

Mathematics
- Child demonstrates that, when counting, the last number indicates how many objects were counted.

- Child measures the length and height of people or objects using standard or non-standard tools.

Vocabulary

answer	responder	compare	comparar
fewer	menos	height	altura
higher	más alto	learn	aprender
question	pregunta		

Differentiated Instruction

 Extra Support

Making Good Choices

If...children have difficulty attending to the activity, **then...**reinforce good behavior by pointing out children who attend. For example, say: *I really like the way Julio is listening. Realmente me gusta la manera en que está escuchando Julio.*

⭐ **Enrichment**

Math Time

Challenge children to compare the heights of several classroom objects.

Accommodations for 3's

Math Time

If...children have trouble counting the cubes, **then...**use fewer cubes to start and slowly increase the number.

 Special Needs

Cognitive Challenges

Some children may not be able to learn as fast or count as many objects as their classmates. With practice, the child will learn.

Focus Question
How can I compare things?
¿Cómo puedo comparar cosas?

 Learning Goals

Language and Communication
• Child names and describes actual or pictured people, places, things, actions, attributes, and events.

Science
• Child uses senses to observe, classify, investigate, and collect data.

Vocabulary

alike	parecido	compare	comparar
different	diferente	rough	áspero
smooth	suave	sort	clasificar
texture	textura		

Differentiated Instruction

 Extra Support

Oral Language and Academic Vocabulary
If...children cannot name colors, then...name a color, and have children point to a fruit of that color.

Enrichment

Observe and Investigate
Challenge children to sort five or six classroom objects into two groups according to their textures.

Accommodations for 3's

Oral Language and Academic Vocabulary
If...children have trouble using words to describe and classify objects, then...encourage them to group the items according to how they feel to the touch and to think of descriptive words based on their grouping.

Science Time

  large group 20 minutes

Personal Safety Skills Model proper safety procedures by keeping hands away from the mouth, eyes, and face while investigating. Caution children not to taste or eat any of the food items they are working with.

Oral Language and Academic Vocabulary

☑️ **Can children compare the characteristics of fruits?**

Point to the *Math and Science Flip Chart*, page 33. Say: *When you sort objects, you group them by a characteristic. A characteristic is a quality the item has, such as color or texture. These fruits are sorted by color, size, and kind. Cuando clasifican objetos, los comparan y agrupan los que tienen las mismas características. Una característica una cualidad de algo, como el color o la forma. Estas frutas están clasificadas según el color, el tamaño y el tipo.* Ask children to find the apples. *Ask: How many colors of grapes do you see? What colors are they? ¿Cuántos colores de uvas ven? ¿Cuáles son esos colores?*

Math and Science Flip Chart, p. 33

● Talk about how each fruit feels when you touch it with your skin. Explain that this quality is called *texture*. Have children compare the texture, or feel, of an apple to the texture of a kiwi or a pineapple. Point to two different grapes for children to compare. Ask: *How are these grapes alike, or similar? How are they different? ¿En qué son parecidas estas manzanas? ¿En qué son diferentes?*

ELL Hold up two red cubes. Say: *These cubes are alike. They are the same color.* Then hold up a red cube and a yellow cube. Say: *These cubes are different colors.* Continue holding up pairs of cubes and having children tell whether the cubes are the same or different colors.

Observe and Investigate

☑️ **Can children sort materials according to texture?**

Provide children with small bowls of different baking materials, including flour, salt, sugar, and corn meal. Label each material. Say: *These are materials used in baking. That is a characteristic they share. What are some other ways these materials are similar?* (color, size, dry) *Estos materiales se usan para hornear. Ésa es su característica en común. ¿En qué otra cosa se parecen estos materiales? (color, tamaño, textura)* Have children feel each material and describe its texture. Say: *When you feel something with your skin, one characteristic you feel is texture. Some things feel smooth or rough or scratchy. These are textures. Cuando dicen cómo se siente algo al tocarlo, están contando cuál su textura. Las cosas pueden ser suaves, ásperas o rugosas. Ésas son texturas.* Allow children *to feel each material and describe the texture.* Encourage children to use words such as *smooth, rough, fluffy, soft, grainy.*

● Ask children to sort the materials into two groups: smooth and rough. Encourage children to touch each material again to check their sorting. Ask children to name other things that could be placed in each group because of their textures. Ask: *What are other things that feel smooth? rough? ¿Qué otras cosas son suaves? ¿Y ásperas?*

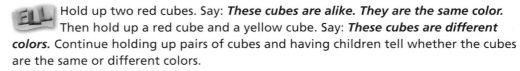

Center Time

▶ **Center Rotation** Center Time includes teacher-guided activities and independent activities. Refer to the **Learning Centers** on pages 100–101 for independent activity ideas.

 small group | **30 minutes**

Math and Science Center

Center Tip

☑ **Can children compare textures made by different objects?**

Materials disposable items with a variety of textures such as tree bark, sponge, potato, scrubber; paper, paint, paint brushes

Comparing Textures Introduce the items, and have children feel them and describe their textures. Tell children they will use paint with the objects to make prints on paper that will show textures.

- Demonstrate for children how to dip a brush into paint and dab a small amount of paint on one of the items. Then model making a print by applying the painted surface of the item to the paper.

- Have children describe which objects made smooth prints and which objects made prints that show bumps. Help children label each print with the name of the object.

If...children have difficulty showing rough textures in the paint, **then...**help them use the proper amount of paint.

Learning Goals

Language and Communication
• Child names and describes actual or pictured people, places, things, actions, attributes, and events.

Emergent Literacy: Writing
• Child experiments with and uses some writing conventions when writing or dictating.

Science
• Child uses senses to observe, classify, investigate, and collect data.

 Writing

Ask children to draw a picture of something they have found in nature. Invite them to label the item they drew. Children can use invented spelling or scribble writing for sounds they do not know.

Purposeful Play

☑ **Observe to see if children work until objects are sorted according to characteristics.**

Children choose an open center area for free playtime. Encourage them to sort different classroom objects according to different characteristics, such as texture, color, purpose, and so on.

Let's Say Good-Bye

 large group | **15 minutes**

 Read Aloud Revisit "What's In the Box?"/"¿Qué hay en la caja?" for your afternoon Read Aloud. Ask children what they learned about fruits and vegetables.

 Home Connection Refer to the Home Connections activities listed in the Resources and Materials chart on page 97. Remind children to explain to their families how they can be "nature spies." Sing the "Good-Bye Song" as children prepare to leave.

Focus Question
How can I compare things?
¿Cómo puedo comparar cosas?

 Learning Goals

Social and Emotional Development
• Child maintains concentration/attention skills until a task is complete.

Language and Communication
• Child names and describes actual or pictured people, places, things, actions, attributes, and events.

Emergent Literacy: Reading
• Child blends onset and rime to form a word without pictoral support.
• Child describes, relates to, and uses details and information from books read aloud.

Vocabulary

answers   respuestas   compare   comparar

observe   observar

Differentiated Instruction

 Extra Support
Oral Language and Vocabulary
If...children respond with a single word or phrase, **then...**offer cues to help them use complete sentences. For example, if a child answers the question "What might the girl discover in the woods?" with the word *leaves,* say: *Yes. The girl might discover leaves. Sí, la niña podría descubrir hojas.* Then have the child repeat the complete sentence.

★ **Enrichment**
Oral Language and Vocabulary
Challenge children to choose a characteristic such as shape or color. Have them draw a variety of items that share the characteristic. Ask children to label their pictures with a word that describes the characteristic, such as *round* or *green.*

 Opening Routines and Transition Tips
For **Opening Routines** and **Transition Tips** turn to pages 178–181 and visit **DLMExpressOnline.com** for more ideas.

 Read **"Pam and Sam"/**"Pam y Sam" from the *Teacher's Treasure Book*, page 195, for your morning Read Aloud.

Language Time

 large group 15 minutes

Social and Emotional Development Remind children of the importance of sticking with a task until it is completed.

Oral Language and Vocabulary

✓ **Can children listen and participate during a group activity?**

Noticing Nature Remind children about the girl who is a nature spy. Ask: *If you were a nature spy, what might you observe on the playground? At a park? Si fueran espías de la naturaleza, ¿qué podrían observar en el patio? ¿Y en un parque?*

● Model using a complete sentence to answer questions. Ask: *What might the girl discover in a pond? ¿Qué podría descubrir la niña en un estanque?* Supply the answer: *She might discover a frog. Podría descubrir una rana.* Then ask: *What might the girl observe about the frog? ¿Qué características de la rana podría observar la niña?* Discuss characteristics such as size, color, and so on.

● Ask children to suggest things the girl might discover in the woods or on the beach and what she might observe about each object. Encourage children to answer using complete sentences.

ELL Help children understand the use of comparatives. Display two objects in different sizes, such as balls. Say: *Let's compare these balls. One ball is big. The other ball is bigger.* Ask: *Which ball is bigger?* Continue with objects such as books (thin/thinner), blocks (tall/taller), and toy vehicles (small/smaller).

Phonological Awareness

✓ **Can children blend onset and rime to say familiar words?**

Onset and Rime Display the Dog Puppets. Say: *Let's play a word game with our friends, the puppets. Vamos a jugar a un juego de palabras con los perritos.* Have one puppet say /d/, and then have the other puppet say -og. Say: *Let's put the parts together: /d/ -og. What word does that make? Unamos las partes: /d/ -og. ¿Qué palabra se forma?* Repeat, having the puppets say the word parts and asking children to blend to say words such as: /k/ -at, cat; /f/ -ox, fox; /h/ -en, hen; /p/ -ig, pig.

Nature Spy
Espía de la naturaleza

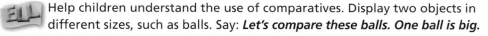

Center Time

▶ **Center Rotation** Center Time includes teacher-guided activities and independent activities. Refer to the **Learning Centers** on pages 100–101 for independent activity ideas.

 small group 60–90 minutes

Library and Listening Center

☑ **Can children use varied vocabulary to describe objects found in nature?**

Materials *Photo Library* CD-ROM or books with illustrations of natural objects: plants, animals, water, and land; drawing paper; crayons

Nature Discoveries Invite children to make discoveries about nature.

- Have children look at photographs of items found in nature.

- Ask children to each draw one thing they discover and to label the drawing. Then have them describe their illustration to a partner.

Center Tip

If...children have difficulty describing objects, **then...**offer prompts by asking questions about the size, shape, or color of the object.

ABC Center

☑ **Note children's ability to form letters and to identify the sound each one makes.**

Materials ABC Picture Cards *Kk* and *Nn*, aluminum pie plates, play sand, tools for "writing" (for example, plastic knife, straw, unsharpened pencil)

Sand Writing Give each child a pie plate with a shallow layer of sand in it and a writing tool. Tell children they can write in the sand.

- Say: *Use your tool to make uppercase and lowercase* **Kk** *in the sand. Say the name of the letter and the sound it makes. Then "erase" the letter by smoothing out the sand.* *Usen su herramienta para hacer una Kk mayúscula y una minúscula en la arena. Digan el nombre de la letra y el sonido que tiene. Luego, "borren" la letra alisando la arena.*

- Have children repeat the activity with *Nn*.

- Help children listen for onset and rime in one-syllable words beginning with *Kk* or *Nn*; for example, *kit* or *nap*.

Center Tip

If...children have difficulty identifying the /k/ or /n/ sound, **then...**prompt them by pointing to an illustration on the letter card and asking: *What is this? What sound do you hear at the beginning of [word]?* *¿Qué es esto? ¿Qué sonido escuchan al comienzo de [palabra]?*

Language and Communication
- Child names and describes actual or pictured people, places, things, actions, attributes, and events.

Emergent Literacy: Reading
- Child independently engages in pre-reading behaviors and activities (such as, pretending to read, turning one page at a time).

Emergent Literacy: Writing
- Child writes some letters or reasonable approximations of letters upon request.

Differentiated Instruction

 Extra Support

Library and Listening Center
If...children have difficulty identifying objects other than plants and animals as natural objects, **then...**ask questions to prompt understanding. For example, point to an illustration of a river, and ask: *Did a human make this river, or is it found in nature?* *¿Un ser humano hizo este río o se encuentra en la naturaleza?*

 Enrichment

Library and Listening Center
Challenge children to use illustrations to make comparisons between natural objects they observe. Ask them to draw a picture that shows a comparison, such as trees that are *tall* and *taller*.

Accommodations for 3's

ABC Center
If...children have difficulty forming a letter, **then...**put your hand over the child's, and form the letter together. Then have the child form the letter independently.

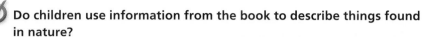

Focus Question

How can I compare things?
¿Cómo puedo comparar cosas?

 Learning Goals

Emergent Literacy: Reading
• Child identifies the letter that stands for a given sound.

• Child describes, relates to, and uses details and information from books read aloud.

Vocabulary

answers   respuestas   discover   descubrir

observe   observar

 Differentiated Instruction

 Extra Support

Learn About Letters and Sounds
If... If children have difficulty saying the /n/ sound, **then...**demonstrate the correct position of the tongue. Say these words slowly and have children repeat after you: *not, net, on.*

Enrichment

Read Aloud
Ask children to use the photographs to retell the story to a partner.

Special Needs

Vision Loss
If the child has peripheral vision, make sure he or she is seated so that peripheral vision is optimized and that lighting is appropriate and does not cause a "glare" effect.

Literacy Time

📖 **Read Aloud**

✓ Do children use information from the book to describe things found in nature?

Build Background Say: *Nature is all around us. What is something we might observe outside? What color (shape, size) is this object?* La naturaleza nos rodea. ¿Qué podríamos observar afuera? ¿De qué color (figura, tamaño) es este objeto?

Listen for Understanding Display *Nature Spy/Espía de la naturaleza,* and read the title aloud.

● Say: *Listen to find out what the girl observes outside.* Escuchen con atención para descubrir qué cosas observa la niña cuando sale. Read the book aloud. To build print awareness, track the text as you read.

Respond to the Story Browse the book as you discuss it with children.

● Model using complete sentences to answer questions. Ask: *What does she discover about a spider web?* ¿Qué ve la niña en la telaraña? *She discovers a spider web has a pattern.* La niña ve dibujos en la telaraña.

● Continue to browse the book, pausing to have children describe the girl's discoveries. Ask: *What shape is the frog's eye?* ¿Qué forma tienen los ojos de las ranas? or *What colors do you see in the leaves?* ¿De qué colores son las hojas? Guide children to answer each question with a sentence.

ELL Use Pattern Blocks to review shape and color words. Display a block, and identify its shape and color. For example, say: *This is a red circle.* Have children repeat the sentence. When all shapes have been identified, ask children to find a specific block, such as the green square.

Learn About Letters and Sounds

✓ Can children identify the sounds /k/ and /n/?

Review the Letters Kk and Nn Display the *ABC Picture Card* Kk.

● Review the letter name and the sound it makes. Say: *Name a word that starts with /k/.* Digan una palabra que empiece con /k/.

● Refer to the Letter Formation Guide on page 189 to review the formation strokes for *K* and *k.* Say: *Let's use our fingers to make capital K in the air. Now let's make lowercase k.* Vamos a usar nuestros dedos para escribir la K mayúscula en el aire. Ahora, hagamos la k minúscula. Repeat with the *ABC Picture Card* Nn.

● Say: *Listen carefully. If I say a word that starts with /n/, nod your head. If the word starts with /k/, keep your head still.* Escuchen atentamente. Si digo una palabra que empieza con /n/, muevan su cabeza. Si digo una palabra que empieza con /k/, déjenla quieta. Say these words: *kitten, no, kid, name, nest, king.*

Nature Spy
Espía de la naturaleza

ABC Picture Cards

Math Time

 Can children count objects from 1 to 10?

Knock It Down! Invite children to play a game that involves building and knocking down towers of objects.

- Using safe, stackable objects, build a tower of no more than ten objects for the class. Say: *Look at this tower I made. I wonder how tall it is. Let's count the number of objects in this tower.* *Miren esta torre. Contemos cuántos objetos hay en esta torre.* Slowly count the objects with children.

- Then invite children to knock down the tower. Say: *Let's knock down this tower! After we knock it down, let's count the number of objects again. Is it the same number?* *¡Derribemos esta torre! Después de derribarla, contemos los objetos nuevamente. ¿Es la misma cantidad?*

- Invite children to build a tower taller than yours. Ask: *How many objects are in your tower?* Have children count the objects and knock down their towers, comparing the number of objects before and after.

𝕩𝕩𝕩 Social and Emotional Development

Making Good Choices

 Can children participate in a discussion by listening and responding?

Circle Time Discuss circle time activities in your classroom. Ask: *What do you like to do during circle time? ¿Qué les gusta hacer durante la hora del círculo?* Display the *Making Good Choices Flip Chart,* page 19. Model using a puppet to review the chart.

- Ask: *Can you tell us what these children are doing during circle time? ¿Pueden decir qué hacen estos niños durante la hora del círculo?* Have the puppet answer: *The children are showing special items to the class and sharing their ideas with their classmates. Los niños están mostrando algunas cosas especiales y compartiendo sus ideas con los compañeros.*

- Ask: *What do good listeners do at sharing time? Use the puppet to tell us.* *¿Cómo se comporta un buen oyente durante el tiempo de compartir? Usen el perrito títere para responder.* Have children take turns using the puppet to identify characteristics of good listeners. Guide children to discuss respectful listening, taking turns, and sitting quietly.

ELL Explain that friends share ideas and feelings by talking about something that interests them or about themselves. Say: *I'll share something about myself. I like to (read).* Ask children to use this sentence frame to share something about themselves.

large group · 15 minutes

Building Blocks

Online Math Activity
Introduce Workin' on the Railroad, in which children learn about non-standard measurement.

Making Good Choices Flip Chart, p. 19

✓ Learning Goals

Social and Emotional Development
- Child maintains concentration/attention skills until a task is complete.

Mathematics
- Child demonstrates that, when counting, the last number indicates how many objects were counted.

Vocabulary

circle	círculo	count	contar
listener	oyente	objects	objetos
sharing	compartir	tower	torre

Differentiated Instruction

✋ Extra Support
Making Good Choices
If...children have difficulty describing a good listener, **then...**ask *yes/no* questions such as: *Does a good listener look at the speaker? Does a good listener talk when someone is sharing? ¿Un buen oyente mira a la persona que está hablando? ¿Un buen oyente habla cuando alguien está compartiendo algo?*

⭐ Enrichment
Making Good Choices
Challenge children to act out various good listening habits.

Accommodations for 3's
Math Time
If...children have difficulty building towers, **then...**help them with building, but allow them to knock down the tower.

Focus Question

How can I compare things?
¿Cómo puedo comparar cosas?

 Learning Goals

Mathematics
• Child measures the length and height of people or objects using standard or non-standard tools.

Science
• Child follows basic health and safety rules.

Vocabulary

arm	brazo	length	largo
longer	más largo	same	igual
shorter	más corto		

Differentiated Instruction

 Extra Support
Math Time
If...children have difficulty predicting the lengths of objects, **then...**ask them just to compare by measuring.

Enrichment
Math Time
Ask children to visually compare the lengths of each other's strings.

Accommodations for 3's
Math Time
If...children struggle during the Math Time activity, **then...**work with small groups, using fewer objects that are easy to measure.

 Special Needs
Delayed Motor Development
If the child has severe motor delays, you may wish to assign a peer buddy to help the child with measuring.

Math Time

 large group 20 minutes

Personal Safety Skills Model safe and appropriate use of scissors, and supervise children as they use them.

 Can children compare lengths of objects?

As Long As My Arm Have children compare the lengths of objects to the lengths of their arms.

● Gather string and scissors. Help each child cut string to the length of his or her arm from finger to shoulder.

● Using a string cut to the length of your arm, model how to measure a few items. Say: *I am going to place this string beside this object. Let's compare the two. The string is longer than the object.* *Colocaré esta cuerda al lado de este objeto. Vamos a comparar. La cuerda es más larga que el objeto.*

● Repeat with objects that are shorter than and the same length as the string.

● Tell children to find objects in the room that are longer than their arm. Say: *Can you find objects in the room that are longer than your arm?* *¿Pueden encontrar objetos en la clase que sean más largos que su brazo?*

● Then ask children to find objects that are the same length as or shorter than their arms.

● Encourage children to predict the lengths of objects before they measure them with the string. Model by saying: *I think this block is shorter than the length of my arm. Let's find out.* *Creo que este bloque es más corto que mi brazo. Comprobémoslo.*

● Observe that children use appropriate vocabulary when comparing lengths (*shorter, longer, same*). Help children avoid using *smaller* or *bigger*.

ELL Be sure English Language Learners understand the meanings of the words *longer, shorter, same*. Point to one of two objects, and have children say "longer" or "shorter."

● For additional suggestions on how to meet the needs of children at the Beginning, Intermediate, Advanced, and Advanced-High levels of English proficiency, see pages 184–187.

Center Time

▶ **Center Rotation** Center Time includes teacher-guided activities and independent activities. Refer to the **Learning Centers** on pages 100–101 for independent activity ideas.

  small group 30 minutes

✓ Learning Goals

Emergent Literacy: Writing
• Child experiments with and uses some writing conventions when writing or dictating.

Mathematics
• Child measures the length and height of people or objects using standard or non-standard tools.

Math and Science Center

	Center Tip
☑ **Can children find items as tall as they are?** **Materials** string, scissors **As Long As I Am Tall** Show children how they can use part of their body to measure something. Spread your hand as wide as it will go, and use it to measure a desk. Say: *If we use a body part for measuring, we have our measuring tool with us wherever we go. If we want to find something that is as long as we are tall, though, it is easier to first use string to measure our height.* *Si usamos una parte del cuerpo para medir, tenemos nuestra herramienta de medición con nosotros en cualquier lugar. Sin embargo, si queremos encontrar algo del mismo largo que nuestra altura, es más fácil usar primero una cuerda para medirnos.* Help each child cut string to the length of his or her body. Give the child the string, and challenge the child to find classroom objects that are the same length as the string. • Say: *Use your string to find objects that are as long as you are tall.* *Usen la cuerda para encontrar objetos que tengan el mismo largo que su altura.* Encourage children to work together to find objects.	**If…**children have difficulty holding up the length of the string, **then…** have them work with partners.

Writing

Recap the day. Invite children to recall what they did during circle time. Record their ideas on separate lines on chart paper. Read the sentences back as you track the print.

Purposeful Play

☑ **Observe children finding objects as long as they are tall.**

Children choose an open center for free playtime. Encourage children to stand next to objects to find some as tall as they are.

Let's Say Good-Bye

 large group  15 minutes

 Read Aloud Revisit "Pam and Sam"/"Pam y Sam" for your afternoon Read Aloud. Ask children what they learned about comparing lengths.

 Home Connection Refer to the Home Connections activities listed in the Resources and Materials chart on page 97. Remind children to tell families what they notice when they play outside. Sing the "Good-Bye Song" as children prepare to leave.

Let's Start the Day

Focus Question

How can I compare things?
¿Cómo puedo comparar cosas?

 Learning Goals

Social and Emotional Development
• Child maintains concentration/attention skills until a task is complete.

Language and Communication
• Child names and describes actual or pictured people, places, things, actions, attributes, and events.

Emergent Literacy: Reading
• Child blends onset and rime to form a word without pictoral support.

Vocabulary

big	grande	different	diferente
object	objeto	size	tamaño
small	pequeño		

Differentiated Instruction

 Extra Support

Oral Language and Vocabulary
If...children have difficulty using complete sentences when describing objects, **then...** restate the idea in a complete sentence, and have the child echo the sentence.

Enrichment

Phonological Awareness
Challenge partners to take turns quickly blending onset and rime in words such as *cat*, *bat*, *mat*, and *sat*.

Accommodations for 3's

Oral Language and Vocabulary
If...children get stuck trying to describe differences, **then...**ask them to compare the heights of two classroom objects. *Ask: Which object is bigger (smaller)? ¿Qué objeto es más grande (más pequeño)?*

 Opening Routines and Transition Tips

For **Opening Routines** and **Transition Tips** turn to pages 178–181 and visit DLMExpressOnline.com for more ideas.

Read **"Wally Worm's World"/**"El mundo del gusano Wally" from the *Teacher's Treasure Book,* page 212, for your morning Read Aloud.

Language Time

XXX Social and Emotional Development Encourage children to stay focused during group activities.

Oral Language and Vocabulary

✓ **Can children use varied vocabulary to describe and compare objects?**

All About Size Display two books that are similar but different sizes. Ask: *How are these books the same? How are they different? ¿En qué se parecen estos libros? ¿En qué se diferencian?*

• Display *Oral Language Development Card 36.* Ask: *What do you see? Observe the elephants carefully. What do you notice? Use a sentence to describe one elephant. Now describe the other elephant. ¿Qué ven? Observen los elefantes. ¿Qué notan aquí? Usen una oración para describir uno de los elefantes. Ahora, describan el otro elefante.*

• Review the suggestions on the back of the card.

ELL Use hand gestures to reinforce understanding of the opposites *big* and *small*. Point to the large elephant. Stretch your arms out wide, and say: *This elephant is bigger.* Point to the small elephant. Put your thumb and index finger together, and say: *This elephant is smaller.* Ask children to use hand gestures to describe other big and small animals.

Phonological Awareness

✓ **Can children blend word parts to pronounce familiar words?**

Onset and Rime Display *Rhymes and Chants Flip Chart,* page 19. Say: *Listen as I read "Let's Compare." Escuchen mientras leo "¡A comparar!".*

• Say: *I will say a word, and then we will put its parts together. Voy a decir una palabra y luego vamos a unir sus partes.* Say: *The word is can. Let's put the parts together to make can: /k/ -an, can. La palabra es can. Vamos a unir las partes para formar can: /k/ -an.* Then say: *Now listen to this word: /f/ -an. Let's put the parts together: /f/ -an, fan. Ahora, escuchen esta palabra: /f/ -an. Unamos las partes: /f/ -an, fan.*

• Repeat to blend onset and rime for the words *man, pan, Dan,* and *ran.*

Oral Language Development Card 36

Rhymes and Chants Flip Chart, p. 19

Center Time

> ▶ **Center Rotation** Center Time includes teacher-guided activities and independent activities. Refer to the **Learning Centers** on pages 100–101 for independent activity ideas.

small group 60–90 minutes

Refer to the **Learning Centers** on pages 100–101 for independent activity ideas.

Learning Goals

Language and Communication
• Child names and describes actual or pictured people, places, things, actions, attributes, and events.

Mathematics
• Child measures the length and height of people or objects using standard or non-standard tools.

Pretend and Learn Center

 Track that children observe and describe similarities and differences in objects.

Materials dishpan, play sand, variety of rocks, small shovels, hand lenses

Be a Rock Hunter Prepare by placing the rocks in the dishpan and covering them with sand. Tell children that they will pretend to be rock hunters.

• Have children take turns using shovels to hunt in the sand to discover two rocks.

• Ask children to use a hand lens to observe the rocks they find. Say: ***Find one way the rocks are similar and one way they are different. Tell a friend what you notice.*** *Observen en qué se parecen y en qué se diferencian esas rocas. Cuéntenle a un amigo lo que descubren.*

• Help children listen for onset and rime in words such as *pan* and *sand*.

Center Tip

If...children finish before Center Time is over, **then...**suggest they draw pictures to show how their rocks are the same or different.

Construction Center

 Note children's ability to use comparative adjectives as they describe their towers.

Materials building blocks, drawing paper, crayons

Build It Big! Say: ***You can build towers with blocks.*** *Podemos construir torres con bloques.*

• Have each child build two towers. Say: ***Make one tower taller than the other***. *Hagan una torre más alta que la otra.*

• Ask children to tell a friend about their towers, using the words *taller* and *shorter*.

• Have children draw their towers. Remind children that their drawings should show that the towers are different sizes.

Center Tip

If...a child makes both towers the same size, **then...**give the child another block. Say: ***Add this block to one tower. Now look at your towers. Which tower is taller? Which tower is shorter?*** *Agrega este bloque a una torre. Ahora, mira tus torres. ¿Qué torre es más alta? ¿Qué torre es más baja?*

Differentiated Instruction

 Extra Support

Pretend and Learn Center
If...children have difficulty identifying similarities and differences, **then...**model an example, such as: ***I notice that both rocks are shiny. I notice that this rock is flatter than the other rock.*** *Veo que las dos rocas son brillantes. Veo también que esta roca es más lisa que la otra.*

⭐ Enrichment

Pretend and Learn Center
Challenge children to observe and note differences and similarities in another set of objects, such as shells, feathers, or leaves.

Accommodations for 3's

Construction Center
If...three-year-olds say *more big* or *more small* instead of using comparative adjectives, **then...** restate their response, using the correct form of the adjective. Have children echo the sentence.

♥ Special Needs

Behavioral Social/Emotional
When working in centers, keep the groups small, so the child does not have to wait a long time for her/his turn, as this could lead to outbursts.

Circle Time

Focus Question
How can I compare things?
¿Cómo puedo comparar cosas?

 Learning Goals

Emergent Literacy: Reading
• Child identifies the letter that stands for a given sound.
• Child describes, relates to, and uses details and information from books read aloud.

Vocabulary

compare	*comparar*	detective	*detective*
rough	*áspero*	smooth	*suave*
tools	*instrumentos*		

Differentiated Instruction

 Extra Support

Read Aloud
If...children have difficulty counting words in the book title, **then...**write a three-word sentence on chart paper, such as *Dogs can run.* Read the sentence, pointing to each word. Then assign one word each to three children. Reread the sentence, and have each child stand as you say his or her word. Count the children. Then count the words in the sentence.

⭐ **Enrichment**

Learn About Letters and Sounds
Invite children to have fun with tongue twisters that feature /n/ or /k/, such as: **Ned noticed Nat's napkin. Can Ken catch Kate's kite?**

Accommodations for 3's

Learn About Letters and Sounds
If...three-year-olds have difficulty distinguishing the sounds of /n/ and /m/, **then...**work with onsets and rime to review the two sounds. Exaggerate the beginning consonant as you have children repeat after you: /n/ -et, *net;* /m/ -et, *met;* /n/ -ine, nine; /m/ -ine, mine.

Literacy Time

📖 Read Aloud

✅ Do children use information from the book to describe and compare learning methods?

Build Background Say: *We're going to read about being detectives.* *Vamos a leer un libro sobre cómo ser detectives.*

● Ask: *What is a detective? How do detectives learn things?* *¿Qué es un detective? ¿Cómo descubren cosas los detectives?*

Listen for Understanding Display *Let's Investigate/Soy detective,* page 17, and read the title. Build print awareness by pointing out that the words in the title are separated by a space. Say: *Let's count the words in the title—1, 2. Contemos las palabras del título: 1, 2.*

● Browse the book. Pause to ask questions about the photographs, such as: *How are these children learning about things? What tool is this child using to learn more?* *¿Cómo aprenden algunas cosas estos niños? ¿Qué instrumento usa este niño para aprender más sobre las rocas?* Read the book aloud, tracking the print as you read.

Respond to the Story Discuss the story. Ask: *How do the children learn new things? How do we learn new things in our classroom? How are the children in the story like the girl in* Nature Spy? *How are they different? ¿Qué hacen los niños del libro para aprender nuevas cosas? ¿Cómo aprendemos nuevas cosas en nuestra clase? ¿En qué se parecen los niños del cuento a la niña de Espía de la naturaleza? ¿En qué se diferencian?* Revisit several photographs, and ask children to compare what is going on in the photograph to what is going on in the classroom. Ask: *Is the activity in the photograph the same as or different from what you do? ¿Es diferente o parecida la actividad que ven en esta fotografía a las que ustedes hacen?*

ELL To help children understand the story opposites *smooth* and *rough,* give them experience with the two textures. Display a smooth rock for children to touch. Say: *This rock is smooth.* Then have children touch a rough rock. Say: *This rock is not smooth. It is rough.*

Learn About Letters and Sounds

✅ Can children write *Kk* and *Nn* and identify the sounds of the letters?

Learn About the Letters *Kk* and *Nn* Display the ABC *Picture Cards* for *Kk* and *Nn.*

● Hold up the *Kk* card. Ask: *What is this letter? What sound does it make? ¿Qué letra es esta? ¿Qué sonido tiene?* Say: *Use your finger to write uppercase K on the table. Now write lowercase k. Usen su dedo para escribir la K mayúscula en la mesa. Ahora, escriban la k minúscula.* Repeat for uppercase *N* and lowercase *n.*

● Act out words that begin with the sound /n/ or /k/, such as *nod, kick, nap, knock,* and *carry.* Have children guess what word you are miming and tell what sound they hear at the beginning of the word.

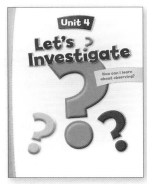

Let's Investigate,
Soy detective
p. 17

ABC Picture Cards

Math Time

Observe and Investigate

✓ **Can children compare their heights?**

Line Up by Height Invite children to line up by height, and discuss who is tallest and shortest in the group.

- Divide children into small groups. Guide them to line up in order by height.

- Ask: *Is the tallest person at the end of the line? Is the shortest person at the other end of the line? Did the group line up correctly?* *¿Está la persona más alta al final de la fila? ¿Está la persona más baja al comienzo de la fila? ¿Está el grupo correctamente ordenado en la fila?*

- Be sure not to present being short or tall as either a positive trait or a negative trait.

   Model comparing by using the phrase *as tall as* _____ to describe children in the class.

 large group 15 minutes

⅋ Social and Emotional Development

Making Good Choices

✓ **Are children able to sustain good listening habits during group activities?**

Listen and Learn Display the *Making Good Choices Flip Chart*, page 19. Discuss the illustration. Use the Dog Puppets to act out a scenario based on the chart.

Puppet 1: I don't really like turtles, so I stopped listening before Victor was finished talking about his pet turtle.

Puppet 2: Victor knows a lot about turtles. I learned a lot from him.

Puppet 1: What did you learn?

Puppet 2: I learned what kind of foods turtles eat. Do you know?

Puppet 1: No, I don't know. I should have listened until Victor was finished talking, but sometimes it's hard for me.

Puppet 2: Sometimes it's hard for me, too, but I always learn something if I listen until someone is done speaking.

- Invite children to take turns using the puppets to act out other scenarios, such as sharing things, drawing a picture, putting away materials, and so on.

   If children use the incorrect form of a verb, restate their response using the correct form. For example, if a child says, "I am learn about snakes," say: *Yes, you are learning about snakes.*

Time to Share
Tiempo de compartir

Making Good Choices
Flip Chart, p. 19

✓ **Learning Goals**

Social and Emotional Development
- Child maintains concentration/attention skills until a task is complete.

Mathematics
- Child measures the length and height of people or objects using standard or non-standard tools.

Vocabulary

height	altura	learn	aprender
listen	escuchar	shortest	más bajo
speak	hablar	tallest	más alto

Differentiated Instruction

 Extra Support

Making Good Choices

If...some children have difficulty sustaining attention when another child is speaking, **then**...review with them previous class discussions about good listening habits.

 **Enrichment**

Making Good Choices

Challenge children to use the Dog Puppets to discuss the importance of finishing tasks such as cleaning brushes after painting. Have one child's puppet pretend to be someone who leaves a brush without cleaning it, and the other child's puppet be the person who wants to use the brush next. Then have children trade roles.

Accommodations for 3's

Observe and Investigate

If...children have difficulty with the concepts of tall and short, **then**...provide visual support by asking a child to stand next to you. Say: *Grown-ups are tall. Most children are shorter than grown-ups.* *Los adultos son altos. La mayoría de los niños son más bajos que los adultos.*

Learning Goals

Language and Communication
• Child names and describes actual or pictured people, places, things, actions, attributes, and events.

Emergent Literacy: Reading
• Child describes, relates to, and uses details and information from books read aloud.

Social Studies
• Child identifies similarities and differences among people.

Vocabulary

alike	parecido	cold	frío
different	diferente	hot	calor
region	lugar	world	mundo

Differentiated Instruction

Extra Support

Oral Language and Academic Vocabulary
If...children have difficulty identifying similarities and differences, **then...**model an example by saying: *These children run the way you do. These children wear clothing that is different from yours. Estos niños corren como ustedes. Estos niños llevan ropa que es diferente de la de ustedes.*

Enrichment

Oral Language and Academic Vocabulary
Challenge children to draw self-portraits. Have them dictate sentences that tell how they are different from other children and how they are the same.

Social Studies Time

large group 20 minutes

Social and Emotional Development Model listening attentively to children's responses.

Oral Language and Academic Vocabulary

Do children understand that people live in places near and far away?

• Say: *We live in a big world. Where we live, the weather is (cold) now. Some parts of the world are the same as where we live, but other parts are different. El mundo es muy grande. Donde vivimos, ahora hace (calor). En algunos lugares pasa lo mismo que aquí, pero en otros lugares es diferente.*

• Ask: *Do you wear the same clothing when it is hot as you do when it is cold? Do you do the same things? ¿Usan la misma ropa cuando hace calor que cuando hace frío? ¿Hacen las mismas cosas?*

ELL Build children's vocabulary by helping them understand weather words. Use the *Photo Library* CD-ROM to display photographs of various types of weather. Display a weather photograph, and describe the weather. For example, say: *It is cold. It is raining.* Then have children independently describe the image, or repeat after you.

• For additional suggestions on how to meet the needs of children at the Beginning, Intermediate, Advanced, and Advanced-High levels of English proficiency, see pages 184–187.

Understand and Participate

Can children recognize and describe differences and similarities among people of various regions of the world?

All Kinds of People Prepare by gathering books with photographs of contemporary children around the world. Include children from tropical places such as Brazil and cold regions such as Alaska. Say: *People live in many different places. We live in a (warm) place. Las personas viven en muchos lugares distintos. Nosotros vivimos en un lugar (cálido).*

• Display a photograph of children in a cold climate. Say: *These children live in a cold place. Estos niños viven en un lugar frío.* Ask: *How are they like children here? How are they different? How are the places alike? How are they different? ¿En qué se parecen a los niños que viven en aquí? ¿En qué se diferencian? ¿En qué se parecen estos lugares? ¿En qué se diferencian?*

• Discuss the clothing and activities portrayed in the photograph. Help children make comparisons to their own clothing and to the things they do. Repeat activity with photographs of children in a warm climate.

Center Time

▶ **Center Rotation** Center Time includes teacher-guided activities and independent activities. Refer to the **Learning Centers** on pages 100–101 for independent activity ideas.

 small group · 30 minutes

Learning Goals

Social and Emotional Development
- Child uses classroom materials carefully.
- Child maintains concentration/attention skills until a task is complete.

Emergent Literacy: Reading
- Child describes, relates to, and uses details and information from books read aloud.

Emergent Literacy: Writing
- Child experiments with and uses some writing conventions when writing or dictating.

Library and Listening Center

✓ **Can children recognize and describe differences and similarities between their family traditions and traditions around the world?**

Materials books that feature photographs of holiday celebrations in a variety of cultures, drawing paper, crayons

Celebrate Around the World Ask: *Do you like holidays? What is one holiday you celebrate with your family? ¿Les gustan los días festivos? ¿Qué día festivo celebran con su familia?*

- Browse books with children, and lead a discussion about ways people around the world celebrate.

- Ask children to draw a picture that shows a celebration that is different from any of their own. Say: *Tell a friend how the celebration is different. Digan a un amigo en qué se diferencia la celebración.*

Center Tip

If...children have difficulty identifying differences between their celebrations and ones shown in the books, **then...** ask questions that help children focus on unique characteristics of the celebration. For example, ask: *What are these people wearing? What are they eating? ¿Qué tienen puesto estas personas? ¿Qué están comiendo?*

 Writing

Ask children to draw pictures that show them celebrating with their families. Have children write or dictate a sentence that tells what they are celebrating.

Purposeful Play

✓ **Observe children's ability to complete the task of putting away materials.**

Children choose an open center for free playtime. Remind them that when they finish playing at the center, they should complete the task of putting away any materials they used.

Let's Say Good-Bye

 large group · 15 minutes

 Read Aloud Revisit "Wally Worm's World"/"El mundo del gusano Wally" for your afternoon Read Aloud. Ask children what they learned about comparing things.

 Home Connection Refer to the Home Connections activities listed in the Resources and Materials chart on page 97. Remind children to tell their families about holiday celebrations around the world. Sing the "Good-Bye Song" as children prepare to leave.

DAY 4

Focus Question

How can I compare things?
¿Cómo puedo comparar cosas?

 ## Learning Goals

Language and Communication
• Child names and describes actual or pictured people, places, things, actions, attributes, and events.

Emergent Literacy: Reading
• Child blends onset and rime to form a word without pictoral support.

Vocabulary

big	grande	different	diferente
object	objeto	opposite	opuesto
size	tamaño	small	pequeño

 ## Differentiated Instruction

✋ Extra Support

Phonological Awareness
If...children have difficulty combining sounds, **then...**have the other puppet combine the sounds to say the word, and have children repeat.

⭐ Enrichment

Oral Language and Vocabulary
Challenge children to name and write a list of words with opposite meanings.

Accommodations for **3's**

Phonological Awareness
If...three-year-olds have difficulty separating onset from rime, **then...**use the puppets to model breaking apart the sounds. If children want to, they can repeat the sounds after the puppets say them.

Let's Start the Day

 ▶ **Opening Routines and Transition Tips**
For **Opening Routines** and **Transition Tips** turn to pages 178–181 and visit **DLMExpressOnline.com** for more ideas.

📖 Read **"Goldilocks and the Three Bears"/**"Ricitos do Oro y los tres osos" from the *Teacher's Treasure Book*, page 172, for your morning Read Aloud.

large group   20 minutes

Language Time

👫 **Social and Emotional Development** Encourage children to silently check in with themselves from time to time to be sure they are still focused on the activity.

Oral Language and Vocabulary

✓ **Can children compare and contrast objects based on their characteristics?**

Making Comparisons Talk about things that are different and things that are the same. Remind children that when they hear words that are opposites, they are usually comparing two things.

● Ask: *What words is the opposite of heavy? What is the opposite of hard?* ¿Cuál es el opuesto de pesado? ¿Cuál es el opuesto de duro? (Accept reasonable answers.)

● Then say the following words one at a time, asking children to say a word with the opposite meaning: *up, big, hot, young, cold.*

ELL To reinforce the concepts of comparing, play a game with children. Ask them to say a word that they know has an opposite meaning. Tell them you will say the word that means the opposite of the one they say. Have them repeat the word pairs.

● For additional suggestions on how to meet the needs of children at the Beginning, Intermediate, Advanced, and Advanced-High levels of English proficiency, see pages 184–187.

Phonological Awareness

✓ **Can children form rhyming words without using pictures?**

Onset and Rime Display the Dog Puppets. Tell children that they are going to play a sound game with the puppets. Have one puppet say the word *big*. Have the second puppet say the initial sound separately and then the rime: /b/ -*ig*, big. Have children repeat. Have the first puppet say *rig*. Ask children what sound the word starts with. Then ask what part of *rig* rhymes with *big*. Say: **Let's put the word parts together to make big and rig:** /b/ -*ig*, big; /r/ -*ig*, rig. **Both words have the sound -ig.** Unamos las partes de la palabra para formar big y rig. /b/ -ig, big; /r/ -ig, rig. Las dos palabras tienen el sonido -ig.

● Repeat to blend onset and rime for *pig, wig,* and *fig*.

Center Time

▶ **Center Rotation** Center Time includes teacher-guided activities and independent activities. Refer to the **Learning Centers** on pages 100–101 for independent activity ideas.

small group 60–90 minutes

Creativity Center

Center Tip

✓ **Observe children's understanding of the concept of differences.**

Materials miscellaneous craft materials such as buttons, empty spools of thread, safety pins, pipe cleaners, beads, paper plates, etc.

Comparing Big and Small Have children talk about stories they know that include very big or very small characters, for example, "Thumbelina" or "Jack and the Beanstalk."

- Discuss the advantages and disadvantages of being very small or very big. Ask: **What could you do if you were very, very big or very, very small? How does being big help the character in the story? How does being small help the character?** *¿Qué harían si fueran enormemente grandes o muy, muy pequeños? ¿Por qué ser grande es de ayuda para el personaje del cuento? ¿Cómo ayuda ser pequeño al personaje?* Tell children they will make objects for very small people or animals. These can be pieces of furniture, tools, toys, or clothes.

- If possible, provide Connecting Cubes to help children envision a scale that would be appropriate for their objects. Encourage children to name and describe the objects they create. Have them tell what the object is, who will use it, and how it will be used.

If...children have difficulty seeing advantages and disadvantages of extremes in size, **then...**make a two-column chart, and help children list the pros and cons for each extreme.

Pretend and Learn Center

Center Tip

✓ **Can children create experiences with dramatic representation?**

Materials chairs, backpacks, books; clothes props (hats, glasses, etc.)

Suddenly Being Big Explain that children will role-play what it might be like to suddenly become a giant.

- Have small groups make up a role-play in which one character suddenly is a giant. The other children will role-play how others react to the sudden change. Have children preform their plays.

- Discuss what it felt like to be around someone who had suddenly grown so big, or what it was like to be the giant. What did children like about the change? What did they dislike?

If...children see only the negative side of having a giant friend or relative, suggest some positive aspects, such as "A giant friend could help you see over a crowd," or "If your sister were a giant, she could protect you during a thunderstorm."

Learning Goals

Language and Communication
- Child names and describes actual or pictured people, places, things, actions, attributes, and events.

Fine Arts
- Child uses and experiments with a variety of art materials and tools in various art activities.
- Child expresses ideas, emotions, and moods through individual and collaborative dramatic play.

Differentiated Instruction

 Extra Support
Creativity Center
If...children have difficulty thinking of what to make, **then...**ask them what items they use every day, and encourage them to make tiny versions of those objects.

 Enrichment
Pretend and Learn
Challenge children to compare/contrast big and small characters from favorite stories or movies.

Accommodations for 3's
Pretend and Learn
If...three-year-olds have difficulty making up their own role-plays, **then...**have them role-play a story they already know, such as "Little Red Riding Hood."

Focus Question

How can I compare things?

¿Cómo puedo comparar cosas?

Literacy Time

large group   15 minutes

 Read Aloud

Learning Goals

Emergent Literacy: Reading

• Child identifies the letter that stands for a given sound.

• Child describes, relates to, and uses details and information from books read aloud.

• Child asks and answers questions about books read aloud (such as, "Who?" "What?" "Where?").

Vocabulary

anxious	ansioso	autumn	otoño
cleverness	ingenio	exhausted	exhausto
fragile	frágil	furiously	furioso
hammering	construir	scrambled	embrollado
slithered	deslizarse		

Differentiated Instruction

👋 Extra Support

Read Aloud

If...children have difficulty summarizing the lessons of the story, **then...**ask questions to guide them, such as *Why did the first pig build his house out of straw? ¿Por qué el primer cerdito construyó su casa con paja?*

⭐ Enrichment

Read Aloud

Challenge children to make up another version of the story with a different ending.

Accommodations for 3's

Learn About Letters and Sounds

If...three-year-olds have difficulty recognizing words that begin with the sounds of *Nn* and *Kk*, **then...**provide picture cards, and have children point to corresponding words.

☑ **Can children compare story elements?**

Build Background Explain that when you compare objects or people, you think about ways they are similar and ways they are different. Tell children that you will read a make-believe story about a wolf and three little pigs.

● Ask: *Have you heard a story about three little pigs? Was it real or make-believe? How do you know?* ¿Han oído alguna vez un cuento sobre tres cerditos? ¿Era real o imaginario? ¿Cómo lo saben?

● Say: *This story is about three pigs who are brothers. As I read, listen for ways the brothers are alike and ways they are different.* Este cuento es sobre tres cerditos que son hermanos. A medida que leo, escuchen atentamente para saber en qué se parecen los hermanos y en qué se diferencian.

Listen for Enjoyment Display the flannel-board items for "The Three Little Pigs,"/"Los tres cerditos" and read the story title.

● Read the story, dramatizing the voices of the wolf and the pigs, and using the flannel-board charaters to act out events.

● Pause to allow children to ask questions and to note how each pig deals with the task of building a house.

Respond to the Story Talk about the story, including the personalities of the pigs Ask: *How are the little pigs similar? How are they different? How do you know? What do you think the first and second pigs learned from their experiences with the wolf?* ¿En qué se parecen los cerditos? ¿En qué se diferencian? ¿Cómo lo saben? ¿Qué creen que aprendieron el primer y el segundo cerdito de su experiencia con el lobo?

● Reread each of the sentences in the story that contain the vocabulary words. Ask children to use their own words to restate what they think the sentence is about.

ELL Help children use context to understand phrases such as *clean away* and *stand up to*. If children have difficulty with the vocabulary, see if they know synonyms of the words. For example, if they don't know the word *fragile*, ask if they know the word *delicate,* or the Spanish cognate *frágil.*

Learn About Letters and Sounds

☑ **Can children recognize words that begin with the sound of *Nn* or *Kk*?**

Learn About the Letters *Nn* and *Kk* Use the *ABC Picture Cards* to review the letters *Nn* and *Kk*. Divide the class. Ask one group to raise their hands when they hear a word that begins with /k/ and the other group to raise their hands when they hear a word that begins with /n/. Slowly read these words: *kite, nose, kayak, kitten, nut, ketchup, noon, keep, kitchen, night, kick, need, note, kit, nap, kettle.* For future work, note any words that give children difficulty.

Teacher's Treasure Book, p. 255

ABC Picture Cards

Math Time

Oberve and Investigate

 Can children compare the lengths of objects?

Missing Step Remind children of the activity in which they lined up by height. Explain that today they will look at cube stairs lined up by height.

● Prepare a set of stairs made of 1 to 5 Connecting Cubes. Ask children: ***Are these stairs in order by height? How can you tell?*** *¿Qué longitud tienen sus zapatos? ¿Me pueden mostrar con sus manos ¿Están estos escalones ordenados según su altura? ¿Cómo lo saben?*

● Have children cover their eyes while you remove one of the steps. Have children uncover their eyes. Say: ***Look carefully at the stairs. What is the length of the missing stair?*** *Miren estas escaleras. ¿Cuál es la longitud, o largo, del escalón que falta?* Have children turn to each other to tell the length of the missing stair and how they know. Call on children to share their answers and explanations with the class. Count cubes with children to check the length of the missing stair, and replace the missing stair to show children how it fits.

✖✖✖ Social and Emotional Development

Making Good Choices

 Can children sustain attention to complete a task?

Staying Focused Remind children that it is important to stay focused and finish tasks. Display the Dog Puppets. Tell children the puppets are helping each other build a tree house.

First puppet: *I am so hungry! I think I will go make a big sandwich. I'll climb down the ladder and see what I can find to eat.* (He climbs down a ladder and puts the ladder on the ground, and then he walks away from the tree.)

Second puppet: (appearing from the top of the tree) *Hey, where did he go? I thought we were going to build a tree house. Now here I am up in a tree all by myself! I have no way to get down. He left the ladder on the ground! I am stuck! Come back! Where are you? Help!*

● Ask: ***How would you feel if you were left up in a tree by your friend? What should the first puppet have done instead of leaving? What do you think the friends will talk about the next time they start a project together?*** *¿Cómo se sentirían si un amigo los dejara en un árbol? ¿Qué debería haber hecho ¿Sobre qué creen que conversarán los amigos antes de comenzar a trabajar juntos en un nuevo proyecto?*

Focus Question
How can I compare things?
¿Cómo puedo comparar cosas?

Learning Goals

Mathematics

• Child measures the length and height of people or objects using standard or non-standard tools.

Vocabulary

after	después	before	antes
length	largo	objects	objetos
order	ordenar		

Differentiated Instruction

 Extra Support

Math Time

If...children have difficulty ordering objects, **then...**ask yes/no questions about whether the object is longer than another.

 Enrichment

Math Time

Challenge children to tell which objects they think are longest and shortest before the objects are put in order.

Accommodations for 3's

Math Time

If...children have difficulty ordering objects, **then...**help them first make sure that the objects are lined up along the bottom.

 Special Needs

Delayed Motor Development

Give the child some items to compare that he can feel or pick up. Ask a classmate to make a drawing of the comparisons the child makes.

Math Time

large group   15 minutes

Social and Emotional Skills Model with a child allowing time to get materials out as well as time to put them away.

✓ **Can children compare the lengths of objects?**

Order Lengths Invite children to order the lengths of objects in the classroom. Discuss ordering with children. Talk about how things can be ordered from longest to shortest or shortest to longest.

● Provide up to five flat classroom objects. Display them for children.

● Then display the *Math and Science Flip Chart*. Say: **Look at the objects on the chart. They are ordered from longest to shortest.** *Miren los objetos de esta ilustración. Están ordenados del más largo al más corto.*

● Say: **Look at these objects I've found in the classroom. I would like to order these objects from longest to shortest too. How should I begin?** *Miren estos objetos que encontré en la clase. Quisiera ordenar estos objetos también del más largo al más corto. ¿Cómo debería comenzar?* Allow children to offer ideas.

● Say: **Let's begin with the object that looks like it is the longest. Which object looks the longest?** *Comencemos con el objeto que parece ser el más largo. ¿Qué objeto parece ser el más largo?* Children should point to an object. Say: **Let's put this object first.** *Pongamos este objeto primero.*

● Continue with the next object. Say: **Which object is almost as long as the longest object?** *¿Qué objeto es casi tan largo como el objeto más largo?* Once children have identified the object they think is the next longest, place that object beside the first one.

● Continue with the remaining objects. If children find that they have chosen the incorrect object, have them experiment with other objects. Say: **We guessed wrong. Let's put the object back or place it where it belongs to put it in order. Does it belong before or after the object already in place?** *Adivinamos mal. Pongamos el objeto donde corresponde para seguir el orden correcto. ¿Va antes o después del último objeto que pusimos?*

● Repeat the activity by ordering the lengths from shortest to longest.

TIP Remind children to begin comparing objects by lining up one end of the objects before comparing the other ends.

ELL Explain that the word *longer* is used to compare two or more objects and the word *longest* to describe an object that is longer than all the others.

● For additional suggestions on how to meet the needs of children at the Beginning, Intermediate, Advanced, and Advanced-High levels of English proficiency, see pages 184–187.

Ordering Objects
Ordenar objetos

Science and Math Flip Chart, p. 34

Center Time

▶ **Center Rotation** Center Time includes teacher-guided activities and independent activities. Refer to the **Learning Centers** on pages 100–101 for independent activity ideas.

 small group · 30 minutes

Refer to the **Learning Centers** on pages 100–101 for independent activity ideas.

Learning Goals

Emergent Literacy: Writing
• Child writes own name or a reasonable approximation of it.

Mathematics
• Child measures the length and height of people or objects using standard or non-standard tools.

Math and Science Center

✓ **Encourage children to compare the lengths of toys.**

Materials classroom toys

Compare Lengths Provide classroom toys for children to use to compare lengths. Ask children to explain how they can compare the lengths of the toys.

● Say: ***Look at these toys. Choose a toy you like. Find a toy that is longer than the one you chose. Find a toy that is shorter.*** *Miren estos juguetes. Escojan uno que les guste. Ahora, busquen un juguete más largo que el que escogieron. Y luego busquen uno más corto.*

● Challenge children to line up a group of toys by length. Ask them to explain the order of the toy lineups, using words such as *taller, longer,* and *shorter.*

Center Tip

If...children have difficulty with the terms *longer* and *shorter,* **then**...review the terms with them by modeling with the toys.

Free Writing

Recall this week's literature and activities, including "The Three Little Pigs," the *Rhymes and Chants Flip Chart*, and the measurement of objects. Have each child draw a picture of the part of the week he or she liked best and label it with their name. When children finish, have them describe their drawings for the class.

Purposeful Play

✓ **Observe children comparing lengths of toys.**

Children choose an open center for free playtime. Encourage cooperation by having children work together to find ways of comparing the lengths of their favorite toys.

Let's Say Good-Bye

 large group · 15 minutes

 Read Aloud Revisit "Goldilocks and the Three Bears"/"Ricitos de Oro y los tres osos" for your afternoon Read Aloud. Ask children how the three bears are similar and different.

 Home Connection Refer to the Home Connections activities listed in the Resources and Materials chart on page 97. Remind children to show family members how to compare the lengths of things. Sing the "Good-Bye Song" as children prepare to leave.

DAY 5

Let's Start the Day

Focus Question

How can I compare things?
¿Cómo puedo comparar cosas?

 Opening Routines and Transition Tips

For **Opening Routines** and **Transition Tips** turn to pages 178–181 and visit DLMExpressOnline.com for more ideas.

Read **"Little Red Riding Hood"/**"Caperucita Roja" from the *Teacher's Treasure Book,* page 162, for your morning Read Aloud.

 Learning Goals

Social and Emotional Development
• Child maintains concentration/attention skills until a task is complete.

Language and Communication
• Child names and describes actual or pictured people, places, things, actions, attributes, and events.

Emergent Literacy: Reading
• Child blends onset and rime to form a word without pictoral support.

Vocabulary

cloud	nube	mitten	mitón
raindrop	gotas de lluvia		

Differentiated Instruction

Extra Support

Oral Language and Vocabulary
If...children have difficulty thinking of other items that share the same trait, **then...**ask questions such as *What else do you know that is wet like rain?* *¿Qué otra cosa es húmeda como la lluvia?*

Enrichment

Oral Language and Vocabulary
Challenge children to create their own chant about objects with differing characteristics.

Accommodations for 3's

Phonological Awareness
If...three-year-olds have difficulty separating onset and rime, **then...**say each part slowly and have them repeat.

Language Time

 large group — 15 minutes

Social and Emotional Development Encourage children to continue tasks until they are finished.

Oral Language and Vocabulary

✓ **Do children understand contrast?**

Contrasting Display *Rhymes and Chants Flip Chart*, page 19. Reread the chant. Guide children to understand that the chant talks about comparing things that are alike and things that are different. Say: *Can you think of two things that are alike? Can you think of two things that are different? ¿Pueden pensar en dos cosas parecidas? ¿Y en dos cosas diferentes?*

● Review the items shown on the chart with children. Ask children to identify the items, and help them with any items they don't know. Say, for example: *This is a cloud. Clouds are in the sky. Rain and snow fall from clouds. This is a raindrop that falls from a cloud. This is a mitten that can help keep you warm. Ésta es una nube. Las nubes están en el cielo. La lluvia y la nieve caen de las nubes. Ésta es una gota de lluvia que cae de una nube. Éste es un mitón que te ayuda a mantenerte en calor.* Ask children to suggest another item that has the same or different characteristics as an item you point out.

ELL Review describing words with children, especially words that refer to color, size, shape, or texture. Have children suggest synonyms they know for a given word and then words that mean the opposite, if possible.

● For additional suggestions on how to meet the needs of children at the Beginning, Intermediate, Advanced, and Advanced-High levels of English proficiency, see pages 184–187.

Phonological Awareness

✓ **Can children blend onset and rime?**

Onset and Rime Display *Rhymes and Chants Flip Chart*, page 19. Recite the chant. Tell children that you're going to turn the chant into a nonsense chant. Reread the chant, placing exaggerated emphasis on the words *can* and *let's*. Help children blend onset and rime to form the words: /c/ -an, can; /l/ -ets, let's. Then slowly repeat each word, and and ask children to suggest a word that rhymes with it, for example, *pan* or *gets*. Reread the chant, substituting the new word for the old.

Rhymes and Chants Flip Chart, p. 19

Center Time

▶ **Center Rotation** Center Time includes teacher-guided activities and independent activities. Refer to the Learning Centers on pages 100–101 for independent activity ideas.

 small group 60–90 minutes

Writer's Center | Center Tip

✓ **Notice if children use scribbles and writing to add labels to their sentences.**

Materials white paper, crayons or markers, sentence starter written on chart paper: It is as _____ as (a) _____.

Color Spy Remind children that one way to be a nature spy is to notice what colors they see. Give each child a sheet of paper.

- Display the sentence starter, and read it aloud as you trace the words and spaces. Say: *We are going to complete this sentence by talking about colors we have seen.* *Completaremos esta oración hablando sobre los colores que hemos visto.*

- Ask: *What color could you put in the first space? What could you draw in the second space?* *¿Qué color pondrían en el primer espacio? ¿Qué dibujarían en el segundo espacio?* Model how to color in the first blank using a crayon or marker. Then model how to draw an object in the second blank that is the same color as the color in the first blank. For example, if blue is the color chosen for the first blank, draw a blue lake in the second blank.

- Guide children to identify their drawings with labels.

Center Tip

If...children have difficulty copying the sentence starter, **then...**write it out for them.

Creativity Center | Center Tip

✓ **Observe children including clean-up time for their project.**

Materials poster board, magazines for pictures, glue sticks, scissors

Compare and Contrast Collage Remind children that in *Nature Spy*, the photos showed a variety of colors, sizes, and shapes. Review that when we use all our senses, we notice differences in the way things look, smell, taste, feel, and sound.

- Invite children to cut out photos that represent differences. Remind children to think of all their senses as they choose photos.

- Have children arrange their photos into a "Differences and Similarities" collage on poster board. Display collages.

Center Tip

If...children have trouble thinking beyond the sense of sight, **then...**remind them that photos can suggest things we can't see, for example, the loud sound of an orchestra or the sweet smell of a flower.

 Learning Goals

Language and Communication
- Child names and describes actual or pictured people, places, things, actions, attributes, and events.

Emergent Literacy: Writing
- Child participates in free drawing and writing activities to deliver information.

Fine Arts
- Child uses and experiments with a variety of art materials and tools in various art activities.

Differentiated Instruction

 Extra Support
Writer's Center
If...children have difficulty thinking of an object of the corresponding color, **then...**ask them questions to get them started.

★ **Enrichment**
Writer's Center
After children complete the activity, challenge them to exchange drawings with a partner and come up with another object for the second blank.

Accommodations for 3's
Writer's Center
If...three-year-olds have difficulty thinking of objects, **then...**have them work in groups to brainstorm.

Learning Goals

Emergent Literacy: Reading
• Child describes, relates to, and uses details and information from books read aloud.

Vocabulary

closer	más cerca	eye	ojo
look	descubrir	nature	naturaleza
spy	espía		

Differentiated Instruction

 Extra Support

Learn About Letters and Sounds
If...children have difficulty writing the letters *Nn* and *Kk*, **then...**use pencil to lightly draw the letters on paper, and have children trace over the letters with crayons.

 Enrichment

Learn About Letters and Sounds
Challenge children to name and write other words that begin with the sounds /n/ and /k/.

 Special Needs

Speech and Language Delays
Use simple sentences and ask the child to tell you what you just said.

Literacy Time

large group · 15 minutes

📖 **Read Aloud**

✓ **Can children compare photos to understand a book's message?**

Build Background Tell children that you will reread the book *Nature Spy*. Ask them what they remember about the book.

● Ask: **What is one photo you remember? What do you remember about it?** *¿Qué fotografía recuerdan? ¿Cuál es la foto que más les gustó?*

Listen for Understanding Display *Nature Spy/Espía de la naturaleza,* and read the title. Remind the class that the girl in the story likes to go outside and discover new things.

● Display page 18. Say: **On this page, I read, "When you look closely, things look so different." What do the pictures on the page show? If the book didn't explain what these objects were, would you know?** *¿Qué muestran las fotos de estas páginas? Si el libro no explicara qué son los objetos, ¿lo sabrían?*

● Display pages 22 and 23. Say: **Here I read that "Everything has its own shape, color, and size." What are the three photos of?** *Aquí leo: "Cada cosa tiene su color, su forma y su tamaño". ¿De qué son las tres fotografías?*

Respond and Connect When you finish talking about the photos, ask children to compare close-up photos to photos taken from a distance. Ask children if they have ever looked at something very closely and noticed how different it looks from when they looked at it from far away.

ELL Model forming sentences for children, such as **I can see waves in the dog's fur.** Invite children to describe what they notice about the photos. Provide the words for any textures or colors they may not know.

● For additional suggestions on how to meet the needs of children at the Beginning, Intermediate, Advanced, and Advanced-High levels of English proficiency, see pages 184–187.

Learn About Letters and Sounds

✓ **Can children identify objects that begin with *Nn* and *Kk*?**

Learn About the Letters *Nn* and *Kk* Review the letters and sounds of *Nn* and *Kk*. Say: **The word** nose **begins with** n. Have children repeat. Then repeat for the words *nap* and *kite*.

● Play an add-on game. Start with a sentence such as **I took my kite to school.** *Llevo mi kite a la escuela.* Have the next person repeat your sentence and add an object that begins with *n* or *k*. For example: **I took my nose and my kite to school.** *Llevo mi nose y mi kite a la escuela.* Prior to beginning the game, explain that the sentence can be silly or make-believe.

Nature Spy
Espía de la naturaleza

Alphabet Wall Cards

Math Time

Observe and Investigate

☑ **Can children recognize the height and length of objects?**

What's This Step? Show children a set of stairs, and have them find steps of specific heights in the stairs.

● Construct a set of stairs of 1 to 10 connecting cubes.

● Show children where the "five" step is, and count the cubes in that step. Say: **This is five.** *Éste es el cinco.* Then ask: **Where is the six step? How do you know?** *¿Dónde está el escalón seis? ¿Cómo lo saben?* Have children explain to partners how they found the "six" step.

● Count together to check that the next step has six cubes.

● Repeat with steps 7, 9, 8, and 10. Be sure to have children explain how each step was found.

 Provide visual support by using a corresponding counting card to label each step.

✗✗✗ Social and Emotional Development

Making Good Choices

☑ **Do children show willingness to resist distraction?**

Following Through Display the *Making Good Choices Flip Chart*, Time to Share, page 19. Review ways that the children pictured in the chart could be kind to each other.

● Point to the children playing with the truck. Ask: **What could these children do to make the boy with the shell feel better?** *¿Qué podrían hacer estos niños para que el niño con la caracola se sienta mejor?*

● Ask: **If you are talking and someone interrupts you, or leaves the room, how do you feel? What do you do? What do you say? What might you do?** *Si alguien les habla y de repente interrumpe o se va de la sala, ¿Cómo se sentirían? ¿Qué harían? ¿Qué dirían? ¿Cómo pueden actuar?*

● Ask children to share feelings about times when friends or adults have not paid attention to something they were saying. Guide them to see why it is important to pay attention and be a good listener .

Making Good Choices Flip Chart, p. 19

Focus Question
How can I compare things?
¿Cómo puedo comparar cosas?

 Learning Goals

Science
• Child uses senses to observe, classify, investigate, and collect data.

Fine Arts
• Child expresses ideas, emotions, and moods through individual and collaborative dramatic play.

Vocabulary

build	construir	lazy	perezoso
strong	duro	weak	blando
wise	ingenioso		

 Differentiated Instruction

 Extra Support

Observe and Investigate
If...children have trouble planning their scenes, **then...**allow them to use the flannel-board characters to help them work out details.

⭐ **Enrichment**

Oral Language and Academic Vocabulary
Challenge children to compare the three little pigs by using words such as *lazy* and *wise*.

Accommodations for 3's

Observe and Investigate
If...children have difficulty acting out the scene, **then...**ask them guiding questions, such as *What did the first little pig do when the wolf blew down his house? ¿Qué hizo el primer cerdito cuando el lobo derribó su casa?*

💙 **Special Needs**

Speech/Language Delays
Immediately after you introduce a story, tell it again to a small group, and ask children to help you put events in order. This gives the child time to practice putting things in sequence.

Dramatic Play

large group   20 minutes

Personal Safety Skills Model proper handling of outdoor material from the natural world, and show how to wash your hands afterward.

Oral Language and Academic Vocabulary

✓ **Can children describe and compare the characteristics of common objects?**

Ask children what the three houses were made of in "The Three Little Pigs"/"Los tres cerditos." Say: **What did the first pig use to build his house?** *¿Qué usó el primer cerdito para construir su casa?*

• Ask children to describe each material used and to compare the materials. Say: **What is straw like? Is it strong or weak? What is stronger, wood or brick?** *¿Cómo es la paja? ¿Es dura o blanda? ¿Qué es más duro: la madera o el ladrillo?*

• Place children into groups of four, and have each group work together to draw one of the little pigs' houses. Help groups apply a descriptive word to the house they draw, such as *weak, strong, strongest.*

Observe and Investigate

✓ **Can children re-create stories through dramatic representation?**

Review "The Three Little Pigs" with children. Guide them to recall parts of the story. Use the flannel board to facilitate discussion.

Say: **What happened when the wolf went to the first house? the second house?** *¿Qué sucedió cuando el lobo fue a la primera casa? ¿Y cuando fue a la segunda casa?*

• Divide children into the same groups as above, and guide them to plan a re-creation of one scene from "The Three Little Pigs."

• Encourage children to use their drawings as props and to use descriptive words to talk about the houses and the pigs.

• Guide children to use phrases from the story. Ask: **What did the wolf say when he knocked on the pigs' doors? How did the pigs answer?** *¿Qué dijo el lobo cuando golpeó la puerta de cada casa? ¿Cómo respondieron los cerditos?*

ELL Lead children in a brief reenactment of the story using the key memorable phrases. Have them act with you and repeat as you say: **Little pig, little pig, let me in** and **Not by the hair of my chinny, chin, chin.**

• For additional suggestions on how to meet the needs of children at the Beginning, Intermediate, Advanced, and Advanced-High levels of English proficiency, see pages 184–187.

Center Time

> **Center Rotation** Center Time includes teacher-guided activities and independent activities. Refer to the **Learning Centers** on pages 100–101 for independent activity ideas.

 small group · 30 minutes

Learning Goals

Science
- Child uses senses to observe, classify, investigate, and collect data.

Fine Arts
- Child expresses ideas, emotions, and moods through individual and collaborative dramatic play.

Pretend and Learn Center

Center Tip

✓ **Can children create a story through a dramatic representation?**

Materials various stuffed animals, classroom toys such as toy houses

Create a Story Divide the class into groups, and have each group use stuffed animals and classroom toys to create a story similar to "The Three Little Pigs"/"Los tres cerditos."

- Discuss ideas for a story using themes from "The Three Little Pigs," such as small animals trying to get away from a larger animal, or animals building homes for shelter and protection.

- Encourage children to pretend they are the stuffed animals and to use descriptive words in their story.

If...children have difficulty thinking of story ideas, **then**...encourage them to simply act out "The Three Little Pigs" but to add a new ending.

Writing

Review the character of the wolf in "The Three Little Pigs." Ask children to help make a list of words that describe the wolf, such as *mean*, *angry*, and *ugly*.

Purposeful Play

✓ **Can children describe common objects through dramatic representation?**

Children choose an open center area for free playtime. Encourage children to continue to pretend to be the stuffed animals and to describe and compare the objects in their center.

Let's Say Good-Bye

 large group · 15 minutes

 Read Aloud Revisit "Little Red Riding Hood"/"Caperucita Roja" for your afternoon Read Aloud. Ask children what they learned this week about comparing things. Have children listen for descriptive and comparative words in the story, such as *huge* and *big*.

 Home Connection Refer to the Home Connections activities listed in the Resources and Materials chart on page 97. Remind children to tell someone at home about comparing things. Sing the "Good-Bye Song" as children prepare to leave.

Focus Question

How do objects move?
¿Cómo se mueven los objetos?

This week children will think about how objects move, especially objects with wheels. They will make a book showing things that fly, listen to a folktale about the sun and the moon, and move across the floor in different ways as they count aloud.

Social and Emotional Development	DAY 1	2	3	4	5
Child is aware of self in terms of abilities, characteristics and preferences, and respects personal boundaries.	✓				✓
Child identifies self by categories (such as gender, age, family member, cultural group).					✓
Child demonstrates initiative in independent activities; makes independent choices.	✓	✓	✓	✓	✓
Child initiates play scenarios with peers that share a common plan and goal.				✓	

Language and Communication	1	2	3	4	5
Child uses newly learned vocabulary daily in multiple contexts.	✓	✓	✓	✓	✓
Child uses words to identify and understand categories.	✓		✓		✓

Emergent Literacy: Reading	1	2	3	4	5
Child produces words with the same beginning sound.	✓				
Child blends onset and rime to form a word without pictoral support.	✓	✓	✓	✓	✓
Child names most upper- and lowercase letters of the alphabet.	✓	✓	✓	✓	✓
Child identifies the letter that stands for a given sound.		✓			
Child produces the most common sound for a given letter.		✓			
Child describes, relates to, and uses details and information from books read aloud.	✓	✓	✓	✓	✓
Child asks and answers questions about books read aloud (such as, "Who?" "What?" "Where?").	✓		✓	✓	

Emergent Literacy: Writing	1	2	3	4	5
Child participates in free drawing and writing activities to deliver information.				✓	✓
Child uses scribbles, shapes, pictures, symbols, and letters to represent language.		✓	✓		
Child experiments with and uses some writing conventions when writing or dictating.		✓			

Mathematics	DAY 1	2	3	4	5
Child demonstrates that the numerical counting sequence is always the same.				✓	
Child recognizes, names, describes, matches, compares, sorts common two-dimensional shapes (such as circle, square, rectangle, triangle, rhombus).	✓	✓	✓	✓	
Child manipulates (flips, rotates) and combines shapes.	✓				✓

Science	1	2	3	4	5
Child uses senses to observe, classify, investigate, and collect data.	✓				
Child explores and describes different ways objects move.	✓	✓	✓		✓
Child follows basic health and safety rules.			✓		

Social Studies	1	2	3	4	5
Child understands and discusses roles, responsibilities, and services provided by community workers.			✓		

Fine Arts	1	2	3	4	5
Child expresses ideas, emotions, and moods through individual and collaborative dramatic play.			✓	✓	

Physical Development	1	2	3	4	5
Child coordinates body movements in a variety of locomotive activities (such as walking, jumping, running, hopping, skipping, climbing).					✓

Materials and Resources

DAY 1	DAY 2	DAY 3	DAY 4	DAY 5
Program Materials				
• Teacher's Treasure Book • Oral Language Development Card 37 • Rhymes and Chants Flip Chart • Book: *What Do Wheels Do All Day?* • Building Blocks Online Math Activities • Shape Sets • Making Good Choices Flip Chart • Math and Science Flip Chart • Connecting Cubes • Home Connections Resource Guide	• Teacher's Treasure Book • Book: *What Do Wheels Do All Day?* • Dog Puppets • ABC Big Book • Shape Sets • Building Blocks Online Math Activities • Making Good Choices Flip Chart • Math and Science Flip Chart	• Teacher's Treasure Book • Oral Language Development Card 38 • Rhymes and Chants Flip Chart • Concept Big Book 2: *Let's Investigate* • Pattern Blocks • Shape Sets • Building Blocks Online Math Activities • Making Good Choices Flip Chart • Dog Puppets	• Teacher's Treasure Book • Flannel Characters for "Why the Sun and the Moon Live in the Sky" • Building Blocks Online Math Activities • Shape Sets • Dog Puppets • Home Connections Resource Guide	• Teacher's Treasure Book • Rhymes and Chants Flip Chart • Book: *What Do Wheels Do All Day?* • Dog Puppets • Shape Sets • Building Blocks Online Math Activities • Making Good Choices Flip Chart • Photo Library CD-ROM
Other Materials				
• bubbles and wands • paper, crayons, markers • old magazines with photos • glue, scissors, books • recorded music • eight index cards with labels: B, I, N, K, b i, n, k • smooth board for ramp • sandpaper or burlap to cover ramp • toy car • objects that roll (rubber balls, marbles, etc.)	• toy car • cardboard boxes, scraps • paper towel tubes, cardboard circles • yarn, ribbons • crayons, markers • glue, tape, scissors • metal fasteners • books and magazines with images of vehicles w/ wheels • large decorated box • different-colored cutout shapes	• dress-up clothes • cardboard boxes • classroom objects as props • drawing and construction paper • pencils, crayons, markers • large decorated box • puzzle pieces • butcher paper • paint, brushes	• dress-up clothes • classroom objects as props • butcher paper • pencils, crayons, markers • construction paper • masking or colored tape	• cardboard boxes, scraps • paper-towel tubes • glue, tape, scissors • decoration (ribbon) • pencils, crayons, markers • large paper • images of people moving
Home Connection				
• Encourage children to explain the toy car activity to their families and to conclude that the car moved faster on smoother surfaces. Send home the following materials: • Weekly Parent Letter, Home Connections Resource Guide, pp. 43 - 44	• Invite children to practice drawing different shapes at home with their families.	• Remind children to use the job words they learned in complete sentences with their families.	• Encourage children to describe the conflict between the puppets to their families and tell how they would solve it. Send home the following materials: • Storybook 12, Home Connections Resource Guide, pp. 125–128	• Remind children to tell their families about the different words they can use to describe motion, such as *roll* and *jump*.

Assessment

As you observe children throughout the week, you may fill out an Anecdotal Observational Record Form to document an individual's progress toward a goal or signs indicating the need for developmental or medical evaluation. You may also choose to select work for each child's portfolio. The Anecdotal Observational Record Form and Weekly Assessment rubrics are available in the assessment section of DLMExpressOnline.com.

More Literature Suggestions

• **Busy Boats** by Tony Mitton
• **On the Move: Machines At Work** by Henry Pluckrose
• **POP! A Book About Bubbles** by Kimberly Brubaker Bradley
• **Cars and Trucks and Things That Go** by Richard Scarry
• **The Windy Day (Un día con viento)** by Anna Milbourne
• **En marcha** por Sigmar
• **Rosaura en bicicleta** por Daniel Barbot

Daily Planner

	DAY 1	**DAY 2**
Let's Start the Day **Language Time** large group	**Opening Routines** p. 140 **Morning Read Aloud** p. 140 **Oral Language and Vocabulary** p. 140 Bubbles **Phonological Awareness** p. 140 Onset and Rime	**Opening Routines** p. 146 **Morning Read Aloud** p. 146 **Oral Language and Vocabulary** p. 146 How Things Go **Phonological Awareness** p. 146
Center Time small group	**Focus On:** **ABC Center** p. 141 **Creativity Center** p. 141	**Focus On:** **Construction Center** p. 147 **Library and Listening Center** p. 147
Circle Time **Literacy Time** large group	**Read Aloud** *What Do Wheels Do All Day?/¿Qué hacen las ruedas todo el día?* p. 142 **Learn About Letters and Sounds: Learn About the Alphabet** p. 142	**Read Aloud** *What Do Wheels Do All Day* p. 148 **Learn About Letters and Sounds: Learn About the Alphabet** p. 148
Math Time large group	**Observe and Investigate** p. 143 Trapezoids	**Feely Box (Match)** p. 149
Social and Emotional Development large group	**Solving Problems** p. 143	**Explain the Chart** p. 149
Content Connection large group	**Science:** **Oral Language and Academic Vocabulary** p. 144 **Observe and Investigate** p. 144	**Math:** **Hidden Shapes** p. 150
Center Time small group	**Focus On:** **Math and Science Center** p. 145 **Purposeful Play** p. 145	**Focus On:** **Math and Science Center** p. 151 **Purposeful Play** p. 151
Let's Say Good-Bye large group	**Read Aloud** p. 145 **Writing** p. 145 **Home Connection** p. 145	**Read Aloud** p. 151 **Writing** p. 151 **Home Connection** p. 151

DAY 3

Opening Routines p. 152

Morning Read Aloud p. 152

Oral Language and Vocabulary
p. 152 Flying

Phonological Awareness
p. 152 Onset and Rime

Focus On:

Pretend and Learn Center p. 153

Writer's Center p. 153

Read Aloud *Let's Investigate/Soy detective*
p. 154

Learn About Letters and Sounds: Learn About the Alphabet p. 154

Observe and Investigate
p. 155 Feely Box

Role-Play Solving Problems p. 155

Social Studies:

Oral Language and Academic Vocabulary
p. 156 Jobs

Understand and Participate
p. 156 Act Out Jobs

Focus On:

Creativity Center p. 157

Purposeful Play p. 157

Read Aloud p. 157

Writing p. 157

Home Connection p. 157

DAY 4

Opening Routines p. 158

Morning Read Aloud p. 158

Oral Language and Vocabulary
p. 158 Sun and Moon

Phonological Awareness
p. 158 Touch Your /n/-ose

Focus On:

Pretend and Learn Center p. 159

ABC Center p. 159

Read Aloud "Why the Sun and the
Moon Live in the Sky"/"Por qué el Sol y la
Luna viven en el cielo" p. 160

**Learn About Letters and Sounds: Learn
About the Alphabet** p. 160

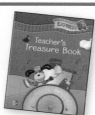

Observe and Investigate
p. 161 Count and Move

Puppet Conflict p. 161

Math:

Step on that Shape! p. 162

Focus On:

Math and Science Center p. 163

Purposeful Play p. 163

Read Aloud p. 163

Writing p. 163

Home Connection p. 163

DAY 5

Opening Routines p. 164

Morning Read Aloud p. 164

Oral Language and Vocabulary
p. 164 How Things Go

Phonological Awareness p. 164

Be a /b/-oat

Focus On:

Construction Center p. 165

Writer's Center p. 165

Read Aloud *What Do Wheels Do
All Day?/¿Qué
hacen las ruedas todo el día?* p. 166

**Learn About Letters and Sounds:
Learn About the Alphabet** p. 166

Observe and Investigate
p. 167 Flip and Turn

What We've Learned p. 167

Outdoor Play Time:

Oral Language and Vocabulary
p. 168 How People Move

Move and Learn
p. 168 Move, Move, Move

Focus On:

Library and Listening Center p. 169

Purposeful Play p. 169

Read Aloud p. 169

Writing p. 169

Home Connection p. 169

Week 4

Moving Along

Learning Centers

Math and Science Center

Measuring Motion
Children measure how and how far an object moves, p. 145

Match Up!
Children match shapes, p. 151

Trace and Match
Children match shapes to tracings, p. 163

Shape Puzzle
Laminate paper shapes (each shape a different color), and cut them into pieces. Children assemble the shape puzzles and name each shape.

Community Roles
Provide pictures of community workers. Children discuss the role of each and how the worker helps the community. Then they create a tool or equipment for a worker.

What Will Fit?
Use boxes of different sizes/ shapes. Children fit as many smaller boxes as they can into the bigger boxes without crushing or bending any.

ABC Center

Practice With *B*
Children make pictures of things beginning with /b/, p. 141

First Letters
Children identify the first letter of body part words, p. 159

Letter Movement
Have children assign a simple movement to each of the letters *B, I, N, K*. Then when you show them a letter card, children make the movement of the letter.

Letter Freeze
Place giant letters *A, S, M, D, P, F, O, L, T, E, G, R, B, I, N, K* on the floor. Children walk slowly through the letters. When you say *Freeze!*, children stop, pick up the letter closest to them, and name the letter and the sound it makes.

Creativity Center

Dancing Bubbles
Children imitate the way bubbles move, p. 141

Jobs Mural
Children create a mural of people working, p. 157

Friends and Me Book
Children use art materials to create a book showing friends doing an interesting activity together. Children invite friends to 'read' the book.

Shape Necklaces
Children trace pattern blocks and cut out shapes as "beads" for a necklace. Punch two holes in each "bead" so children can thread yarn in and out and make a necklace.

Hanging Shapes
Children trace pattern blocks onto construction paper and cut them out. Punch a hole in each shape, and have children string yarn through the hole. Hang mobiles in the room.

Library and Listening Center

Find the Wheels
Children find pictures of vehicles with wheels, p. 147

Moving Around
Children talk about pictures of people moving, p. 169

The Speed of It
Children browse books or magazines about vehicles that move. They discuss how fast or slow each vehicle moves. Each child chooses a vehicle and makes the sound it might produce.

Listen to Big Book
Children listen in pairs to *What Do Wheels Do All Day?* and point out items that go in different categories, such as "two wheels," "fast," "red," and so on.

Construction Center

Build a Vehicle
Children build a vehicle with wheels, p. 147

Build a Rocket Ship
Children build a rocket ship, p. 165

Roll It!
Children use blocks to build a ramp. They experiment with the motion of items as they roll them down the ramp. (toy cars, balls, stuffed animals, etc.).

Will It Hold?
Repeat the bridge activity from Week 2. This time, however, have children experiment with the placement of the boxes to see how this affects the strength of the bridge.

Different Ways
Children discuss different ways to build a bridge out of blocks. They build a bridge out of blocks two different ways.

Writer's Center

Make a Book
Children make a book about things that fly, p. 153

My Vehicle Poster
Children make a poster about a vehicle they have ridden in, p. 165

Label the Shapes
Children write the names of each shape they used in their Shape Mobile. Supply word cards with a picture of each shape for them to trace and match.

Move on Surfaces
Supply a toy car and four small boxes (one empty; the others have a layer to cover the bottom: sand, rice, or clay). Children move the car on each surface and then draw a picture and write a label to tell how the car moved on each surface (bumpy, smooth).

Pretend and Learn Center

At the Airport
Children pretend to be planes, pilots, or passengers, p. 153

Act Out the Sun and the Moon
Children pretend to be the sun and the moon, p. 159

Follow the Leader
Children take turns being the leader and leading others in exploring different kinds of motion (run, creep slowly, etc.).

Pretend Community
Children use dress-up clothes and props to become their favorite community worker. Children act out their jobs within the community.

Flat Tire
Children act out riding to school in a bus. Suddenly all the wheels go flat. (Children make sound of air coming out of the tires.) Then children act out riding in a bus with flat tires! They continue acting out what might happen next.

DAY 1

Let's Start the Day

Focus Question
How do objects move?
¿Cómo se mueven los objetos?

Learning Goals

Language and Communication
- Child uses newly learned vocabulary daily in multiple contexts.

Emergent Literacy: Reading
- Child blends onset and rime to form a word without pictoral support.

Science
- Child explores and describes different ways objects move.

Vocabulary

blow	soplar	bubbles	burbujas
float	flotar	heavy	pesado
light	liviano	move	mover
wand	varita		botella

Differentiated Instruction

Extra Support
Oral Language and Vocabulary
If...children have difficulty thinking of words that describe bubbles, **then...**offer them choices by asking questions such as ***Are bubbles heavy or light? Are they round or shaped like a box?*** *¿Son las burbujas livianas o pesadas? ¿Son redondas o tienen forma de caja?*

Enrichment
Phonological Awareness
Have children separate one-syllable words such as *kite* into onset (/k/) and rime (*-ite*).

Special Needs
Behavioral Social/Emotional
Help the child participate appropriately with peers. Use verbal praise. If the child is upset or aggressive, walk over to her/him, and gently place your hand on her/his shoulder. Use this as the cue to calm down and take a deep breath.

Opening Routines and Transition Tips

For **Opening Routines** and **Transition Tips** turn to pages 178–181 and visit **DLMExpressOnline.com** for more ideas.

Read **"Engine Ninety-Nine"**/"La máquina noventa y nueve" from the *Teacher's Treasure Book,* page 250, for your morning Read Aloud.

Language Time

large group 15 minutes

Social and Emotional Development Remind children that they need to do their best even when tasks are hard.

Oral Language Development Card 37

Oral Language and Vocabulary

Can children describe bubbles and what they do?

Bubbles Mime dipping a bubble wand into a bottle of liquid and blowing through it. Pretend to watch the bubbles as they rise. Ask children to describe what you're doing. Ask: ***Have you every played with bubbles?*** *¿Han jugado alguna vez con burbujas?*

- Display *Oral Language Development Card 37.* Explain or elicit that the child in the picture is blowing bubbles. Ask children what bubbles look like and what they do; encourage children to use descriptive words such as *light* and *shiny.* Then follow the suggestions on the back of the card.
- Provide bubbles and wands for children to investigate and experiment with. Have children describe how the bubbles move and what they look like.

ELL Words with multiple meanings can be troublesome for ELL children. Help children grasp the difference between *light*, the opposite of *heavy*, and *light*, the opposite of *dark*.

Phonological Awareness

Can children combine onset and rime to form words?

Onset and Rime Display *Rhymes and Chants Flip Chart,* "What Makes Them Go?", page 20. Read the chant with children. Explain that you are thinking of one of the things that go. Tell children that the first sound of the word is /b/. Have children repeat the onset. Then explain that the rest of the word is *us*; have children repeat the rime. Say **/b/-*us*** several times in succession. Help children say the whole word, *bus*. Repeat with /sh/-*ip*, /j/-*et*, and /b/-*oat*.

- Play "I'll Start It/You'll Finish It." Point to yourself, and say: /b/. Then point to the children, and guide them to finish the word (-us). Then say the word together: *bus.*

Rhymes and Chants Flip Chart, p. 20

Center Time

Center Rotation Center Time includes teacher-guided activities and independent activities. Refer to the **Learning Centers** on pages 138–139 for independent activity ideas.

small group   60–90 minutes

ABC Center

	Center Tip
✓ **Can children name words that begin with *b*?** ✓ **Can children use onset and rime to form words?** **Materials** paper, pencils, crayons, magazine photos, scissors, glue **Practice with *Bb*** Tell children the words *bus, boat,* and *bubbles* begin with *Bb*. Remind them that they know other words that start with *Bb*. ● Have children draw pictures of objects that begin with *b* or cut pictures out of magazines and glue the pictures onto paper. ● Have children write *B* below each object and then write as much of the rest of the word as they can. Allow children to dictate as needed. ● Separate some of the words into onset and rime (such as /b/ -*ird* for *bird*), and have children identify the word.	**If**...children can't think of many words that start with *b*, **then**...give them clues such as *I'm thinking of an animal that has wings* (bird or bat) or *I'm thinking of a word that rhymes with wig* (big).

Creativity Center

	Center Tip
✓ **Can children move in a way that is similar to the way bubbles move?** ✓ **Can children use vocabulary words to talk about the way bubbles move?** **Materials** recorded music **Dancing Bubbles** Have children move or dance as if they were bubbles that have just been blown out of a wand. ● Find an area of the classroom or school where children can move without bumping into one another or classroom furniture. ● As they listen to appropriate music, ask children to be bubbles. ● Ask children to use vocabulary words to describe how they are moving and what they are like.	**If**...children's movements are too boisterous, **then**...remind them that bubbles are light and float through the air. You may also want to change the music to something quieter or slower.

Learning Goals

Social and Emotional Development
• Child is aware of self in terms of abilities, characteristics and preferences, and respects personal boundaries.

Language and Communication
• Child uses newly learned vocabulary daily in multiple contexts.

Emergent Literacy: Reading
• Child produces words with the same beginning sound.

• Child blends onset and rime to form a word with pictoral support.

Science
• Child explores and describes different ways objects move.

Differentiated Instruction

✋ Extra Support
ABC Center
If...children have a hard time distinguishing /b/ from sounds such as /p/ and /d/, **then**...have them watch the position of your mouth and lips as you say /b/ and the other letters.

⭐ Enrichment
ABC Center
Ask children to think of rhymes for as many of the words as they can.

Accommodations for 3's
ABC Center
If...children have difficulty identifying "Bb" words, **then**...allow them to work with a partner.

Focus Question

How do objects move?
¿Cómo se mueven los objetos?

Language and Communication
• Child uses newly learned vocabulary daily in multiple contexts.

Emergent Literacy: Reading
• Child names most upper- and lowercase letters of the alphabet.

• Child describes, relates to, and uses details and information from books read aloud.

• Child asks and answers questions about books read aloud (such as, "Who?" "What?" "Where?").

Science
• Child explores and describes different ways objects move.

Vocabulary

circle	círculo	pedal	pedal
race	carrera	roll	rodar
spin	girar	tow	remolque
wheels	rueda		

Differentiated Instruction

 Extra Support

Learn About Letters and Sounds

If...it's confusing for children to think about matching four letters at the same time, **then**... use just *Bb* and *Kk* at first, and add in the other letters one at a time as you repeat the activity.

 Enrichment

Read Aloud

Turn to a page in the book with more than one vehicle shown. Ask a child to secretly choose a vehicle on the page and give clues to its identity, such as *It has two wheels* or *Its wheels are big.* Then have the other children guess which vehicle it is. Repeat with other pages and other children.

Literacy Time

📖 Read Aloud

✓ **Can children talk about wheels and how things move?**

✓ **Can children categorize?**

Build Background Introduce the topic of wheels. Ask: **What do wheels look like? Where have you seen wheels?** *¿A qué se parecen las ruedas? ¿Dónde han visto ruedas?*

Listen for Enjoyment Display *What Do Wheels Do All Day?/¿Qué hacen las ruedas todo el día?* and read the title. Explain that the book tells about wheels and things that have wheels. As you read, ask children to think about how the wheels in the book are alike and how they are different. Ask:

● **What is the name of this vehicle? Does it go fast or slow?** *¿Cómo se llama este vehículo? ¿Va rápido o lento?*

● **Who can find a big wheel? Who can find a small wheel?** *¿Quién puede encontrar una rueda grande? ¿Quién puede encontrar una rueda pequeña?* **Which wheels always come in pairs?** *¿Qué ruedas siempre vienen de a dos?*

Respond to the Story Ask children to name their favorite part of the book. Then have them act out one of the wheels in the book and use their bodies to show what it does. Ask: **How was the bicycle wheel like the Ferris wheel? How were they different?** *¿En qué se parecen la rueda de una bicicleta y la rueda de la fortuna? ¿En qué se diferencian?*

ELL Use gestures and intonation to model the meaning of adjectives such as *fast, slow, big,* and *small.* For instance, say: **A jet is FAST!** very quickly, while sliding your hand rapidly through the air. Then say: **A snail is slo-o-o-ow,** while moving your hand slowly across a surface.

● For additional suggestions on how to meet the needs of children at the Beginning, Intermediate, Advanced, and Advanced-High levels of English proficiency, see pages 184–187.

Learn About Letters and Sounds

✓ **Can children identify lowercase and uppercase of *Bb, Ii, Nn,* and *Kk*?**

✓ **Can children associate *Bb, Ii, Nn,* and *Kk* with the sounds /b/, /i/, /n/, and /k/?**

Learn About the Alphabet Display eight index cards. Write each of the capital letters *B, I, N,* and *K* and lowercase forms *b, i, n,* and *k* on a card.

● Show the cards in random order. Have children say the letter and its sound.

● Give each card to a child. Have children move around the area and find the child with the other form of the letter they are holding; the child with *b,* for instance, stands with the child who has *B.*

What Do Wheels Do All Day?
¿Qué hacen las ruedas todo el día?

Math Time

Building Blocks

Online Math Activity

Introduce Mystery Pictures 3: Match New Shapes, in which children make mystery pictures out of shapes that are revealed only one shape at a time. Each child should complete the activity this week.

Observe and Investigate

✓ **Can children identify a trapezoid?**

Trapezoids Have Shape Sets available. Introduce the trapezoid to children.

● Say: *This shape is a trapezoid. Say* **trapezoid** *with me. What do you notice about the trapezoid? Esta figura es un trapecio. Digan trapecio conmigo. ¿Qué observan sobre el trapecio?* Allow children time to answer.

● Guide children to see that the trapezoid has two parallel sides that are always the same distance apart and two sides that are closer at one end than the other. Turn the shape as you describe its features. Say: *Look. The shape stays a trapezoid even as I turn it. Observen. Aunque la giremos, la figura sigue siendo un trapecio.*

● Repeat with a rhombus. Help students recognize that all sides of a rhombus are the same length and a rhombus has two pairs of parallel sides.

ELL Provide visual support by holding a shape show with children. Name the shapes together with children, and demonstrate how figures stay the same shape when you change their orientation.

⅄⅄⅄ Social and Emotional Development

Making Good Choices Flip Chart, p. 20

Making Good Choices

✓ **Can children understand what it means to keep trying?**

Solving Problems Display the *Making Good Choices Flip Chart*, page 20. Ask: *What do you do when tasks are hard? Do you give up right away? Do you keep trying? ¿Qué hacen cuando tienen una tarea difícil? ¿Se rinden o siguen intentando?* Guide children to understand that it's best to keep trying even when it isn't easy. Ask:

● *Which children in the picture are trying hard? How can you tell? How do you think they are feeling about themselves? ¿Qué niños de la imagen vuelven a intentarlo? ¿Cómo se dan cuenta? ¿Cómo creen que se sienten?*

● *Which child has stopped trying? How do you think this child is feeling? What other things could he be doing? How could other children help? ¿Qué niño ha dejado de intentar? ¿Cómo piensan que se siente ese niño? ¿Qué otras cosas podría hacer? ¿Cómo podrían ayudarlo los otros niños?*

ELL Reinforce the concepts of same and different. Ask questions such as: *How are my shoes the same as yours? How are they different?* Compare shoe sizes, colors, and styles with several children, guiding children to recognize same and different characteristics.

✓ Learning Goals

Social and Emotional Development
● Child demonstrates initiative in independent activities; makes independent choices.

Language and Communication
● Child uses newly learned vocabulary daily in multiple contexts.

Mathematics
● Child recognizes, names, describes, matches, compares, sorts common two-dimensional shapes (such as circle, square, rectangle, triangle, rhombus).
● Child manipulates (flips, rotates) and combines shapes.

Vocabulary

easy	fácil	happy	feliz
hard	difícil	rhombus	rombo
sad	triste	same	igual
trapezoid	trapecio	try	intentar

Differentiated Instruction

✋ Extra Support
Observe and Investigate
If...children have trouble distinguishing a rhombus and a trapezoid, **then...**emphasize that all sides of a rhombus are the same length and all sides of a trapezoid are not.

⭐ Enrichment
Making Good Choices
Ask what words such as *happy* and *sad* are called. Explain that they are opposites. Help children list opposites and draw pictures to show the words.

Accommodations for 3's
Observe and Investigate
If...children struggle with the trapezoid shape, **then...** guide their fingers around the sides of the shape, pointing out that the sides and corners are not all the same.

Learning Goals

Science
• Child uses senses to observe, classify, investigate, and collect data.
• Child explores and describes different ways objects move.

Vocabulary

fast	rápido	measure	medida
motion	movimiento	pull	tirar
push	empujar		
round and round	dar vueltas		
slow	lento	straight	recto
zigzag	zigzag		

Differentiated Instruction

Extra Support
Observe and Investigate
If...children have difficulty moving the car down the ramp, **then...**show them how to give the car a gentle push.

Enrichment
Oral Language and Academic Vocabulary
Challenge children to use other phrases that describe motion, such as *up and down, back and forth,* and *in and out.*

Accommodations for 3's
Observe and Investigate
If...children have difficulty understanding zigzag motion, **then...**draw both straight and zigzag lines on the board, and explain that zigzag lines change direction frequently.

Special Needs
Speech/Language Delays
Offer visual and verbal demonstrations of what you want the child to do. Sometimes, children with language/speech delays don't participate because they don't understand what is expected.

Science Time

  large group 20 minutes

Social and Emotional Skills Model self-help skills by asking for assistance for certain tasks.

Oral Language and Academic Vocabulary

✓ **Can children describe different ways objects, including people, can move?**
How Do Things Move? Point to the playground equipment in the photo. Say: ***When you play on this equipment, your body moves in different ways.*** *Cuando juegan con estos juegos, su cuerpo se mueve de varias maneras.*

● Explain that when something moves, it is in motion. Talk about different kinds of motion. Say: ***One way to talk about motion is to describe its speed. Things move quickly or slowly. Another way to talk about motion is direction. Things move straight or around or up or down.*** *Una manera de hablar del movimiento es describir su velocidad. Las cosas se mueven lentamente o rápidamente. Otra manera es describir la dirección. Las cosas pueden moverse hacia adelante, dar vueltas o ir de arriba a abajo.* Have children point use gestures to identify how they would move if they played on the playground equipment. Encourage them to describe motion using speed and direction words such as *fast, slow, straight, round and round,* and *zigzag.* Say: ***Sometimes we can move different ways on the same equipment.*** *A veces, en el mismo juego podemos movernos de distintas maneras.* Have children descibe how they move as they slowly climb the steps of a twisted slide and then move quickly downward.

ELL Walk straight across the room and say: ***I am walking straight.*** Then walk in a zigzag. Explain that you walked in a zigzag. Finally, walk round and round, and name that motion. Play a game of "Follow the Leader."

Observe and Investigate

✓ **Can children investigate and conclude that toy cars move faster on smooth surfaces than on rough surfaces?**

Create a simple ramp by leaning a smooth board on books. Gather a toy car and rough materials, such as burlap or sandpaper, to place on the ramp. Discuss how the car will move down the ramp. Have a child demonstrate. Say: ***We will change the surface of the ramp to see if the motion changes.*** *Vamos a cambiar la rampa para ver si cambia el movimiento.*

● Have children feel the smooth ramp. Roll the toy car down again, asking children to pay attention to the toy's speed and how it moves. Then place a rough material on the ramp. Have children feel the rough material and describe its texture. Ask children to predict how the car will move now. Roll the car down the ramp, and have children observe how the motion of the car changes. Have children feel the different materials, and help them conclude that the car moves faster on a smoother surface.

Math and Science Flip Chart, p. 35

Center Time

▶ **Center Rotation** Center Time includes teacher-guided activities and independent activities. Refer to the **Learning Centers** on pages 138–139 for independent activity ideas.

small group   30 minutes

Math and Science Center

☑ **Can children measure and describe the motion of objects?**

Materials Connecting Cubes, books, wooden board; various movable objects such as rubber balls, marbles, toy cars, cylinder, and so on

Measuring Motion Set a ramp on the floor with barriers, allowing enough space for objects to move to a stop. Tell students they will measure and describe the motion of the objects.

- Have children hold an object at the top of the ramp and then release the object so it rolls gently down the ramp. Help children mark where the object stops moving and use Connecting Cubes to measure the distance from the bottom of the ramp to that spot.

- Challenge students to describe and compare the objects according to how far they rolled. Which ones rolled far? Which didn't roll far at all?

Center Tip

If...children have difficulty controlling the objects, **then...**have them decrease the angle of the ramp.

✓ Learning Goals

Language and Communication
• Child uses words to identify and understand categories.

Science
• Child uses senses to observe, classify, investigate, and collect data.

• Child explores and describes different ways objects move.

Writing

Have children talk about things that are easy and things that are hard. Make a two-column list on chart paper or an interactive whiteboard, heading the columns *Things That Are Easy* and *Things That Are Hard* and writing each activity in the correct column. Add sketches where appropriate. Read the list aloud with children.

Purposeful Play

☑ **Can children mimic and describe the sounds made by certain objects?**

Children choose an open center area for free playtime. Have children investigate the sounds made by different objects and then mimic the sounds and describe them with words.

Let's Say Good-Bye

large group   15 minutes

 Read Aloud Revisit "Engine Ninety-Nine"/"La máquina noventa y nueve" for your afternoon Read Aloud. Give children the onset and rime of a one-syllable word, and have them figure out what the word is.

 Home Connection Refer to the Home Connections activities listed in the Resources and Materials chart on page 135. Remind children to tell their families something they learned about wheels and things that have wheels. Sing the "Good-Bye Song" as children prepare to leave.

DAY 2

Focus Question

How do objects move?
¿Cómo se mueven los objetos?

✓ Learning Goals

Social and Emotional Development
• Child demonstrates initiative in independent activities; makes independent choices.

Language and Communication
• Child uses newly learned vocabulary daily in multiple contexts.

Emergent Literacy: Reading
• Child blends onset and rime to form a word without pictoral support.

Emergent Literacy: Writing
• Child uses scribbles, shapes, pictures, symbols, and letters to represent language.

Science
• Child explores and describes different ways objects move.

Vocabulary

pedal	pedalear	pull	tirar
push	empujar	roll	rodar
spin	girar	tow	remolcar
wheels	ruedas		

Differentiated Instruction

 Extra Support

Phonological Awareness
If...children have trouble blending onset and rime, **then...**use motions to help children identify the words. For instance, if children struggle to blend /p/-*ull*, act out pulling a wagon while the puppets say the sounds.

⭐ **Enrichment**

Phonological Awareness
If children can easily blend onset and rime to form one-syllable words such as *pull* and *car,* have them try blending onset and rime with two-syllable words such as *pedal* and *wagon.*

Let's Start the Day

▶ **Opening Routines and Transition Tips**
For **Opening Routines** and **Transition Tips** turn to pages 178–181 and visit DLMExpressOnline.com for more ideas.

📖 Read **"My Little Red Wagon"/**"Mi cochecito rojo" from the *Teacher's Treasure Book,* page 247, for your morning Read Aloud.

Language Time

large group 15 minutes

 Social and Emotional Development Tell children to look for lots of different ways to solve problems as they go through the day.

Oral Language and Vocabulary

✓ **Can children associate vocabulary words with the motions they describe?**
How Things Go Push a toy car across the meeting area. Ask children what you are doing to make the car go. Elicit that you are pushing the car. Have children imitate your movements.

● Display *What Do Wheels Do All Day?/¿Qué hacen las ruedas todo el día?* Read the selection aloud. Guide children to act out the motions associated with the vocabulary words.

● Say *Roll!* ¡Rodar! and have children act out a wheel that is rolling. Repeat with other vocabulary words.

Phonological Awareness

✓ **Can children blend onset and rime to form one-syllable words?**
/d/-*ogs* Say: *Two visitors are in our classroom. Their names begin with /d/ and end with -ogs. Hay dos visitantes en el salón de clases. Su nombre empieza con /d/ y termina con -ogs.* Say the sounds several times in succession until children identify the word *dogs.* Then display the Dog Puppets. Have the first puppet say the onset of a word, and have the second puppet supply the rime, as in /p/ -*ush.* Help children identify the complete words. Use one-syllable vocabulary words from the *Big Book* (/p/ -*ull,* /r/ -*oll,* /t/ -*ow*), and other short, simple words of your choosing.

ELL The sounds /l/ and /r/ aren't used in all languages. Give children plenty of practice in hearing and producing these sounds in words such as *roll.*

● For additional suggestions on how to meet the needs of children at the Beginning, Intermediate, Advanced, and Advanced-High levels of English proficiency, see pages 184–187.

What Do Wheels Do All Day?
¿Qué hacen las ruedas todo el día?

Center Time

Center Rotation Center Time includes teacher-guided activities and independent activities. Refer to the **Learning Centers** on pages 138–139 for independent activity ideas.

 small group 60–90 minutes

Construction Center

 Can children build a vehicle with wheels?

 Can children talk about how things with wheels move?

Materials cardboard boxes and scraps, paper towel tubes, paper or cardboard circles to use as wheels, yarn, ribbons, crayons or markers, scissors, glue, tape, metal fasteners

Build a Vehicle Ask children to use the materials to build a vehicle with wheels that moves on roads.

- The vehicle can be a real one (bicycle, car, bus, and so on) but can also be imaginary.
- Have children describe their vehicles and how they move.
- Set up roads with blocks and have children move their vehicles along the roads.

Center Tip

If...children have trouble sharing the roads with others, **then...**help them make and post stop signs and speed limit signs to remind each other of the rules.

Library and Listening Center

 Can children talk about how vehicles with wheels are alike and how they are different?

Materials paper, crayons or markers, pencils, picture books and magazines that have pictures of vehicles with wheels

Find the Wheels Have children look through the books and magazines to find pictures of vehicles with wheels.

- Have children tell a classmate or teacher about the vehicles and how they move.
- Ask children how the vehicles are alike and different.
- Encourage children to draw the vehicles they like best.

Center Tip

If...children are not sure of the names of the vehicles (for example, *van*), **then...** give them the names in onset-rime form (for example, /v/ -*an*), and have them identify the name from the parts.

Learning Goals

Language and Communication
- Child uses newly learned vocabulary daily in multiple contexts.

Emergent Literacy: Reading
- Child describes, relates to, and uses details and information from books read aloud.

Emergent Literacy: Writing
- Child uses scribbles, shapes, pictures, symbols, and letters to represent language.

Science
- Child explores and describes different ways objects move.

Differentiated Instruction

Extra Support
Construction Center
If...children have trouble describing how vehicles move, **then...**put together a short list of describing words (e.g., *fast, slow, roll, spin*...) and have children choose words that apply.

Enrichment
Library and Listening Center
Have children identify vehicles that do *not* have wheels. Encourage them to find these vehicles in the books and to compare and contrast them with vehicles that do have wheels.

Accommodations for 3's
Construction Center
If...children lack the small motor skills necessary to put vehicles together on their own, **then...** help them cut, tape, or glue, encouraging them to tell you in words what they want their vehicle to look like.

Circle Time

Learning Goals

Language and Communication
• Child uses newly learned vocabulary daily in multiple contexts.

Emergent Literacy: Reading
• Child names most upper- and lowercase letters of the alphabet.

• Child describes, relates to, and uses details and information from books read aloud.

Science
• Child explores and describes different ways objects move.

Vocabulary

pedal	pedalear	roll	rodar
spin	girar	tow	remolque
wheels	ruedas		

Differentiated Instruction

 Extra Support

Read Aloud

If....children have trouble with the concepts of *same* and *different*, **then...**model them visually with a pencil and a marker. Tell children that they are the *same* because both are long and used to write with. Then say that they are *different* because one writes in color and the other doesn't. Repeat with other objects.

 Enrichment

Learn About Letters and Sounds
Challenge children to use their knowledge of the alphabet to predict when the page they're looking for will be next (e.g., predicting when you reach *Hh* that *Ii* will be the next page).

 Special Needs

Hearing Impairment
Remember to consistently work on the child's residual hearing. Circle time may have too much noise distraction. So, if you think s/he did not hear you, explain a concept, and take a few minutes to review it with her/him individually.

Literacy Time

large group · 15 minutes

📖 Read Aloud

✅ **Can children categorize vehicles with wheels?**

✅ **Do children recognize the relationship between words and pictures in a book?**

Build Background Make two lists on the board, one headed *Things That Have Wheels* and the other *Things That Don't Have Wheels.*

- Have children name things that have wheels (e.g., cars, trucks, scooters). Write each vehicle name in the appropriate column.

- Repeat for things that don't have wheels (e.g., bears, apples, sleeping bags).

Listen for Understanding Display *What Do Wheels Do All Day?/¿Qué hacen las ruedas todo el día?* and read the title. Run your hand under the words as you read the book. Point out that the words and the pictures work together to teach readers about wheels and how things with wheels move. As you read, ask questions such as:

- *How does a [bicycle] move? ¿Cómo se mueve un/a [bicicleta]?*

- *What vehicles move in the same way as a [bicycle]? ¿Qué vehículos se mueven como un/a [bicicleta]?*

- *What vehicles move in a different way? ¿Qué vehículos se mueven de manera diferente?*

Respond to the Story Have children name vehicles with two wheels/with four wheels/that go fast/that are slow. Use the book as a reference.

 TIP If time permits, reinforce the idea of categories by using chart paper or an interactive whiteboard to list vehicles by group. For example, *Vehicles with 4 Wheels* includes cars and wagons, and *Vehicles with 2 Wheels* includes scooters and bicycles. Use pictures and words to create the lists.

 ELL Help children distinguish between plural nouns and singular nouns and how these affect the verb. For instance, we say *A car* (singular) *has four wheels*, but *Cars* (plural) *have four wheels.* Have children listen for and say both of these forms during this lesson.

Learn About Letters and Sounds

✅ **Do children recognize the letters *Bb, Ii, Kk,* and *Nn* when they see them in a book?**

✅ **Can children associate the letters *Bb, Ii, Nn,* and *Kk* with the appropriate sounds?**

Learn About The Alphabet Use the *ABC Big Book.* Go through the pages one at a time, asking children to stop you when they see the letter *Bb.*

- Have children name objects pictured that begin with *Bb,* emphasizing the initial /b/ when children say the words.

- Repeat with *Ii, Kk,* and *Nn.*

What Do Wheels Do All Day?

¿Qué hacen las ruedas todo el día?

ABC Big Book

large group | 15 minutes

Math Time

Observe and Investigate

✓ **Can children match shapes?**

Feely Box (Match) Remind children that they can move their fingers to feel things. Invite children to feel shapes to match them to other shapes.

- Cut a hole in a large, decorated box. Place a trapezoid from the Shape Set into the box. Display five shapes from another Shape Set, including a trapezoid that matches the one in the box.

- Say: *Place your fingers in the box and feel around the shape inside. Can you tell what the shape is? Metan la mano en la caja y toquen una figura con los dedos. ¿Pueden decir qué figura es?*

- Have a child point to and name the shape that matches the one inside the box. Ask: *How did you figure out the shape? ¿Cómo supieron qué figura era?* Repeat with other children and different shapes.

- Retain the Feely Box for a variation on this activity tomorrow.

ELL Associate shape words with the actual shapes, and connect English shape words to the shape words in the child's primary language when possible. Also include the terms *match* and *shape*.

Building Blocks

Online Math Activity

Introduce Memory Geometry 3: Shapes-a-Round, in which children play a version of the traditional concentration game by matching shapes with the same or different orientations. Each child should complete the activity this week.

✸✸✸ Social and Emotional Development

Making Good Choices

✓ **Can children explain what it means to keep trying?**

Explain the Chart Display the *Making Good Choices Flip Chart* page 20. Bring out one of the Dog Puppets. Explain that the puppet knows that the page is called *Keep Trying* but isn't sure what that means.

- Have children take turns explaining the idea of trying even when things are hard, using the picture on the chart as a reference.

- When appropriate, have the puppet ask questions to clarify.

ELL Help children learn feeling words by having them make appropriate facial expressions when they say the words (for example, scowling for *angry* and pretending to cry for *sad*). You can also have children play a game in which one child names a feeling word and the others repeat it, making the corresponding face.

Making Good Choices Flip Chart, p. 20

✓ Learning Goals

Social and Emotional Development
• Child demonstrates initiative in independent activities; makes independent choices.

Language and Communication
• Child uses newly learned vocabulary daily in multiple contexts.

Mathematics
• Child recognizes, names, describes, matches, compares, sorts common two-dimensional shapes (such as circle, square, rectangle, triangle, rhombus).

Vocabulary

angry	enojado	feel	sentir
fingers	dedos	happy	feliz
hard	difícil	moving	movimiento
proud	orgulloso	sad	triste
try	intentar		

Differentiated Instruction

✋ **Extra Support**

Making Good Choices

If...children are uncertain what to say to the puppet, **then...**have the puppet ask about a specific situation, for instance, *I was drawing a picture but it didn't look right, so I crumpled it up. Do you think that was a good thing to do? What else might I have done? Estaba haciendo un dibujo pero no lo hice bien, entonces lo rompí: ¿Estuvo bien eso? ¿Qué podría haber hecho?*

⭐ **Enrichment**

Making Good Choices

Ask children to categorize the children pictured on the chart into those who look as if they are continuing to try and those who look as if they are not trying anymore.

Accommodations for 3's

Observe and Investigate

If...children have difficulty naming the shapes, **then...**reduce the number of shapes, making sure the shapes are clearly different.

Focus Question
How do objects move?
¿Cómo se mueven los objetos?

Learning Goals

Mathematics

• Child recognizes, names, describes, matches, compares, sorts common two-dimensional shapes (such as circle, square, rectangle, triangle, rhombus).

Vocabulary

hexagon	hexágono
octagon	octógono
parallelogram	paralelogramo
rhombus	rombo
shape	figura
trapezoid	trapecio

Differentiated Instruction

Extra Support
Math Time

If...children have difficulty thinking of the shapes as "hidden," **then...**ask them where they have seen the shapes before.

Enrichment
Math Time

Encourage children to think of other shapes not shown on the flip chart and where they may have seen them.

Accommodations for 3's
Math Time

If...children have trouble thinking of things with the shape, **then...**provide examples.

Math Time

large group · 20 minutes

✓ **Can children identify shapes in everyday objects?**

Hidden Shapes Invite children to play Hidden Shapes. Tell children some shapes have disappeared and hidden themselves in things they see every day. Tell children they are going to think about where they may have seen the shapes before.

● Display the *Math and Science Flip Chart,* page 36.

● Point to a shape. Ask: **What is this shape?** *¿Qué figura es ésta?* Help children identify the shape.

● Say (for example): **This is an octagon. It has eight sides. Look at the sides. Run your fingers around the eight sides.** *Ésta figura es un octógono. Tiene ocho lados. Miren los lados. Pasen sus dedos alrededor de los ocho lados.*

● Discuss with children where they may have seen the shape "hidden." Ask: **This shape hides in something you might see every day. Have you seen this shape before? Where?** *Esta figura se esconde en algunos de los objetos que pueden ver todos los días. ¿Han visto esta figura anteriormente? ¿En dónde?* Guide children to think of a stop sign or another common object with the octagon shape.

● Repeat with the other shapes on the chart.

● Be sure to suggest other places the child might find the shape in everyday objects.

ELL Work with children to practice pronouncing shape names. Teach them to clap with each syllable as they say them. Clap and say: */rom/ /bus/, /trap/ /a/ /zoid/,* and so on.

● For additional suggestions on how to meet the needs of children at the Beginning, Intermediate, Advanced, and Advanced-High levels of English proficiency, see pages 184–187.

Shapes!
¡Formas!

Math and Science Flip Chart , p. 36

Center Time

Center Rotation Center Time includes teacher-guided activities and independent activities. Refer to the **Learning Centers** on pages 138–139 for independent activity ideas.

 small group 30 minutes

Math and Science Center

✓ **Can children match shape sets?**

Materials different colored shape sets

Match Up! Prepare several different colored shape sets. Mix them up, and spread them across a work table for children. Tell children to find as many matching shapes as they can.

- Give children plenty of time to find matches.
- Encourage children to work in pairs.

Center Tip

If...children have difficulty finding matches, **then** provide individual support.

Purposeful Play

✓ **Can children group objects according to a common attribute?**

Children choose an open center for free playtime. Have them look at the objects in the center and try to put them into groups that go together.

Learning Goals

Emergent Literacy: Reading
- Child identifies the letter that stands for a given sound.

Emergent Literacy: Writing
- Child experiments with and uses some writing conventions when writing or dictating.

Mathematics
- Child recognizes, names, describes, matches, compares, sorts common two-dimensional shapes (such as circle, square, rectangle, triangle, rhombus).

Writing

Tell children that they will help you make two lists, one of things that begin with *b* and one of things that don't begin with *b*. Write headers on chart paper, and have children suggest ideas for each column. Write the words. Sketch pictures if appropriate. Conclude by reading the lists aloud.

Let's Say Good-Bye

 large group 15 minutes

Read Aloud Revisit the story "My Little Red Wagon"/"Mi cochecito rojo" for your afternoon Read Aloud. Ask children to listen for times when someone or something in the story moves.

Home Connection Refer to the Home Connections activities listed in the Resources and Materials chart on page 135. Tell children to look for things with wheels as they are on their way home. Sing the "Good-Bye Song" as children prepare to leave.

Let's Start the Day

Focus Question

How do objects move?
¿Cómo se mueven los objetos?

 Learning Goals

Social and Emotional Development
• Child demonstrates initiative in independent activities; makes independent choices.

Language and Communication
• Child uses newly learned vocabulary daily in multiple contexts.

Emergent Literacy: Reading
• Child blends onset and rime to form a word without pictoral support.

Science
• Child explores and describes different ways objects move.

Vocabulary

airplane	avión
fly	volar
jet	avión a reacción
machine	máquina
wings	alas

Differentiated Instruction

 Extra Support
Phonological Awareness
If...children have trouble blending the words in the lesson, **then...**have children use onset and rime to blend words that are very familiar to them, such as their names.

 Enrichment
Phonological Awareness
Encourage children to memorize parts of the rhyme. Ask them to work in a small group to act out the various things that move while saying the words (for example, moving like a boat while saying the line about a boat sailing).

Opening Routines and Transition Tips

For **Opening Routines** and **Transition Tips** turn to pages 178–181 and visit **DLMExpressOnline.com** for more ideas.

 Read **"Going on a Bear Hunt"/**"Vamos a cazar un oso" from the *Teacher's Treasure Book,* page 201, for your morning Read Aloud.

Language Time

 large group · 15 minutes

Social and Emotional Development Tell children that they solve problems every day. Ask them to think about what problems they have had. Ask: **What did you do to solve your problem? Did you talk to a friend? Did you ask an adult for help?** *¿Cómo resolvieron su problema? ¿Hablaron con un amigo? ¿Le pidieron ayuda a un adulto?*

Oral Language and Vocabulary

✓ **Can children use vocabulary words to talk about flying and airplanes?**

Flying Ask children to name and act out things that can fly.

• Display *Oral Language Development Card 38*. Ask children what they see in the picture. Follow up by asking what they think it's like to fly in an airplane and how they think airplanes stay in the air. Then follow the suggestions on the back of the card.

ELL Help children with multiple meanings. The word *fly* can be a verb, but it can also be a noun. Help children become used to both meanings by saying sentences such as **The fly has eyes,** and **A bird can fly.**

• For additional suggestions on how to meet the needs of children at the Beginning, Intermediate, Advanced, and Advanced-High levels of English proficiency, see pages 184–187.

Phonological Awareness

✓ **Can children blend onset and rime to form words?**

Onset and Rime Display *Rhymes and Chants Flip Chart,* page 20. Read the poem aloud. Tell children you will say some of the ways things can go, but that you'll say the words in two parts. Demonstrate by saying /s/ and then saying *-ails*. Repeat the sounds several times, bringing them closer together until children recognize the word as *sails*. Repeat with /r/-*olls*, /bl/-*asts*, /fl/-*ies*, and /dr/-*ives*.

Oral Language Development Card 38

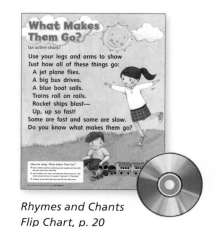

Rhymes and Chants Flip Chart, p. 20

Center Time

▶ **Center Rotation** Center Time includes teacher-guided activities and independent activities. Refer to the **Learning Centers** on pages 138–139 for independent activity ideas.

 small group 60–90 minutes

Pretend and Learn Center

☑ **Can children use vocabulary words to talk about their play?**

☑ **Can children solve problems on their own or with help from an adult?**

Materials dress-up clothes, cardboard boxes, classroom objects to use as props

At the Airport Have children pretend to be airplanes or pilots and airplane passengers.

● Have children use a large empty space. Help them set up a runway where airplanes can land and take off.

● Have them use vocabulary words to tell you and other children what they are doing.

● Remind children to share the space and to try their best to solve any problems that might arise.

Center Tip

If...sharing the space becomes problematic, **then...**tell children that airports have an air traffic controller whose job it is to tell pilots when they can land and take off. Encourage children to take turns being the controller.

Writer's Center

☑ **Can children identify objects and animals that can fly?**

☑ **Can children use vocabulary words to talk about things that fly and how they move?**

Materials paper, pencils, crayons or markers, stapler

Make a Book Remind children that they named and acted out things that could fly. Now they will make a book about things fly.

● Have children draw pictures of something that flies (helicopter, airplane, bee). Ask them to write as much of the name as they can.

● Repeat with other objects. Ask children what they know about these objects/ animals. Encourage use of new vocabulary words.

● Have children label their drawings with their names. Help children use construction paper to make a cover, and staple into book form.

Center Tip

If...children can't write the name of a given animal or object on their own, **then...**write the name on a card, and have children copy it.

Refer to the **Learning Centers** on pages 138–139 for independent activity ideas.

✓ Learning Goals

Social and Emotional Development
• Child demonstrates initiative in independent activities; makes independent choices.
• Child initiates interactions with others in work and play situations.

Science
• Child explores and describes different ways objects move.

Fine Arts
• Child expresses ideas, emotions, and moods through individual and collaborative dramatic play.

Differentiated Instruction

Extra Support
Pretend and Learn Center
If...children are not talking much about their play, **then...**ask them direct questions such as *How does your plane move? What are some things your plane uses to stay in the air?* ¿Cómo se mueve su avión? ¿Qué cosas usa su avión para mantenerse en el aire?

Enrichment
Writer's Center
Ask children to order their book pages in a way that makes sense to them. Then have them explain the order to you.

Accommodations for 3's
Writer's Center
If...children name and draw objects that do not fly, **then...**explain that those objects would be interesting to draw and write about, but that this book is for things that fly. Then suggest two or three objects, including one that flies (such as *egg, helicopter, chair*), and have them choose the one that can fly.

Circle Time

Focus Question

How do objects move?
¿Cómo se mueven los objetos?

✓ Learning Goals

Emergent Literacy: Reading

- Child blends onset and rime to form a word without pictoral support.
- Child names most upper- and lowercase letters of the alphabet.
- Child describes, relates to, and uses details and information from books read aloud.
- Child asks and answers questions about books read aloud (such as, "Who?" "What?" "Where?").

Vocabulary

alike	parecido	answers	respuestas
compare	comparar	detective	detective
different	diferente	float	flotar
observe	observar	rough	áspero
scale	balanza	smooth	suave
tools	herramientas		

Differentiated Instruction

 Extra Support

Read Aloud

If...children are uncertain of the meanings of words such as *heavy, rough,* and *smooth,* **then...**provide some small objects with these characteristics for children to feel and handle.

 Enrichment

Learn About Letters and Sounds

Have children locate the letters *Bb, Ii, Kk,* and *Nn* in books and magazines.

Literacy Time

📖 Read Aloud

✓ **Can children identify how objects are alike and different?**

Build Background Ask children to name some things they have learned about or learned how to do. Then ask:

- *How did you learn those things? ¿Cómo aprendieron esas cosas?*

- *Who learned by listening? Who learned by watching? Who learned by doing something? ¿Quién aprendió escuchando? ¿Quién aprendió mirando? ¿Quién aprendió haciendo algo?*

Listen for Understanding Display *Let's Investigate/Soy Detective,* and read the title. Explain that *investigate* is a long word that means "study" or "learn about." Explain that this book tells about different ways of learning things. Read the book aloud.

- Have children answer questions in the text, such as *What else can you compare? ¿Qué más pueden comparar?* and *Would you rather carry a bag full of apples or a bag full of grapes? ¿Preferirían cargar una bolsa llena de manzanas o una bolsa llena de uvas?*

- Have children give reasons for their answers.

Respond to the Story Ask children to identify things in the story that were alike and things that were different. Point out or elicit that sometimes two things can be alike *and* different.

💡 **TIP** Children may find it easier to do the Respond to the Story activity if you flip through the pages once more after explaining the assignment, using the pictures to help refresh children's memories.

Learn About Letters and Sounds

✓ **Can children identify letters and sounds?**

Learn About the Alphabet Write the letter *Bb* on the board. Have children name the letter, write it in the air, and say the sound /b/.

- Say several onset-rime combinations with *Bb,* such as /b/ -at, /b/ -ug, and /b/ -oot. Have children identify the complete words.

- Repeat with *Nn* and *Kk,* using *not, name, nose,* and *key, kick, kite.*

- Finally, repeat with *Ii,* using words with /i/ as the start of the rime (/t/ -ick, /s/ -it, /r/ -ing).

ELL Synonyms can be difficult for children whose native language is not English. *Let's Investigate,* for example, uses the words *small, rock,* and *pail.* Native speakers, however, might use *little, stone,* or *bucket* instead. Be sure ELL children understand that the words have the same meanings.

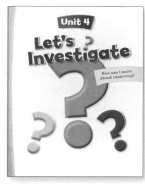

Let's Investigate
Soy Detective

Online Math Activity
Children can complete Mystery Pictures 3 and Memory Geometry 3 during computer time or Center Time.

Math Time

Observe and Investigate

 Can children match shapes?

Feely Box Remind children that they move their fingers to feel things. Invite children to feel and move shapes.

- Use the box that was used for the Feely Box activity on Day 2.

- Place children in pairs. Say: *Place your fingers in the box and feel around the shape inside. Can you name what the shape is? Tell your partner the name of the shape in the box and how you figured out the name.* *Metan las manos en la caja y toquen con los dedos la figura que hay adentro. ¿Pueden decir qué figura es? Díganle a su compañero el nombre de la figura que hay en la caja y explíquenle cómo lo supieron.*

- When children guess the shape and remove it from the box, have them turn the shape, and ask them what the name of the shape is then.

- Have children take turns placing a shape in the box and having their partner tell the name of the shape and how he or she figured it out.

ELL Continue to connect shape words to the shape words in the child's primary language whenever possible. Remember to include the terms *name* and *shape*.

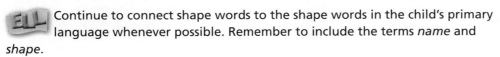 Social and Emotional Development

Making Good Choices

 Can children show perseverance?

Role-Play Solving Problems Display the *Making Good Choices Chart: Keep Trying.* Put on one puppet, and give the other puppet to a child.

- Have your puppet try to put together puzzle pieces. Give up after one try.

- Use your own voice to ask if the other puppet has anything to say to your puppet. Guide children to conclude that the puppet should try again.

- Have your puppet try two or three more times and eventually succeed. Repeat with other activities pictured on the chart. If possible, have two children do the role-play, each taking one puppet.

- After each role-play, ask: *What happened this time? How do they feel? What would you tell them to do next time?* *¿Qué pasó esta vez? ¿Cómo se sintieron los perritos? ¿Qué les dirían que hagan la próxima vez?*

Making Good Choices Flip Chart, p. 20

Focus Question
How do objects move?
¿Cómo se mueven los objetos?

Learning Goals

Language and Communication
• Child uses words to identify and understand categories.

Science
• Child follows basic health and safety rules.

Social Studies
• Child understands and discusses roles, responsibilities, and services provided by community workers.

Fine Arts
• Child expresses ideas, emotions, and moods through individual and collaborative dramatic play.

Vocabulary

community	comunidad	job	trabajo
helper	ayuda	hurt	lastimar
safe	seguro	work	trabajar

Differentiated Instruction

✋ Extra Support
Oral Language and Academic Vocabulary
If...children have trouble thinking of job titles, **then...**remind them of the unit on community helpers. Have children name community helper jobs such as firefighter and police officer.

⭐ Enrichment
Oral Language and Academic Vocabulary
Have children categorize the list of jobs another way (such as *jobs for which people wear uniforms* and *jobs for which people don't wear uniforms*).

♥ Special Needs
Cognitive Challenges
Learning about community helpers will help the child throughout her/his life. As you discuss jobs, don't forget to include some that the child may be familiar with, such as a physical therapist or a speech therapist.

Social Studies Time

large group   20 minutes

Personal Safety Skills Ask children to name some things they do that help them stay safe. Then explain that even if children do hurt themselves, there are many people who can help them. Help them understand that these people include family members, as well as workers such as nurses and doctors.

Oral Language and Academic Vocabulary

✓ **Can children identify jobs that people can have?**

Jobs Tell children that being a nurse or a doctor is a job. Add that you have a job, too—you are a teacher. Ask children what other kinds of jobs people can have. Help children use the words in sentences, such as *A firefighter puts out fires. El bombero apaga el fuego.*

● Make a chart of jobs children name, dividing the jobs into two categories, such as *jobs that people do outdoors* and *jobs that people do indoors.*

● Review the completed list with children.

Understand and Participate

✓ **Can children act out what people do when they have certain jobs?**

Act Out Jobs Tell children that they will be acting out some of the jobs listed on the chart.

● Have children choose a job on the list.

● Have them take turns doing things that a person with that job would ordinarily do (for instance, a child being a truck driver would pretend to drive, while a child taking on the role of a chef would pretend to cook).

ELL The word ending *-er* often indicates someone who holds a job: firefight*er*, driv*er*, bak*er*, writ*er*. Help children say sentences such as *A builder is a person who builds*, making sure they understand how these *-er* words are formed.

● For additional suggestions on how to meet the needs of children at the Beginning, Intermediate, Advanced, and Advanced-High levels of English proficiency, see pages 184–187.

Center Time

▶ **Center Rotation** Center Time includes teacher-guided activities and independent activities. Refer to the **Learning Centers** on pages 138–139 for independent activity ideas.

  small group 30 minutes

Creativity Center

Center Tip

 ✓ **Can children identify what people do when they have certain kinds of jobs?**

Materials butcher paper, paint and paintbrushes

Jobs Mural Have children create a mural that shows people working at many different kinds of jobs.

- Have children choose jobs from the list in the lesson you just completed.

- Ask children to paint a group mural with pictures of people doing the jobs from the list.

- Have children tell a classmate or an adult what each person is doing and what kind of a job he or she has.

If...you have more than five or six children in the center, **then...**consider splitting the groups into smaller groups, each creating its own mural. This will ease congestion and may help children be more cooperative.

Purposeful Play

✓ **Can children solve problems and talk about how problems can be solved?**

Children choose an open center for free playtime. Remind children to pay attention to how they solve problems that arise as they play.

Let's Say Good-Bye

  large group 15 minutes

 Read Aloud Revisit the story "Going on a Bear Hunt"/"Vamos a cazar un oso" for your afternoon Read Aloud. Have children listen for words that begin with /i/.

 Home Connection Refer to the Home Connections activities listed in the Resources and Materials chart on page 135. Tell children to look for people doing different kinds of jobs as they make their way home. Sing the "Good-Bye Song" as children prepare to leave.

✓ Learning Goals

Social and Emotional Development
- Child demonstrates initiative in independent activities; makes independent choices.

Emergent Literacy: Writing
- Child uses scribbles, shapes, pictures, symbols, and letters to represent language.

Social Studies
- Child understands and discusses roles, responsibilities, and services provided by community workers.

Writing

Ask children to think of a job they would like to have. Have them draw a picture of themselves dressed like a person who would do that job. Then have them write the name of the job and tell why they would like to do it. Take dictation as needed.

Focus Question
How do objects move?
¿Cómo se mueven los objetos?

Learning Goals

Social and Emotional Development
• Child demonstrates initiative in independent activities; makes independent choices.

Language and Communication
• Child uses newly learned vocabulary daily in multiple contexts.

Emergent Literacy: Reading
• Child blends onset and rime to form a word without pictoral support.

Vocabulary

folktale	cuento folclórico
made-up	inventado
make-believe	imaginario
moon	Luna
real	real
sky	cielo
sun	sol

Differentiated Instruction

 Extra Support
Phonological Awareness
If...it's difficult for children to identify the body part you're naming, **then...**touch a body part and give children three choices of words, such as touching your neck and saying /n/-eck, /h/-and, and /sh/-in. Have children nod their heads when you say the correct word.

 Enrichment
Phonological Awareness
Have children play the game with a partner or in a small group. They should take turns giving directions by separating the words into onset and rime: *Touch your /ch/-eek. Tóquense la /ch/ -eek.*

Let's Start the Day

▶ **Opening Routines and Transition Tips**
For **Opening Routines** and **Transition Tips** turn to pages 178–181 and visit DLMExpressOnline.com for more ideas.

 Read **"What's in the Box?"/**"¿Qué hay en la caja?" from the *Teacher's Treasure Book* page 253, for your morning Read Aloud.

Language Time

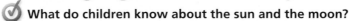 **Social and Emotional Development** Tell children that there are usually lots of different ways to solve problems. Say: *Let's see who really tries to solve problems in different ways today! ¡Vamos a ver hoy quién intenta resolver los problemas de diferentes maneras!*

Oral Language and Vocabulary

✓ **What do children know about the sun and the moon?**

Sun and Moon Ask children to name things that we can see in the sky. Elicit or explain that two of the biggest things we can see in the sky are the sun and the moon. Ask children to tell what they know about these objects.

● Display the flannel board characters for "Why the Sun and the Moon Live in the Sky"/"Por qué el Sol y la Luna viven en el cielo". Explain that the sun and the moon do not really live in the sky. They are not alive. This is a made-up, or make believe, story that explains why the sun and the moon are in the sky instead of on the ground. Explain that this story is a folktale that people have told for many years. Have children explain the difference between a make-believe story and a story that is real. Read the story, acting out the various parts.

Phonological Awareness

✓ **Can children identify names for body parts from the onset and rime?**

Touch Your /n/ -ose Explain that children will play a game. Say: *Touch your /n/ -ose. Tóquense la /n/ -ose.* Separate the onset and rime of *nose,* and then touch your nose and have children follow your lead. Say: */n/ -ose is* nose. **Touch your /n/ -ose means** touch your nose. *Tóquense la /n/ -ose quiere decir tóquense la nose.* Then repeat, using these body parts: /f/ -eet, /l/ -eg, /h/ -air, /h/ -ead, /ch/ -in, /m/ -outh, /ch/-est, /n/-ee (knee), /n/ -eck, and /th/ -umb.

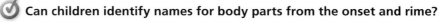 Preview the words you'll use in the Phonological Awareness activity to increase children's ability to play the game. It's fine to review the body parts before introducing the game, or you can do the preteaching earlier in the day.

● For additional suggestions on how to meet the needs of children at the Beginning, Intermediate, Advanced, and Advanced-High levels of English proficiency, see pages 184–187.

Center Time

> **Center Rotation** Center Time includes teacher-guided activities and independent activities. Refer to the **Learning Centers** on pages 138–139 for independent activity ideas.

small group   60–90 minutes

Pretend and Learn Center

☑ Can children act out a narrative?

Materials dress-up clothes, other objects to use as props

Act Out the Sun and the Moon Ask children how they think the sun and the moon came to be in the sky. Have them work in pairs or small groups to act out their idea of what might have happened.

- Have children take on the roles of Sun, Moon, and any other characters they want or need.

- Remind children to work together to plan and act out the story.

- Encourage children to use props and costume materials.

Center Tip

If...children want more elaborate costume or set pieces, **then...**provide materials and space for children to create these pieces.

ABC Center

☑ Can children identify the first letters of body part words?

Materials butcher paper, pencils, markers or crayons

First Letters Have children identify and write the initial letters of body parts.

- Have children lie on butcher paper. Trace their outlines or help classmates do it for one another.

- Have children identify body parts on their body tracings. Help them isolate the initial sound of each part and associate it with the correct letter.

- Ask them to write the initial letter of each body part in the correct place, such as *h* for *head*.

Center Tip

If...children can't identify the first letter of a body part word, **then...**encourage them to ask classmates for help before coming to you.

✓ Learning Goals

Language and Communication
- Child uses newly learned vocabulary daily in multiple contexts.

Emergent Literacy: Reading
- Child names most upper- and lowercase letters of the alphabet.

Emergent Literacy: Writing
- Child participates in free drawing and writing activities to deliver information.

Fine Arts
- Child expresses ideas, emotions, and moods through individual and collaborative dramatic play.

Differentiated Instruction

 Extra Support

ABC Center

If...children have a hard time isolating the initial sound of each word, **then...**have children say the word *nose*, elongating the initial /n/ so it sounds like *nnnnnose*. Then have children repeat the word, but stop them before they move on to the *ose* part of the word. Repeat with *nnnnnneck* and *lllllleg*. Have children use this procedure to find the initial letter of other words.

 Enrichment

ABC Center

Encourage children to write as much of each body part as they can, not just the first letter. Help by saying each word slowly and carefully several times.

Accommodations for 3's

ABC Center

If...children can't form the letters on their own, **then...**guide them to first write the letters in the air and then write the letters in pencil on the body tracing.

Focus Question

How do objects move?
¿Cómo se mueven los objetos?

 Learning Goals

Emergent Literacy: Reading
• Child names most upper- and lowercase letters of the alphabet.

• Child describes, relates to, and uses details and information from books read aloud.

• Child asks and answers questions about books read aloud (such as, "Who?" "What?" "Where?").

Vocabulary

moon	Luna	oceans	Tierra
sky	cielo	sun	Sol
water	agua		

Differentiated Instruction

 Extra Support

Learn About Letters and Sounds
If...children have trouble recalling what a given letter looks like, **then...**write it on the board, or display a card showing that letter.

Enrichment

Learn About Letters and Sounds
Have children form letters from previous units (such as *Ee, Rr,* and *Tt*) as well as from this unit.

Accommodations for 3's
Read Aloud
If...children have trouble telling real from make-believe, **then...**model the difference by saying: *In the story, Water talks to the Sun. In our world, water can't talk, so the story is not real; it's made-up, or make-believe. En el cuento, la Luna habla con el Sol. En nuestro mundo, la Luna no puede hablar; entonces, el cuento no es real: es inventado o imaginario.*

Literacy Time

 large group 15 minutes

 Read Aloud

 Can children explain how they know that a story is made-up or make-believe?

Build Background Remind children that "Why the Sun and the Moon Live in the Sky" is a made-up story about the sun and the moon.

● Briefly review what children know about the sun and the moon (for example, the sun is hot; the moon is a long way from Earth, the sun and the moon are not living things).

Listen for Enjoyment Display the flannel board characters for "Why the Sun and the Moon Live in the Sky,"/"Por qué el Sol y la Luna viven en el cielo" and read the title. Say: *I am going to read this story again. When I finish, tell us about your favorite part. Voy a leer este cuento otra vez. Cuando termine, cuenten su parte favorita.*

Respond to the Story Invite children to talk about the story. Then ask children how they know the story is made-up and not real.

 TIP Most children will enjoy acting out the story. You can have one child play the role of Sun, another be Moon, and a third be Water, or you can ask all the members of the class to play all the parts, making appropriate gestures and facial expressions from their seats. Encourage children to say the dialogue with you.

ELL This is a good opportunity for children to teach the class the words for *sun, moon,* and *water* in their home languages. This will expose native speakers of English to the sounds of other languages and can help ELL children feel like experts.

Learn About Letters and Sounds

Can children form letters and associate them with sounds?

Learn About the Alphabet Have children use their bodies to form the letters *B, I, K,* and *N*.

● Say a letter (*Bb, Ii, Kk,* or *Nn*) and point to two or three children.

● Have those children arrange their bodies into the shape of that letter. They may choose upppercase or lowercase.

● Have the rest of the children say the letter and its sound. Repeat with other children and the remaining letters.

Teacher's Treasure Book, p. 319

Online Math Activity

Children can complete Mystery Pictures 3 and Memory Geometry 3 during computer time or Center Time.

large group · 15 minutes

Math Time

Observe and Investigate

 Can children count and move simultaneously?

Count and Move Invite children to count and move together.

- Say: *Let's count and move! Imagine you are climbing the stairs. ¡A contar y a moverse! Imaginen que están subiendo las escaleras.* Have children march in place to mimic climbing stairs. Say: *Let's count as we climb the stairs. One stair, two stairs, three stairs... Contemos a medida que subimos la escalera. Un escalón, dos escalones, tres escalones...* Continue counting with children up to 10.

- Then say: *Next, let's creep forward and then creep back. Count and move with me! A continuación, arrastrémonos hacia adelante y luego hacia atrás. ¡Cuenten y muévanse conmigo!* Have children creep forward and back to the count of 10.

- Discuss with children what kind of movements they like, such as crouching, hopping, and marching. Experiment with these types of movements in this activity. Have children say the movement word as they move.

ELL Reinforce the word *stairs* by having children climb a real set of stairs if possible.

large group · 15 minutes

✗✗✗ Social and Emotional Development

Making Good Choices

 Can children suggest solutions to a problem?

Puppet Conflict Display the Dog Puppets. Have them "dance" near each other. Then have them collide. Have the puppets talk about it and decide to be more careful, but then have them collide again, knocking one of them over.

- Have the puppet who was knocked over say: *That's it! I am NOT going to play with you anymore because you're not very nice! ¡Ya basta! ¡NO voy a jugar más con ustedes porque no son amables!*

- Ask children how to help solve the problem. Ask: *How do the puppets feel now? What could they do next? What might they do next time they play? ¿Cómo se sienten los títeres? ¿Qué podrían hacer ahora? ¿Qué pueden hacer la próxima vez que jueguen?*

ELL Give children practice with helping verbs such as *can* and *should* and their position in sentences. Children can tell the puppets, for example, *You should dance farther apart* or *You can look at each other when you dance.*

Making Good Choices Flip Chart, p. 20

Differentiated Instruction

 ✋ **Extra Support**

Making Good Choices
If...children have trouble identifying solutions, **then...**offer them choices, such as *Which will help solve the problem? How about standing farther apart when you dance or not looking where you're going when you dance? ¿Qué ayudará a resolver el problema: quedarse lejos cuando bailan o no mirar adónde van cuando bailan?*

⭐ **Enrichment**

Observe and Investigate
Count and move to 30. Encourage students to count with you as they move.

Accommodations for 3's

Making Good Choices
If...children are more interested in talking about the problem (for example, *They went bang!*) than in thinking of solutions, **then...**let them talk for a minute or so about what they saw, allowing them to feel that they've been heard; then redirect them to thinking about solutions.

Focus Question
How do objects move?
¿Cómo se mueven los objetos?

Learning Goals

Mathematics
• Child recognizes, names, describes, matches, compares, sorts common two-dimensional shapes (such as circle, square, rectangle, triangle, rhombus).

Vocabulary

find   encontrar   step   paso
triangle   triángulo

Differentiated Instruction

 Extra Support

Math Time
If...children struggle finding the shapes, **then...** review a shape's attributes while children feel the shape.

 Enrichment

Math Time
Have children look around the classroom or in books for examples of shapes in unusual places.

Accommodations for 3's

Math Time
If...children seem reluctant to find and step on the shapes, **then...**step on a shape yourself, and ask children if it is the correct shape and how they know.

 Special Needs

Delayed Motor Development
A child who can't walk can play a variation of the game. Attach shapes of varying textures to a mat or poster for the child to hold. As the other children are stepping on a shape, the child can find and touch the shape.

Math Time

  large group   15 minutes

Social and Emotional Development Model different phrases children can use if they bump into each other during an activity, such as *excuse me* and *I'm sorry.*

Can children identify shapes?

Step on That Shape! Invite children to find a shape and step on it. Tell children they can move to the shapes in different ways. They can take big or little steps, or they can hop or jump to the shapes.

● Make several large shapes, like those in the Shape Set, on the floor using construction paper, masking tape, or colored tape. Make sure the shapes are clearly visible.

● Distribute a variety of shapes around the area.

● Work with groups of five children. Say: *I am looking for a rectangles. Where is a rectangle? Is there one beside the triangle? Is there one behind the square? Find that shape!* *Estoy buscando un rectángulo. ¿Dónde hay un rectángulo? ¿Está al lado del triángulo? ¿Está detrás del cuadrado? ¡Encuentren esa figura!*

● Give children time to locate the shape on the floor. Ask: *How do you know the shape you stepped on is a rectangle?* *¿Cómo saben que la figura sobre la que están parados es un rectángulo?*

● Ask the rest of the group if they are correct. Say: *Did they step only on the rectangles? Help them find the rectangles!* *¿Se pararon sobre el rectángulo? ¡Ayúdenlos a encontrar el rectángulo!*

● Repeat the activity until all groups have stepped on shapes.

ELL Invite children to participate in a game of "Follow the Leader" in which they must perform the motion you say, such as jump, hop, big step, or little step, to reach a target shape. Model a few examples.

● For additional suggestions on how to meet the needs of children at the Beginning, Intermediate, Advanced, and Advanced-High levels of English proficiency, see pages 184–187.

Center Time

 small group   30 minutes

Math and Science Center

✓ **Children match shapes to tracings of shapes.**

Materials paper, markers or crayons, shape sets

Trace and Match Ask children to trace shapes and then have a partner match the shapes to their tracings.

- Say: *Trace each shape from the set on a large sheet of paper. Then give your shapes and tracings to a partner.* *Dibujen el contorno de cada figura en una hoja de papel grande. Luego, den sus figuras y dibujos a un compañero.*

- Guide children to match the shape to the tracing. Say: *Can you match the shapes to the traced shape? Which shape looks as if it matches the tracing? Do you need to move the shape to make it match?* *¿Pueden hacer coincidir las figuras con el dibujo? ¿Qué figura parece que coincide con el dibujo? ¿Tienen que mover la figura para que coincida?*

Center Tip

If...children have difficulty matching the traced shape, **then...**demonstrate by placing a shape over a tracing and flipping or turning the shape. Talk about whether the shape matches.

Learning Goals

Language and Communication
- Child uses newly learned vocabulary daily in multiple contexts.

Emergent Literacy: Writing
- Child participates in free drawing and writing activities to deliver information.

Mathematics
- Child recognizes, names, describes, matches, compares, sorts common two-dimensional shapes (such as circle, square, rectangle, triangle, rhombus).

Writing

Have children write and draw about their favorite part in "Why the Sun and the Moon Live in the Sky." Encourage children to write all the words and letters they can.

Purposeful Play

✓ **Observe children matching shapes.**

Children choose an open center for free playtime. Encourage children to draw pictures over or color in the traced shapes and to say the shape names as they color.

Let's Say Good-Bye

 large group   15 minutes

 Read Aloud Revisit the story "What's in the Box?"/"¿Qué hay en la caja?" for your afternoon Read Aloud. Ask children to think about whether the story could be real and explain why they think so.

 Home Connection Refer to the Home Connections activities listed in the Resources and Materials chart on page 135. Have children tell their families what happened in "Why the Sun and the Moon Live in the Sky." Sing the "Good-Bye Song" as children prepare to leave.

Let's Start the Day

Focus Question
How do objects move?
¿Cómo se mueven los objetos?

 Learning Goals

Social and Emotional Development
• Child demonstrates initiative in independent activities; makes independent choices.

Language and Communication
• Child uses newly learned vocabulary daily in multiple contexts.

Emergent Literacy: Reading
• Child blends onset and rime to form a word without pictoral support.

Science
• Child explores and describes different ways objects move.

Vocabulary

blast	retumbar	drive	manejar
fly	volar	roll	rodar
sail	navegar		

Differentiated Instruction

 Extra Support

Oral Language and Vocabulary
If...children have a hard time remembering the meanings of movement words, **then...**have them repeat each word several times along with a motion that describes it.

 Enrichment

Oral Language and Vocabulary
Have children add new lines to the poem, naming other objects and how they move, such as *a balloon floats* and *a top spins*.

▶ **Opening Routines and Transition Tips**
For **Opening Routines** and **Transition Tips** turn to pages 178–181 and visit DLMExpressOnline.com for more ideas.

📖 Read **"The Piñata"**/*"La Piñata"* from the *Teacher's Treasure Book,* page 175, for your morning Read Aloud.

Language Time

 large group 15 minutes

 Social and Emotional Development Tell children to pay attention to any problems they have today. Ask them to think about good ways they can solve problems.

Oral Language and Vocabulary

✓ **Can children use and understand words that tell about movement?**

How Things Go Remind children that they have been learning about how things move.

● Display "What Makes Them Go?" on the *Rhymes and Chants Flip Chart,* page 20. Read the poem aloud. Read it again, having children use their legs and arms to act out how each object moves, as the poem's opening directs. Finally, read it one more time, and have children use their bodies to move through the circle area as if they were those vehicles. Ask children to use words to describe the motions (for example, *sails, flies, drives*).

Phonological Awareness

✓ **Can children blend words when given onset and rime?**

Be a /b/ -oat Continue the activity above, in which children act out how various vehicles move. This time, however, name the vehicles in onset-rime form—that is, tell children to move like a /b/ -oat or a /tr/ -ain—and help them determine which vehicle you are naming. You can include vehicles that are not named in the rhyme, such as *car* and *bike.*

ELL Children who know the word *ship* may be confused by the term *rocket ship.* Help children understand what *rocket ship* refers to and how it connects to the idea of a ship that goes on water.

● For additional suggestions on how to meet the needs of children at the Beginning, Intermediate, Advanced, and Advanced-High levels of English proficiency, see pages 184–187.

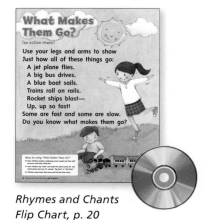

What Makes Them Go?
(an action chant)

Use your legs and arms to show
Just how all of these things go:
A jet plane flies.
A big bus drives.
A blue boat sails.
Trains roll on rails.
Rocket ships blast—
Up, up so fast!
Some are fast and some are slow.
Do you know what makes them go?

Rhymes and Chants Flip Chart, p. 20

Center Time

▶ **Center Rotation** Center Time includes teacher-guided activities and independent activities. Refer to the **Learning Centers** on pages 138–139 for independent activity ideas.

 small group 60–90 minutes

Construction Center

 Listen as children talk about how rockets move and where rockets can go.

Materials cardboard scraps, cardboard tubes, recycled materials, glue, scissors, tape, craft materials such as ribbons

Build a Rocket Ship Have children create rocket ships out of cardboard and other recycled materials. Have children talk about where rockets will go and how they move.

- Give each child a tube from a paper towel roll.

- Have children add features to their rocket and decorate the rockets. Encourage collaboration and sharing of materials.

Center Tip

If...there aren't enough tubes to go around, **then**...have children work with a partner.

Writer's Center

 Monitor children as they name, draw, and describe vehicles.

Materials large sheets of paper, pencils, crayons or markers

My Vehicle Poster Have children think of vehicles they have ridden on or in. Give each child a large sheet of paper to serve as a poster. Then have children draw and write about each vehicle somewhere on the poster.

- Have children write as much on their own as they can.

- Have children tell an adult or a classmate about the vehicles, particularly how the vehicles move.

Center Tip

If...children want their vehicles to look more realistic, **then**...provide magazines, and invite children to cut and glue pictures of the vehicles they want.

Learning Goals

Language and Communication
- Child uses newly learned vocabulary daily in multiple contexts.

Emergent Literacy: Writing
- Child participates in free drawing and writing activities to deliver information.

Science
- Child explores and describes different ways objects move.

Differentiated Instruction

 Extra Support
Writer's Center
If...children forget the name of a vehicle, **then**...give them a hint by saying a word that rhymes with it or by supplying the first letter or sound.

Enrichment
Construction Center
Have children dictate or write a story about their rocket ship and what it does.

Accommodations for 3's
Construction Center
If...children begin to construct things that are not rockets, **then**...help them incorporate the objects into stories about rockets (for example, if the child starts building a house, point out that a rocket might fly to Mars and land near a house).

 Special Needs
Vision Loss
Make cardboard cutouts of vehicles so the child can feel the edges of the cutouts, can choose and arrange them, and then can glue them onto poster board. Then the child can dictate his/her information about how the vehicles move for an adult to add to the poster.

Focus Question

How do objects move?
¿Cómo se mueven los objetos?

Learning Goals

Language and Communication
• Child uses words to identify and understand categories.

Emergent Literacy: Reading
• Child names most upper- and lowercase letters of the alphabet.
• Child describes, relates to, and uses details and information from books read aloud.

Science
• Child explores and describes different ways objects move.

Vocabulary

blast	retumbar	drive	mover
fly	volar	roll	rodar
sail	navegar		

Differentiated Instruction

 Extra Support

Learn About Letters and Sounds
If...children can't reliably remember the sound that goes with a given letter, **then...**have children write the letter in the air while saying the sound; for example, have them write a lowercase n while saying /nnnnnnn/.

 Enrichment

Learn About Letters and Sounds
Have children say not only the sound that goes with the letter but also a word that begins with that sound (for example, /b/, bat for b).

Accommodations for 3's

Read Aloud
If...children name vehicles without thinking about the categories *with wheels* and *without wheels*, **then...**have them simply name vehicles and help them determine afterward which category is the correct one for each.

Literacy Time

 Read Aloud

large group · 15 minutes

✓ **Can children identify ways that vehicles move?**

✓ **Can children sort vehicles into those with wheels and those without?**

Build Background Remind children that this week they have learned about many vehicles and how they move.

● Help children name vehicles that have wheels.

● Then help them name vehicles that do not have wheels.

Listen for Understanding Display *What Do Wheels Do All Day?/¿Qué hacen las ruedas todo el día?* and read the title. Remind children that they have heard this book before.

● Tell them to watch for pictures of things that move.

● Instruct them to listen for words that tell how things move.

Respond and Connect Help children make a list of all the ways they know that things move. Read the completed list with children, and compliment children on their knowledge and recall.

ELL Children may have an idea of a vehicle or movement word but not remember the English term. You can have children act out the idea or describe it in some other way. If you can determine the word, provide its beginning sounds to jog children's memories.

● For additional suggestions on how to meet the needs of children at the Beginning, Intermediate, Advanced, and Advanced-High levels of English proficiency, see pages 184–187.

Learn About Letters and Sounds

✓ **Can children associate letters with their sounds?**

Learn About the Alphabet Write the letters *Bb, Ii, Kk,* and *Nn* on the board. Have children name them and supply their sounds.

● Introduce a game with the letters. Hold a ball in front of the child next to you and say **Nn.** The child gives the sound for *Nn*, takes the ball, and repeats with the next child, choosing a different letter. Repeat as many times as scheduling permits.

What Do Wheels Do All Day?
¿Qué hacen las ruedas todo el día?

Building Blocks

Online Math Activity

Children can complete Mystery Pictures 3 and Memory Geometry 3 during computer time or Center Time.

Math Time

Observe and Investigate

☑ **Can child recognize that shapes are the same even when turned or flipped?**

Flip and Turn Discuss movement with children. Ask them to turn their bodies and explain that they are still the same no matter how they are turned. Tell children shapes can be flipped and turned around too.

- Display shapes from the Shape Set. Say: *Look at these shapes. What is the name of each shape? Miren estas figuras. ¿Cuál es el nombre de cada figura?* Have children name the shapes with you.

- Display a square. Say: *What if I turned this square around? What happens to the shape? Is it still a square? ¿Qué pasa si giro este cuadrado? ¿Qué sucede con la figura? ¿Sigue siendo un cuadrado?* Point out to children that the shape is the same. Say: *Even though the square is turned around, it still has four equal sides and four equal angles. Aunque lo giremos, el cuadrado todavía tiene cuatro lados iguales y cuatro ángulos iguales.*

- Repeat by flipping and sliding the square.

- Give each child a shape from the Shape Set. Ask children to turn their shapes around, flip them over, and slide them to see that the shapes stay the same.

✗✗✗ Social and Emotional Development

Making Good Choices

☑ **Can children talk about how they can solve problems and explain what they do to help classmates solve problems?**

What We've Learned Display *Making Good Choices Flip Chart*, page 20. Have children talk about the scenario in the picture again. Ask:

- *What have you learned this week about solving problems? ¿Qué aprendieron esta semana sobre resolver problemas?*

- *How can you help other children remember strategies for solving problems? ¿Cómo pueden ayudar a otros niños recordando estrategias para resolver problemas?* Wrap up by telling children that they can be proud of what they've learned.

ELL To help ELL children participate in the discussion, preview the *Keep Trying* picture with children. Remind them of the vocabulary words they'll need in order to describe the picture. You can do this just before introducing the chart or earlier in the day.

Making Good Choices Flip Chart, p. 20

 Learning Goals

Social and Emotional Development
- Child identifies self by categories (such as gender, age, family member, cultural group).
- Child demonstrates initiative in independent activities; makes independent choices.

Mathematics
- Child manipulates (flips, rotates) and combines shapes.

Vocabulary

angry	enojado	easy	fácil
flip	dar vuelta	happy	feliz
hard	duro	proud	orgulloso
sad	triste	same	igual
try	intentar	turn	giro

Differentiated Instruction

✋ **Extra Support**

Making Good Choices

If...the chart doesn't spark discussion for some children, **then...**do a role-play with puppets as you did on the previous day. It may be that children need cues that are more immediate and more kinesthetic or auditory.

⭐ **Enrichment**

Making Good Choices

Ask children to collaborate on a story that tells about someone who has a big problem. How do the child and the classmates solve the problem? Write the words they dictate, and have children draw pictures.

Accommodations for 3's

Observe and Investigate

If...children struggle to recognize shapes, **then...**review the shapes with them, allowing them to hold and trace shapes with their fingers. Invite them to close their eyes as you say the name of the shape.

Social and Emotional Development
• Child is aware of self in terms of abilities, characteristics and preferences, and respects personal boundaries.

Language and Communication
• Child uses newly learned vocabulary daily in multiple contexts.

• Child uses words to identify and understand categories.

Physical Development
• Child coordinates body movements in a variety of locomotive activities (such as walking, jumping, running, hopping, skipping, climbing).

Vocabulary

climb	trepar	crawl	arrastrarse
hop	dar pisadas	jump	saltar
run	correr	walk	caminar

Differentiated Instruction

 Extra Support

Oral Language and Academic Vocabulary
If...children have trouble comparing how they move with how objects and vehicles move, **then...**ask leading questions such as **What makes a car go?** (engine; wheels); **Do you have an engine/a set of wheels?** ¿Cómo funciona un auto? (motor; ruedas) ¿Tienen un motor/ ruedas?

 Enrichment
Move and Learn
Have children determine which ways of moving are fastest and which are slowest from among running, walking, crawling, jumping, and hopping.

Accommodations for 3's
Move and Learn
If...children don't yet have the coordination needed to hop, **then...**have them hop while holding onto an adult's hand or a piece of playground equipment.

Outdoor Play Time

Health Skills Ask children to talk about how they stay healthy. Help them see that one good way to stay healthy is to exercise, or move the body.

Oral Language and Academic Vocabulary
 Can children use vocabulary words to describe how they move?

How People Move Remind children that they have learned a lot about how vehicles and other objects move. Explain that today they will be thinking about how their own bodies move.

● Ask children to describe ways they can move, using words such as *run* and *jump*. Elicit as many vocabulary words as possible; introduce the rest.

● Ask volunteers to act out each of these motions. Be sure children see the differences between pairs like *walk/run* or *jump/hop*.

ELL Encourage children to act out a new motion even if they don't know the English word that names the activity. Provide a hint, such as the first letter or sound of the activity, if you think the child is familiar with the word and simply can't recall it at the moment.

Move and Learn
Can children associate ways of moving with words?

Move, Move, Move Have children play outdoors. Encourage them to run, jump, and engage in other types of movement. From time to time, call out a direction, such as *Jump! ¡Salten!*

● When children hear the direction, they should immediately stop what they are doing and move around by jumping until they hear you call out *Stop!*

● Cycle through the vocabulary words. Note which words are harder for children to understand than others. Repeat these words more than the others.

● Follow up by asking children how their movements are like those of a vehicle and how they are different.

 TIP It is fine to include other movement words. Be certain that you have introduced each of these words to children before beginning this part of the activity, however.

Center Time

> **Center Rotation** Center Time includes teacher-guided activities and independent activities. Refer to the **Learning Centers** on pages 138–139 for independent activity ideas.

Library and Listening Center

Center Tip

✓ Observe how children use vocabulary words that describe how people move.

Materials *Photo Library* CD-ROM, books that show people moving, paper, pencils, crayons and markers

Moving Around Display relevant photos from the CD-ROM, and have children look through the books to find pictures of people moving.

- Ask children to identify the way the people are moving, using vocabulary words from the previous activity.

- Have children draw people moving and label the pictures with the way they are moving (run, walk, jump, swing, skip, and so on).

If...your classroom has a computer that is connected to the Internet, **then**...work with children to find pictures of people running, jumping, and so on.

Learning Goals

Language and Communication
• Child uses newly learned vocabulary daily in multiple contexts.

Emergent Literacy: Reading
• Child describes, relates to, and uses details and information from books read aloud.

Emergent Literacy: Writing
• Child participates in free drawing and writing activities to deliver information.

Writing

Have children choose something they especially liked doing today. Have them draw and write about it. Encourage them to share their work with others.

Purposeful Play

✓ Monitor whether children move in ways that are appropriate for the situation.

Children choose an open center for free playtime. Have them pay attention to how they move their bodies.

Let's Say Good-Bye

large group   15 minutes

 Read Aloud Revisit the story "The Piñata"/"La Piñata" for your afternoon Read Aloud. Have children listen for people moving.

 Home Connection Refer to the Home Connections activities listed in the Resources and Materials chart on page 135. Remind children to practice different ways of moving when they get home. Sing the "Good-Bye Song" as children prepare to leave.

In general, the purpose of assessing young children in the early childhood classroom is to collect information necessary to make important decisions about their developmental and educational needs. Because assessment is crucial to making informed teaching decisions, it is necessarily a vital component of *DLM Early Childhood Express.* The guidelines and forms found online allow the teacher to implement assessment necessary in the pre-kindergarten classroom.

Effective assessment is an ongoing process that always enhances opportunities for optimal growth, development, and learning. The process of determining individual developmental and educational needs tailors early childhood education practices and provides a template for setting individual and program goals.

Pre-kindergarten assessment should be authentic; that is, it should be a natural, environmental extension of the classroom. Assessments should be incorporated into classroom activities whenever possible, not completed as separate, pull-out activities in which the teacher evaluates the student one-on-one. Whenever possible, assessment should evaluate children's real knowledge in the process of completing real activities. For example, observing children as they equally distribute snacks would be a better assessment of their ability to make groups than observing an exercise in which children group counters would be.

It is also important to note that assessments should be administered over time, as environmental influences can greatly impact single outcomes. If a pre-kindergarten child is tired or ill, for example, the child may not demonstrate knowledge of a skill that has actually been mastered. It is also important to consider the length of assessment for children of this age, as attention spans are still developing and can vary greatly based on environmental influences. Most assessments should be completed within half an hour.

If possible, use multiple types of assessment for the same content area when working with pre-kindergarten children. Some children may be able to demonstrate mastery kinesthetically if they are not able to use expressive language well; others may not process auditory instruction adequately, but will be able to complete an assessment after observing someone model the task. It is vital that the assessment process should never make the child anxious or scared.

Informal Assessment

INFORMAL assessments rely heavily on observational and work-sampling techniques that continually focus on child performance, processes, and product over selected periods of time and in a variety of contexts.

ANECDOTAL assessments are written descriptions that provide a short, objective account of an event or an incident. Only the facts are reported—where, what, when, and how. Anecdotal records are especially helpful when trying to understand a child's behavior or use of skills. These recordings can be used to share the progress of individual children and to develop and individualize curriculum.

The Anecdotal Observational Record Form can be used at any time to document an individual child's progress toward a goal or signs indicating the need for developmental or medical evaluation. Observations can reflect the focused skills for the week, but are not limited to those skills. You may pair the form with video or audio recordings of the child to complete an anecdotal record.

Anecdotal Observational Record Form

CHECKLISTS are lists of skills or behaviors arranged into disciplines or developmental domains and are used to determine how a child exhibits the behaviors or skills listed. Teachers can quickly and easily observe groups of children and check the behaviors or skills each child is demonstrating at the moment.

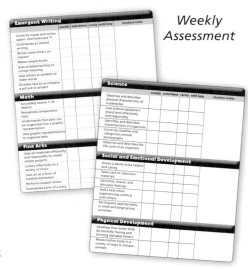

Weekly Assessment

Weekly Assessments measure progress toward specific guidelines that are addressed in the weekly curriculum. The Performance Assessment Checklist measures progress toward the guidelines of the entire curriculum. It is intended to be used three times per year.

Performance Assessment Checklist

When using either type of checklist, it is important to remember that the skills and behaviors on the list are only guidelines. Each child is unique and has his or her own developmental timetable. It is also important to remember that the checklist only documents the presence or absence of a specific skill or behavior during the time of observation. It does not necessarily mean the skill is consistently present or lacking, though consistency may be noted when the skill has been observed over time.

PORTFOLIO assessments are collections of thoughtfully selected work samples, or artifacts, and accompanying reflections indicative of the child's learning experiences, efforts, and progress toward and/or attainment of established curriculum goals. They are an authentic, performance-based method to allow teachers to analyze progress over time. As children choose work samples for their portfolios, they become involved in their own learning and assessment and begin to develop the concept of evaluating their own work.

Although early childhood activities tend to focus on processes as opposed to products, there are numerous opportunities to collect samples of children's work. Items to collect include drawings, tracings, cuttings, attempts to print their names, and paintings. You may also include informal assessments of a child's ability to recognize letters, shapes, numbers, and rhyming words.

Formal Assessment

FORMAL assessments involve the use of standardized tests. They are administered in a prescribed manner and may require completion within a specified amount of time. Standardized tests result in scores that are usually compared to the scores of a normative group. These tests generally fall into the following categories: achievement tests, readiness tests, developmental screening tests, intelligence tests, and diagnostic tests.

Assessing Children with Special Needs

Children with special needs may require a more thorough initial assessment, more frequent on-going assessments, and continuous adaptation of activities. Assessment is essentially the first task for the teacher or caregiver in developing the individualized instruction program required for children with disabilities.

Assessing Children Who Are English Language Learners

Whenever possible, assessments should be given in both the child's first language and in English.

Celebrate the Unit

I Spy Day

Children and families find clues on a scavenger hunt

- To prepare for an I Spy Day scavenger hunt, go on a nature walk. As children explore nature, record their observations for use in writing some classroom scavenger clues.

- Have children draw large detective tools on cardstockto use as invitations for the families to join the class on I Spy Day. Help children attach the invitation text to the tool.

- Help each child make a "hand lens," using paper towel tubes, two rings of cardboard, and circles of clear plastic. Help children glue the plastic circle on one ring of cardboard and then glue on the second ring so the plastic is between the two circles. Cut two slits in the top of the cardboard tube, and help children slip the "lens" into the two slits.

- Organize the classroom into four areas. Display children's work from each of the four weeks. Focus each area on one of the weekly themes and that week's focus question:

  How can I learn more about things? How can I use tools to investigate?

  How can I compare things?How do objects move?

- Think of simple clues, such as"I spy something floating in a bucket." Before the scavenger hunt, place a strip of paper at each clue location. When the hunt begins, call out a clue. When a child locates the strip of paper from that clue, then call out the next clue.

- Allow children to use both their handmade hand lenses and real hand lenses to explain how they explore, compare, and investigate items in the four areas.

- End the scavenger hunt with a clue that leads to a variety of nature snacks, such as:

  Nature mix: raisins, dried cranberries, sesame sticks

  Ants on a Log: celery sticks with cream cheese spread and raisins or blueberries

  Bugs in dirt: crackers (dirt), raisins (beetles), sprinkles (ants), gummy worms

Evaluate and Inform

- Review the informal observation notes you recorded for each child during the four weeks of the unit. Identify areas in which individual children will need additional support.

- Send a summary of your observation notes home. Encourage parents to respond to the summary with questions or comments.

- Review dated samples of children's work in their portfolios. Copy samples to send home to families along with the observation summary.

- Send home the Unit 4 My Library Book for children to read with their families.

Día del "Veo-Veo"

Los niños y familias exploran pistas en un juego de búsqueda

- Como preparación para un juego de búsqueda durante el Día del "Veo-Veo", lleve a la clase a dar un paseo por la naturaleza. Mientras los niños exploran y comentan las cosas que hay en la naturaleza, anote sus observaciones para usarlas al escribir algunas pistas.

- Guíe a los niños para que dibujen en una cartulina los instrumentos que usan los detectives, en tamaño grande. Use los instrumentos como fondo de las invitaciones que enviará a las familias para que participen en el Día del Veo-Veo de la clase. Ayude a los niños a adjuntar el texto de la invitación al dibujo del instrumento.

- Ayude a cada niño detective a fabricar una "lupa" con tubos de toallas de papel, dos anillos de cartulina y círculos de plástico transparente. Ayude a los niños a pegar el círculo de plástico sobre un anillo de cartulina y luego a pegar el otro anillo del otro lado, de tal manera que el plástico quede entre los dos anillos. Haga dos cortes en la parte superior del tubo de cartón y ayude a los niños a encajar la "lupa" en los dos cortes.

- Organice el salón de clases en cuatro áreas. Exhiba el trabajo que los niños. Enfoque cada área en uno de los temas semanales y en la pregunta de enfoque de esa semana:

   ¿Qué puedo aprender observando las cosas? ¿Qué instrumentos puedo usar para investigar? ¿Cómo puedo comparar cosas? ¿Cómo se mueven los objetos?

- Piense en pistas sencillas, por ejemplo, "Veo algo flotando en una cubeta." Justo antes del juego, coloque una tirita de papel de color en el sitio donde está ubicada cada pista. Cuando comience el juego de búsqueda, diga la primera pista en voz alta. Cuando un niño halle la tira de papel de esa pista, entonces diga la siguiente pista.

- Permita que los niños usen tanto sus lupas hechas a mano como lupas reales para explicar cómo exploran, comparan e investigan los objetos de las cuatro áreas.

- Finalice el juego de búsqueda con una pista que los lleve a una variedad de bocaditos naturales. Algunas ideas para preparar bocaditos son las siguientes:

   Mezcla natural: pasas de uva, arándanos rojos secos, palitos de sésamo

   Hormigas sobre un tronco: tallos de apio con queso crema y pasas

   Insectos y polvo: trocitos de galletas integrales saladas (polvo), pasas de uva (escarabajos), chispas (hormigas), dulces con forma de gusano

Evaluar e informar

- Repase las notas de la observación informal que realizó sobre cada niño durante las cuatro semanas de la unidad. Identifique las áreas en las que algunos niños en particular necesitarán apoyo adicional.

- Envíe a casa un resumen de sus notas de observación. Anime a los padres a responderle con preguntas o comentarios.

- Revise las muestras fechadas del trabajo de los niños. Haga copias de algunas de estas muestras y envíelas a las familias junto con el resumen de sus observaciones.

- Dé a los niños el librito de la Unidad 4 para leer con sus familias.

Appendix

About the Authors

NELL K. DUKE, ED.D., is Professor of Teacher Education and Educational Psychology and Co-Director of the Literacy Achievement Research Center at Michigan State University. Nell Duke's expertise lies in early literacy development, particularly among children living in poverty, and integrating literacy into content instruction. She is the recipient of a number of awards for her research and is co-author of several books including *Literacy and the Youngest Learner: Best Practices for Educators of Children from Birth to 5* and *Beyond Bedtime Stories: A Parent's Guide to Promoting Reading, Writing, and Other Literacy Skills From Birth to 5.*

DOUG CLEMENTS is SUNY Distinguished Professor of Education at the University of Buffalo, SUNY. Previously a preschool and kindergarten teacher, Clements currently researches the learning and teaching of early mathematics and computer applications. He has published over 100 research studies, 8 books, 50 chapters, and 250 additional publications, including co-authoring the reports of President Bush's National Mathematics Advisory Panel and the National Research Council's book on early mathematics. He has directed twenty projects funded by the National Science Foundation and Department of Education's Institute of Education Sciences.

JULIE SARAMA Associate Professor at the University at Buffalo (SUNY), has taught high school mathematics and computer science, gifted and talented classes, and early childhood mathematics. She directs several projects funded by the National Science Foundation and the Institute of Education Sciences. Author of over 50 refereed articles, 4 books, 30 chapters, 20 computer programs, and more than 70 additional publications, she helped develop the Building Blocks and Investigations curricula and the award-winning Turtle Math. Her latest book is *Early Childhood Mathematics Education Research: Learning Trajectories for Young Children.*

WILLIAM TEALE is Professor of Education at the University of Illinois at Chicago. Author of over one hundred publications on early literacy learning, the intersection of technology and literacy education, and children's literature, he helped pioneer research in emergent literacy. Dr. Teale has worked in the area of early childhood education with schools, libraries, and other organizations across the country and internationally. He has also directed three U.S. Department of Education-funded Early Reading First projects that involve developing model preschool literacy curricula for four-year-old children from urban, low-income settings in Chicago.

Contributing Authors

Kimberly Brenneman, PhD, is an Assistant Research Professor of Psychology at Rutgers University. She is also affiliated with the Rutgers Center for Cognitive Science (RuCCS) and the National Institute for Early Education Research (NIEER). Brenneman is co-author of *Preschool Pathways to Science (PrePS): Facilitating Scientific Ways of Thinking, Talking, Doing, and Understanding* and is an educational advisor for PBS's *Sid the Science Kid* television show and website. Research interests include the development of scientific reasoning and methods to improve instructional practices that support science and mathematics learning in preschool.

Peggy Cerna is an independent Early Childhood Consultant. She was a bilingual teacher for 15 years and then served as principal of the Rosita Valley Literacy Academy, a Pre-Kindergarten through Grade 1 school in Eagle Pass, Texas. Cerna then opened Lucy Read Pre-Kindergarten Demonstration School in Austin, Texas, which had 600 Pre-Kindergarten students. During her principalship at Lucy Read, Cerna built a strong parental community with the collaboration of the University of Texas, AmeriCorps, and Austin Community College. Her passion for early literacy drove her to create book clubs where parents were taught how to read books to their children.

Dan Cieloha is an educator with more than 30 years' experience in creating, implementing, and evaluating experientially based learning materials, experiences, and environments for young children. He believes that all learners must be actively and equitably involved in constructing, evaluating, and sharing what they learn. He has spearheaded the creation and field-testing of a variety of learning materials including *You & Me: Building Social Skills in Young Children*. He is also president of the Partnership for Interactive Learning, a leading nonprofit organization dedicated to the development of children's social and thinking skills.

Paula A. Jones, M.Ed., is an Early Childhood Consultant at the state and national levels. As a former Early Childhood Director for the Lubbock Independent School District, she served as the Head Start Director and co-founded three of their four Early Childhood campuses which also became a model design and Best Practices Program for the Texas Education Agency. She was a contributing author for the first Texas Prekindergarten Guidelines, served as president for the Texas Association of Administrators and Supervisors of Programs for Young Children, and is a 2010 United Way Champions for Children Award winner.

Bobbie Sparks is a retired educator who has taught biology and middle school science as well as being the K-12 district science consultant for a suburban district. At Harris County Department of Education she served as the K-12 science consultant in Professional Development. During her career as K-12 science consultant, Sparks worked with teachers at all grade levels to revamp curriculum to meet the Texas science standards. She served on Texas state committees to develop the TEKS standards as well as committees to develop items for tests for teacher certification in science.

Opening Routines

Below are a few suggested routines to use for beginning your day with your class. You can rotate through them, or use one for a while before trying a new approach. You may wish to develop your own routines by mixing and matching ideas from the suggestions given.

1. Days of the Week

Ask children what day of the week it is. When they respond, tell them that you are going to write a sentence that tells everyone what day of the week it is. Print "Today is Monday." on the board. If you have a helper chart, have children assist you in finding the name of the day's helper. Print: "Today's helper is Miguel." Ask the helper to come forward and find the Letter Tiles or ABC Picture Cards that spell his or her name.

As the year progresses, you might want to have the helper find the letters that spell the day of the week. Eventually some children may be able to copy the entire sentence with Letter Tiles or ABC Picture Cards.

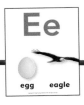

Mm moon   **Ii** iguana icicle   **Gg** giraffe girl   **Uu** umbrella unicycle   **Ee** egg eagle   **Ll** leaf

2. Calendar Search

Print "Today is _____." on the board. Ask children to help you fill in the blank. Print the day of the week in the blank. Invite children to look at the calendar to determine today's date. Write the date under the sentence that tells what day of the week it is. Invite children to clap out the syllables of both the sentence and the date.

Review the days of the week and the months of the year using the "Days of the Week Song"/"Canción de los dias de la semana" and the "Months of the year"/ "Los meses del año."

Ask children what day of the week it was yesterday. When they respond, ask them what day it is today. Place a seasonal sticker on today's date. Have children follow your lead and recite "Yesterday was Monday, September 12. Today is Tuesday, September 13. Tomorrow will be Wednesday, September 14."

3. Feelings

Make happy- and sad-faced puppets for each child by cutting yellow circles from construction paper and drawing happy and sad faces on them. Laminate the faces, and glue them to tongue depressors. Cover two large coffee cans. On one can glue a happy face, and write the sentence "I feel happy today." Glue the sad face to the second can, and write the sentence "I feel sad today."

Give each child a happy- and a sad-faced puppet. Encourage children to tell how they feel today and to hold up the appropriate puppet. Encourage children to come forward and place their puppets in the can that represents their feelings. Later in the year you can add puppets to represent other emotions.

You can vary this activity by using a graph titled "How I Feel Today"/"Como me siento hoy." Have children place their puppets in the appropriate column on the graph instead of in the cans.

4. Pledge of Allegiance/ Moment of Silence

Have children locate the United States flag. Recite the Pledge of Allegiance to the U.S. flag. Then allow a minute for a moment of silence.

Discuss these activities with children, allowing them to volunteer reasons the Pledge of Allegiance is said and other places they have seen the Pledge recited.

5. Coming to Circle

Talk with children about being part of a class family. Tell children that as part of a class family they will work together, learn together, respect each other, help each other, and play together. Explain that families have rules so that jobs get done and everyone stays safe. Let children know they will learn rules for their classroom. One of those rules is how they will come together for circle. Sing "This is the Way We Come to Circle" (to the tune of "This is the Way We Wash Our Clothes").

This is the way we come to circle.
Come to circle, come to circle.
This is the way we come to circle,
So early in the morning.

This is the way we sit right down,
Sit right down, sit right down.
This is the way we sit right down,
So early in the morning.

This is the way we fold our hands,
Fold our hands, fold our hands.
This is the way we fold our hands,
So early in the morning.

Transition Tips

Sing songs or chants such as those listed below while transitioning between activities:

1. I Am Now in Pre-K

To the tune of "I'm a Little Teapot"

I am now in Pre-K,
I can learn.
I can listen. I can take a turn.
When the teacher says so,
I can play.
Choose a center and together we'll play.

2. Did You Clean Up?

To the tune of "Are You Sleeping, Are You Sleeping, Brother John?"

Did you clean up?
Did you clean up?
Please make sure.
Please make sure.
Everything is picked up.
Everything is picked up.
Please. Thank you!
Please. Thank you!

Chant: Red, Yellow, Green
Red, yellow, green
Stop, change, go
Red, yellow, green
Stop, change, go
Green says yes.
And red says no.
Yellow says everybody wait in a row.
Red, yellow, green
Stop, change, go
Red, yellow, green
Stop, change, go

3. The Five Senses Song

To the tune of "If You're Happy and You Know It"

I can see with my eyes every day (clap clap)
I can see with my eyes every day (clap clap)
I can see with my eyes
I can see with my eyes
I can see with my eyes every day (clap clap)
(Repeat with smell with my nose, hear with my ears, feel with my hands, and taste with my mouth.)

4. Eat More Vegetables

To the tune of "Row, Row, Row Your Boat"

Eat, eat, eat more,
Eat more vegetables.
Carrots, carrots, carrots, carrots
Eat more vegetables.
(Repeat with broccoli, lettuce, celery, and spinach.)

5. Circle Time

To the tune of "Here We Go 'Round the Mulberry Bush"

This is the way we come to circle
Come to circle, come to circle.
This is the way we come to circle
So early in the morning.

This is the way we sit right down,
Sit right down, sit right down.
This is the way we sit right down,
So early in the morning.

Play a short game such as one of the following to focus children's attention:

Name That Fruit!

Say: *It's red on the outside and white on the inside. It rhymes with chapel!*

Children answer, "Apple!" and then repeat twice, "Apple/Chapel."

Repeat with other fruits, such as cherry and banana.

I Spy

Use a flashlight to focus on different letters and words in the classroom. Have children identify them.

Monkey See Monkey Do

Choose one child to be the monkey leader. He or she will act out a motion such as twist, jump, clap, or raise hand, and the rest of the monkeys say the word and copy the motion.

Let's Play Pairs

Distribute one *ABC Picture Card* to each child. Draw letters from an additional set of cards. The child who has the matching letter identifies it and goes to the center of his or her choice.

That's My Friend!

Take children's name cards with their pictures from the wall and distribute making sure no one gets his or her own name. When you call a child's name, she or he has to say something positive about the child on the card and end with "That's my friend!"

Name Game

Say: *If your name begins with ____, you may choose a center.* Have the child say his or her name as he or she gets up. Repeat the child's name, emphasizing the beginning sound.

Center Management

Learning Centers provide children with additional opportunities to practice or extend each lesson's skills and concepts either individually or in small groups. The activities and materials that are explored in the centers not only promote oral language but also help develop children's social skills as they work together. The use of these Learning Centers encourage children to explore their surroundings and make their own choices.

Teacher's Role

The Learning Centers allow time for you to:

- Observe children's exploration of the centers.

- Assess children's understanding of the skills and concepts being taught.

- Provide additional support and encouragement to children who might be having difficulty with specific concepts or skills. If a child is having difficulty, model the correct approach.

Classroom Setup

The materials and activities in the centers should support what children are learning. Multiple experiences are necessary for children's comprehension. The centers should also engage them in learning by providing hands-on experiences. Every time children visit a center and practice skills or extend concepts being taught in the lessons, they are likely to broaden their understanding or discover something new.

In order to support children's learning, the materials and activities in the Learning Centers should change every week. It is important that all the children have a chance to explore every center throughout each week. Be sure they rotate to different centers and do not focus on only one activity. You might also consider adding new materials to the centers as the week progresses. This will encourage children to expand on their past work. Modify or add activities or materials based on your classroom needs.

It is crucial that children know what is expected of them in each center. To help children understand the expectation at each center, display an "I can" statement with an illustration or photograph of a student completing the activity. Discuss these expectations with children in advance, and reinforce them as needed. These discussions might include reviewing your typical classroom rules and talking about the limited number of children allowed in each center. Remind them that they may work individually or in small groups.

Library and Listening Center

Children should feel free throughout the day to explore books and other printed materials. Create a comfortable reading area in the room, and fill it with as many children's books as possible. Include a number of informational books that tell why things happen and books of rhymes, poems, and songs, as well as storybooks and simple alphabet books.

Before beginning each unit in the program, bring in books about the specific concepts or themes in a unit. Encourage children to bring in books they have enjoyed and would like to share with classmates. Even though they may not be actually reading, have children visit the area often. Here they can practice their book handling, apply their growing knowledge of print awareness, and look at pictures and talk about them. Have them read the books to you or to classmates.

Big Book literature selections from the program have been recorded and are available as part of the *Listening Library Audio CDs*. After each literature reading, encourage children to listen to the recordings. Provide CD players that work both with and without earphones. This way, individual children may listen to selections without disturbing the rest of the class. You will also be able to play the recordings for the whole class, if you choose. Encourage children to record their own stories and then share these stories with their classmates.

As you set up the Learning Centers, here are a few ideas you might want to implement in your classroom.

- Create a separate Workshop Center sign-up chart for children to use when choosing a center to explore.

- Provide an area for children who want to be alone to read or to simply reflect on the day's activities.

- Separate loud areas and quiet areas.

- Hang posters or art at eye level for the children.

- Place on shelves materials, such as books or art supplies, that are easily accessible to the children.

English Language Learners

Teaching the English Language Learner

Stages of English-Language Proficiency

An effective learning environment is an important goal of all educators. In a supportive environment, all English learners have the opportunity to participate and to learn. The materials in this guide are designed to support children while they are acquiring English, allowing them to develop English-language reading skills and the fluency they need to achieve in the core content areas as well.

This guide provides direction in supporting children in four stages of English proficiency: Beginning, Intermediate, Advanced, and Advanced-High. While children at a beginning level by definition know little English and will probably have difficulty comprehending English, by the time they progress to the intermediate or early advanced levels of English acquisition, their skills in understanding more complex language structures will have increased. These stages can be described in general terms as follows:

BEGINNING AND INTERMEDIATE Children identified at these levels of English-language proficiency demonstrate dramatic growth. During these stages, children progress from having no receptive or productive English to possessing a basic command of English. They are learning to comprehend and produce one- or two-word responses to questions, are moving to phrases and simple sentences using concrete and immediate topics, and are learning to interact in a limited fashion with text that has been taught. They progress to responding with increasing ease to more varied communication tasks using learned material, comprehending a sequence of information on familiar topics, producing basic statements and asking questions on familiar subjects, and interacting with a variety of print. Some basic errors are found in their use of English syntax and grammar.

ADVANCED Children who have reached the Advanced level of English-language proficiency have good comprehension of overall meaning and are beginning to demonstrate increased comprehension of specific details and concepts. They are learning to respond in expanded sentences, are interacting more independently with a variety of text, and in using newly acquired English vocabulary to communicate ideas orally and in writing. They demonstrate fewer errors in English grammar and syntax than at the beginning and early intermediate levels.

ADVANCED-HIGH Children who are identified at this level of English-language proficiency demonstrate consistent comprehension of meaning, including implied and nuanced meaning, and are learning the use of idiomatic and figurative language. They are increasingly able to respond using detail in compound and complex sentences and sustain conversation in English. They are able to use standard grammar with few errors and show an understanding of conventions of formal and informal usage.

It is important to provide an instructional scaffold for phonemic awareness, phonics, words structure, language structures, comprehension strategies and skills, and grammar, usage, and mechanics so that children can successfully learn to read while advancing along the continuum of English acquisition. For example, at the Beginning level, you might ask children for *yes* or *no* answers when answering questions about selection comprehension or grammar. Children at the Advanced-High level should be asked to provide answers in complete and expanded sentences. By the time children achieve an Advanced level, their knowledge of English will be more sophisticated because they are becoming more adept at comprehending English and using techniques such as making inferences or using persuasive language.

The following charts illustrate how to use sentence stems with children at each level of English-language proficiency:

Teaching Sentence Stems

- Write the sentence stems on the board, chart paper, or sentence strips. Choose stems that are appropriate for the four general levels of English proficiency.

- Model using the sentence stem(s) for the comprehension strategy or skill.

- Read each phrase as you insert the appropriate words to express an idea. Have children repeat the sentences after you. For Beginning and Intermediate children, use the stems within the questions you ask them.

Linguistic Pattern: *I predict that* _____.

Beginning	Intermediate	Advanced	Advanced-High
Simple questions about the text. Yes-or-no responses or responses that allow children to point to an object or picture.	Simple questions about the text which allow for one- or two-word responses or give children two options for a response to select from.	Questions that elicit a short response or a complete simple sentence using the linguistic pattern.	Have children make predictions on their own. Children should use the linguistic pattern and respond with a complete complex sentence.

Practicing Sentence Stems

- To give children multiple opportunities to generate the language they have just been taught, have them work in pairs or small groups and utilize cooperative learning participation strategies to facilitate this communicative practice.

- Pair children one level of proficiency above or below the other. For example, have Beginning children work with Intermediate level children.

- Use differentiated prompts to elicit the responses that incorporate the linguistic patterns and structures for the different proficiency levels. See the following sample of prompts and responses.

Beginning	Intermediate	Advanced	Advanced-High
Do you predict _____? *Yes/No*	Do you predict _____ or _____? *I predict* _____.	What do you predict _____? *I predict* _____.	Give a prediction about _____. *I predict* _____.

- Select some common cooperative learning participation strategies to teach to children. Once they have learned some language practice activities, they can move quickly into the various routines. See the examples on the next page.

English Language Learners

My Turn, Your Turn

Children work in pairs.

1. The teacher models a sentence and the whole group repeats, or echoes it.

2. One child generates an oral phrase, and the partner echoes it.

3. Partners switch and alternate roles so that each child has a chance to both generate and repeat phrases.

Talking Stick

Children work in small groups. This strategy allows every child to have an opportunity to speak several times and encourages more reflective or reticent participants to take a turn. Children can "pass" only one time.

1. The teacher charts sentence graphic organizers and linguistic patterns children will use in their responses.

2. The teacher models use of linguistic patterns from the lesson.

3. The teacher asks a question or gives a prompt, and then passes a stick, eraser, stuffed animal, or any other designated object to one child.

4. A child speaks, everyone listens, and then the child passes the object on to the person next to him or her.

5. The next child speaks, everyone listens, and the process continues until the teacher or facilitator gives a signal to return the object.

Think-Pair-Share

This strategy allows children time for processing ideas by building in sufficient wait time to process the question and frame an answer. It is an appropriate strategy to use during small- or large-group discussions or lessons, giving all children a chance to organize their thoughts and have a turn sharing their responses with a partner. It also allows for small group verbal interaction to practice language before sharing with the larger group.

1. After reading or listening to a section of text, the teacher presents a question or task. It is helpful to guide with a specific prompt, modeling the language to be used in the response.

2. Children think about their responses for a brief, designated amount of time.

3. Partners share and discuss their responses with each other.

4. An adaptation can be to have each child share his or her partner's response within a small group to promote active listening.

Teaching Vocabulary

Building the background knowledge and a context for children to learn new words is critical in helping children understand new vocabulary. Primary language can be a valuable tool for preteaching, concept development, and vocabulary. Cognates, or words similar in English counterparts, often provide an opportunity for bridging the primary language and English. Also, children who have background knowledge about a topic can more easily connect the new information they are learning with what they already know than children without a similar context from which to work. Therefore, giving children background information and encouraging them to make as many connections as possible with the new vocabulary word they encounter will help them better understand the selection they are about to read.

In addition to building background knowledge, visual displays such as pictures, graphs, charts, maps, models, or other strategies offer unambiguous access to new content. They provide a clear and parallel correspondence between the visual objects and the new vocabulary to be learned. Thus, because the correlation is clear, the negotiation of meaning is established. Additionally, this process must be constant and reciprocal between you and each child if the child is to succeed in effectively interacting with language.

Included in this guide is a routine for teaching vocabulary words. In addition to this routine, more detailed explanations of the ways to teach vocabulary are as follows:

REAL OBJECTS AND REALIA: Because of the immediate result visuals have on learning language, when explaining a word such as *car,* the best approach is simply to show a real car. As an alternative to the real object, you can show realia. Realia are toy versions of real things, such as plastic eggs to substitute for real eggs, or in this case, a toy car to signify a real car. A large, clear picture of an automobile can also work if it is absolutely recognizable.

If, however, the child has had no experience with the item in the picture, more explanation might be needed. For example, if the word you are explaining is a zoo animal such as an *ocelot,* and children are not familiar with this animal, one picture might be insufficient. They might confuse this animal with a cat or any one of the feline species. Seeing several clear pictures, then, of each individual type of common feline and comparing their similarities and differences might help clarify meaning in this particular instance. When children make a connection between their prior knowledge of the word *cat* with the new word *ocelot,* it validates their newly acquired knowledge, and thus they process learning more quickly.

PICTURES: Supplement story illustrations with visuals such as those found in the *Photo Library CD, ABC Picture Cards,* magazine pictures, and picture dictionaries. Videos, especially those that demonstrate an entire setting such as a farm or zoo, or videos where different animals are highlighted in the natural habitat, for instance, might be helpful. You might also wish to turn off the soundtrack to avoid a flood of language that children might not be able to understand. This way children can concentrate on the visual-word meaning correlation.

PANTOMIME: Language is learned through modeling within a communicative context. Pantomiming is one example of such a framework of communication. Some words, such as *run* and *jump,* are appropriate for pantomiming. Throughout this guide, you will find suggestions for pantomiming words like *sick* by coughing, sneezing, and holding your stomach. If children understand what you are trying to pantomime, they will more easily engage in the task of learning.

Letter Formation Guide

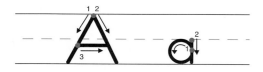

A Starting point, slanting down left
Starting point, slanting down right
Starting point, across the middle: capital *A*

a Starting point, around left all the way
Starting point, straight down,
touching the circle: small *a*

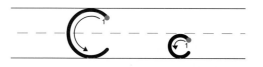

B Starting point, straight down
Starting point, around right and in
at the middle, around right and in
at the bottom: capital *B*

b Starting point, straight down, back
up, around right all the way: small *b*

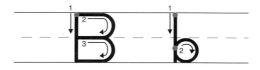

C Starting point, around left to
stopping place: capital *C*

c Starting point, around left to
stopping place: small *c*

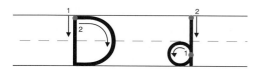

D Starting point, straight down
Starting point, around right and in
at the bottom: capital *D*

d Starting point, around left all the way
Starting point, straight down, touching
the circle: small *d*

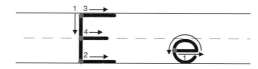

E Starting point, straight down
Starting point, straight out
Starting point, straight out
Starting point, straight out: capital *E*

e Starting point, straight out, up and
around to the left, curving down
and around to the right: small *e*

F Starting point, straight down
Starting point, straight out
Starting point, straight out: capital *F*

f Starting point, around left and straight down
Starting point, straight across: small *f*

G Starting point, around left, curving up and
around
Straight in: capital *G*

g Starting point, around left all the way
Starting point, straight down, touching the
circle, around left to stopping place: small *g*

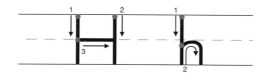

H Starting point, straight down
Starting point, straight down
Starting point, across the middle: capital *H*

h Starting point, straight down, back
up, around right, and straight down: small *h*

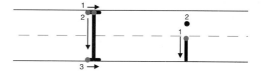

I Starting point, across
Starting point, straight down
Starting point, across: capital *I*

i Starting point, straight down
Dot exactly above: small *i*

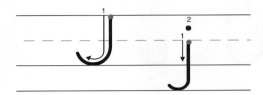

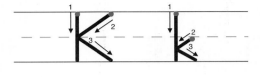

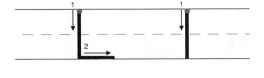

J Starting point, straight down, around left to stopping place: capital *J*

j Starting point, straight down, around left to stopping place
Dot exactly above: small *j*

K Starting point, straight down
Starting point, slanting down left, touching the line, slanting down right: capital *K*

k Starting point, straight down
Starting point, slanting down left, touching the line, slanting down right: small *k*

L Starting point, straight down, straight out: capital *L*

l Starting point, straight down: small *l*

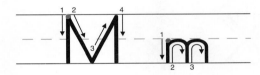

M Starting point, straight down
Starting point, slanting down right to the point, slanting back up to the right, straight down: capital *M*

m Starting point, straight down, back up, around right, straight down, back up, around right, straight down: small *m*

N Starting point, straight down
Starting point, slanting down right, straight back up: capital *N*

n Starting point, straight down, back up, around right, straight down: small *n*

O Starting point, around left all the way: capital *O*

o Starting point, around left all the way: small *o*

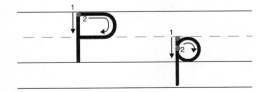

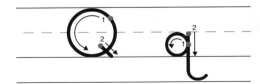

P Starting point, straight down
Starting point, around right and in at the middle: capital *P*

p Starting point, straight down
Starting point, around right all the way, touching the line: small *p*

Q Starting point, around left all the way
Starting point, slanting down right: capital *Q*

q Starting point, around left all the way
Starting point, straight down, touching the circle, curving up right to stopping place: small *q*

R Starting point, straight down
Starting point, around right and in at the middle, touching the line, slanting down right: capital *R*

r Starting point, straight down, back up, curving around right to stopping place: small *r*

Letter Formation Guide

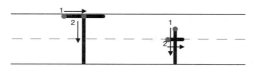

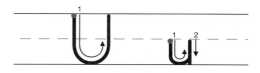

S Starting point, around left, curving right and down around right, curving left and up: capital S

s Starting point, around left, curving right and down around right, curving left and up to stopping place: small s

T Starting point, straight across Starting point, straight down: capital T

t Starting point, straight down Starting point, across short: small t

U Starting point, straight down, curving around right and up, straight up: capital U

u Starting point, straight down, curving around right and up, straight up, straight back down: small u

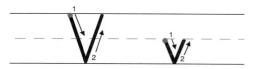

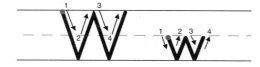

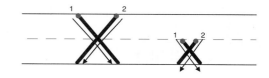

V Starting point, slanting down right, slanting up right: capital V

v Starting point, slanting down right, slanting up right: small v

W Starting point, slanting down right, slanting up right, slanting down right, slanting up right: capital W

W Starting point, slanting down right, slanting up right, slanting down right, slanting up right: small w

X Starting point, slanting down right Starting point, slanting down left: capital X

X Starting point, slanting down right Starting point, slanting down left: small x

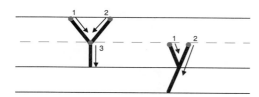

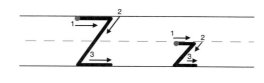

Y Starting point, slanting down right, stop Starting point, slanting down left, stop Starting point, straight down: capital Y

y Starting point, slanting down right Starting point, slanting down left, connecting the lines: small y

Z Starting point, straight across, slanting down left, straight across: capital Z

z Starting point, straight across, slanting down left, straight across: small z

Number Formation Guide

0 Starting point, curving left all the way around to starting point: *0*

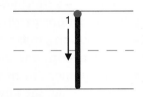

1 Starting point, straight down: *1*

2 Starting point, around right, slanting left and straight across right: *2*

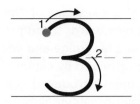

3 Starting point, around right, in at the middle, around right: *3*

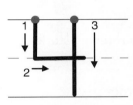

4 Starting point, straight down
Straight across right
Starting point, straight down, crossing line: *4*

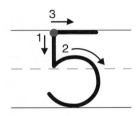

5 Starting point, straight down, curving around right and up
Starting point, straight across right: *5*

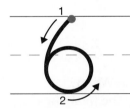

6 Starting point, slanting left, around the bottom curving up, around right and into the curve: *6*

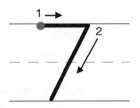

7 Starting point, straight across right, slanting down left: *7*

8 Starting point, curving left, curving down and around right, slanting up right to starting point: *8*

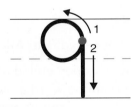

9 Starting point, curving around left all the way, straight down: *9*

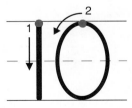

10 Starting point, straight down
Starting point, curving left all the way around to starting point: *10*

Vocabulary Development

Vocabulary development is a key part of **The DLM Early Childhood Express**. Children learn new words through exposure during reading and class discussion. They build language and vocabulary through activities using key words and phrases and by exploring selected vocabulary. After vocabulary words have been introduced, encourage children to use the words in sentences. Again, providing linguistic structures gives children a context for using new vocabulary and building oral language and gives you the opportunity to assess children's understanding of new words. For example, use sentence patterns such as the following:

- A _____ can _____.
- A _____ is a _____.
  (Use this for classification activities. *A tulip is a flower. A rabbit is an animal.*)
- The _____ is _____.
  (Use for describing. *The rabbit is soft.*)

Define words in ways children in your class can understand. When possible, show pictures of objects or actions to help clarify the meanings of words. Provide examples or comparisons to help reinforce the meanings of words and to connect new words to previously learned words. For example, say *The rabbit's FUR is soft like COTTON.* Connect words to categories. For example, say: *Pears are fruits. Are apples fruits? What else is a fruit?* Demonstrate the meaning of words when possible.

During reading, be sure children feel comfortable asking questions and sharing their reactions to what you are reading. Encourage children to share explanations, make predictions, compare and contrast ideas, sequence story events, and describe what you are reading. Encourage children's engagement by modeling reactions and responses while reading. For example, say *I like the part where _____ did _____.* or *This story is about _____.* Support children who are reluctant to speak by using linguistic structures that encourage them to talk about stories and use vocabulary words. You might use the following linguistic structures:

- This story is about _____.
- First _____.
- Next _____.
- Last _____. (Use this for retelling stories.)
- The _____ is the same as _____.
- The _____ is different from _____.
- We read about _____.

Model asking questions before, during, and after reading:

- I wonder what this story is going to be about.
- Who is _____?
- What is _____?
- What did _____ do?
- Why did _____ do _____?
- What happened first? Middle? Last?

Be sure to ask open-ended questions. Unlike questions that simply require a *yes* or *no* or one-word answer, open-ended questions encourage children to think about responses and use new vocabulary in sentences.

Throughout the day, create opportunities for children to talk to each other as they share daily experiences, discuss and explain what they are doing, and talk abut what they are learning.

Vocabulary Words by Topic

Animals

alligator/caimán
ant/horminga
anteater/oso hormiguero
bat/murciélago
bear/oso
beaver/castor
bee/abeja
beetle/escarabajo
bobcat/lince
butterfly/mariposa
camel/camello
cat/gato
chicken/gallina/pollo
chipmunk/ardilla
cow/vaca
crab/cangrejo
deer/venado/ciervo
dog/perro
dolphin/delfin
donkey/burro
dragonfly/libélula
duck/pato
eagle/águila
elephant/elefante
flamingo/flamingo
fly/mosca
fox/zorro
frog/rana
giraffe/jirafa
goat/cabra
gorilla/
grasshopper/saltamontes
hamster/hámster
hippopotamus/hipopótamo
horse/caballo
kangaroo/canguro
koala/coala

ladybug/catarina
leopard/leopardo
lion/león
llama/llama
lobster/langosta
monkey/mono
moose/alce
mosquito/mosquito
mouse/ratón
octopus/pulpo
opossum/zarigüeya
owl/búho
panda/oso panda
parakeet/periquito
peacock/pavo real
pelican/pelicano
penguin/pingüino
pig/cerdo
polar bear/oso polar
porcupine/puerco espín
rabbit/conejo
raccoon/mapache
rhinoceros/rinoceronte
robin/petirrojo
salamander/salamandra
sea horse/caballo de mar
shark/tiburón
sheep/oveja
skunk/mofeta/zorrillo
snake/serpiente
squirrel/ardilla
starfish/estrella de mar
swan/cisne
tiger/tigre
toad/sapo
turkey/pavo
turtle/tortuga
walrus/morsa

whale/ballena
zebra/cebra

Colors and Shapes

blue/azul
green/verde
red/rojo
yellow/amarillo
circle/círculo azul
diamond/diamante
oval/óvalo
rectangle/rectángulo
square/cuadrado
triangle/triángulo

Signs

deer crossing/cruce de venado
handicapped parking/
    estacionamiento para inválidos
railroad crossing/paso del tren
school crossing/cruce escolar
speed limit/limite de velocidad
stop sign/señal de alto
traffic light/semáforo
yield sign/señal de ceder el paso

Earth

beach/playa
blizzard/tormenta de nieve
cloud/nube
coral reef/arrecife de coral
desert/desierto
dry season/temporada seca
fall/otoño
fog/niebla
forest/bosque
geyser/géiser
glacier/glaciar

hail/granizo
hurricane/huracán
ice/hielo
island/isla
lake/lago
lightning/relámpago
mountain/montaña
ocean/océano
plain/llano
rain/lluvia
rain forest/selva tropical
rainy season/temporada de lluvias
rapids/rápidos
river/río
snow/nieve
spring/primavera
stream/arroyo
summer/verano
sun/sol
tornado/tornado
tundra/tundra
volcano/volcán
waterfall/cascada
wind/viento
winter/invierno

Human Body

ankle/tobillo
arm/brazo
body/cuerpo
ear/oreja
elbow/codo
eyes/ojos
feet/pies
fingers/dedos
hair/pelo
hands/manos

Vocabulary Words by Topic

head/cabeza
hearing/oído
heel/talón
hips/caderas
knee/rodilla
legs/piernas
mouth/boca
nose/nariz
sense/sentido
shoulders/hombros
sight/vista
smell/olfato
taste/gusto
teeth/dientes
toes/dedos de los pies
touch/ tacto

Plants

cactus/cactus
carrot/zanahoria
clover/trébol
cornstalk/planta de maíz
dandelion/diente de león
fern/helecho
grapevine/parra
grass/hierba
lettuce/lechuga
lilac bush/lila de monte
marigold/caléndula
moss/musgo
oak tree/árbol de roble
onion/cebolla
orange tree/naranjo
palm tree/palma
pine tree/pino
poison ivy/hiedra venenosa
rice/arroz
rose/rosa

seaweed/alga marina
sunflower/girasol
tomato/tomate
tulip/tulipán
water lily/nenúfar
wheat/trigo

Clothing

belt/cinturón
blouse/blusa
boots/botas
boy's swimsuit/traje de baño para
    niños
coat/abrigo
dress/vestido
earmuffs/orejeras
girl's swimsuit/traje de baño para
    niñas
gloves/guantes
hat/sombrero
jacket/chaqueta
jeans/pantalones vaqueros
mittens/manoplas
pajamas/pijama
pants/pantalones
raincoat/impermeable
robe/bata
scarf/bufanda
shirt/camisa
shoes/zapatos
shorts/pantalones cortos
skirt/falda
slippers/pantuflas
socks/calcetines
sweat suit/chandal
sweater/suéter
tie/corbata
vest/chaleco

Food

apples/manzanas
bacon/tocino
bagels/roscas de pan
bananas/plátanos
beans/frijoles
beef/carne
beets/betabel
blueberries/arándanos
bread/pan
broccoli/brécol
butter/mantequilla
cake/pastel
cantaloupe/cantalupo
carrots/zanahoria
cauliflower/coliflor
celery/apio
cereal/cereal
cheese/queso
cherries/cerezas
chicken/pollo
clams/almejas
cookies/galletas
corn/maíz
cottage cheese/requesón
crackers/galletas saladas
cream cheese/queso crema
cucumbers/pepinos
eggs/huevos
figs/higos
fish/pescado
grapefruit/toronja
grapes/uvas
green peppers/pimientos verdes
ham/jamón
ice-cream cone/cono de helado
jelly/gelatina
lemons/limones

lettuce/lechuga
limes/limas
macaroni/macarrones
milk/leche
mushrooms/champiñones
nuts/nueces
onions/cebollas
orange juice/jugo de naranja
oranges/naranjas
peaches/duraznos
peanut butter/crema de cacahuete
pears/peras
peas/guisantes
pie/tarta
pineapples/piñas
plums/ciruelas
pork chop/chuleta de puerco
potatoes/papas
radishes/rábanos
raisins/pasas
rice/arroz
rolls/panecillos
salad/ensalada
sausage/salchicha
shrimp/camarón
soup/sopa
spaghetti/espaguetis
squash/calabaza
strawberries/fresas
sweet potatoes/camotes
tomatoes/tomates
watermelon/sandía
yogurt/yogur

Recreation

archery/tiro el arco
badminton/bádminton
baseball/béisbol
basketball/baloncesto
biking/ciclismo
boating/paseo en bote
bowling/boliche
canoeing/piragüismo
climbing/montañismo
croquet/croquet
discus/disco
diving/buceo
fishing/pesca
football/fútbol
golf/golf
gymnastics/gimnasia
hiking/excursionismo
hockey/hockey
horseback riding/equitación
ice-skating/patinaje sobre hielo
in-line skating/patines en línea
lacrosse/lacrosse
pole-vaulting/salto con pértiga
running/atletismo
scuba diving/buceo
shot put/lanzamiento de peso
skiing/esquí
soccer/fútbol
surfing/surfing
swimming/natación
T-ball/T-ball
tennis/tenis
volleyball/voleibol
walking/caminar
waterskiing/esquí acuático
weight lifting/levantamiento

School

auditorium/auditorio
book/libro
cafeteria/cafetería
cafeteria table/mesa de cafetería
calculator/calculadora
chair/silla
chalk/tiza
chalkboard/pizarrón
chart paper/rotafolio
classroom/aula
computer/omputadora
construction paper/papel para
     construir
crayons/crayones
desk/escritorio
easel/caballete
eraser/borrador
globe/globo
glue/pegamento
gym/gimnasio
hallway/vestíbulo
janitor's room/conserjería
learning center/centro de
     aprendizaje
library/biblioteca
markers/marcadores
music room/salón de música
notebook paper/papel de cuaderno
nurse's office/enfermería
paint/pintura
paintbrush/pincel
pen/pluma
pencil/lápiz
pencil sharpener/sacapuntas
playground/patio de recreo
principal's office/oficina del
     director

ruler/regla
science room/salón de ciencias
scissors/tijeras
stairs/escaleras
stapler/grapadora
supply room/almacén
tape/cinta adhesiva

Toys

ball/pelota
balloons/globos
bike/bicicleta
blocks/cubos
clay/arcilla
coloring book/libro para colorear
doll/muñeca
doll carriage/careola de muñecas
dollhouse/casa de muñecas
farm set/juego de la granja
game/juego
grocery cart/carro de compras
hats/sombreros
in-line skates/patines
instruments/instrumentos
jump rope/cuerda para saltar
kite/cometa
magnets/imanes
marbles/canicas
puppet/títere
puzzle/rompecabezas
scooter/motoneta
skateboard/patineta
slide/tobogán
stuffed animals/peluches
tape recorder/grabadora
top/trompo
toy cars/carro de juguete
toy trucks/camión de juguete

train set/juego de tren
tricycle/triciclo
wagon/vagón
yo-yo/yó-yó

Equipment

baggage cart/carro para equipaje
baseball/béisbol
bat/bate
mitt/manopla
basketball/pelota de baloncesto
basketball net/canasta
blueprints/planos
computer/computadora
drafting tools/borradores
bow/arco
arrow/flecha
bowling ball/pelota de boliche
bowling pin/bolos de boliche
bridle/freno
saddle/silla de montar
saddle pad/montura
broom/escoba
bulldozer/aplanadora
canoe/canoa
paddle/paleta
cash register/caja registradora
computer/computadora
crane/grúa
dishwasher/lavaplatos
drill/taladro
drum/tambor
drumsticks/palillos
dryer/secadora
dustpan/recogedor
figure skates/patinaje artistico

Vocabulary Words by Topic

football/balón
shoulder pads/hombreras
football helmet/casco
goggles/gafas
golf ball/pelota de golf
golf clubs/palo de golf
tee/tee
hammer/martillo
handcuffs/esposas
badge/placa
hat/gorra
hockey stick/palo de hockey
hockey puck/disco de hockey
ice skates/patines
hoe/azadón
hose/manguera
coat/chaqueta
hat/sombrero
sprinkler/rociador
iron/plancha
ironing board/tabla de planchar
lawn mower/cortacéspedes
mail pouch/bolsa de correo
mirror/espejo
probe/sonda
pick/pico
mop/estropajo
paintbrush/brocha de pintar
piano/piano
pliers/alicates
rake/rastrillo
roller skates/patines
saw/sierra
screwdriver/desarmador
scuba tank/tanque de buceo
mask/máscara
flippers/aletas
shovel/pala

sketch pad/cuaderno para dibujo
palette/paleta
skis/esquís
ski boots/botas para esquiar
poles/palos
soccer ball/balón de fútbol
shoes/zapatos de tenis
stepladder/escalera doble
stethoscope/estetoscopio
surfboard/tabla de surf
tennis ball/pelota de tenis
tennis racket/raqueta de tenis
tractor/tractor
vacuum cleaner/aspiradora
washer/lavadora
water skis/esquís acuáticos
rope/cuerda
life jacket/chaleco salvavidas
watering can/regadera
wheelbarrow/carretilla
wrench/llave inglesa

Home

basement/sótano
bathroom/baño
bathroom sink/lavabo
bathtub/bañera
bed/cama
bedroom/recámara/habitación
blanket/cobija/manta
chair/silla
circuit breaker/cortocircuito
dresser/cómoda
electrical outlet/enchufe
end table/mesa auxiliar
fireplace/chimenea
furnace/horno
kitchen/cocina

kitchen chair/silla de cocina
kitchen sink/fregadero
kitchen table/mesa de cocina
lamp/lámpara
light switch/interruptor de la luz
living room/sala
medicine cabinet/botiquín
nightstand/mesilla de noche
pillow/almohada
refrigerator/refrigerador
shower/ducha
smoke alarm/alarma de incendios
sofa/sofá
stove/estufa
thermostat/termostato
toilet/el baño
water heater/calentador de agua

Occupations

administrative assistant/asistente
    administrativo
air traffic controller/controlador
    aéreo
airline pilot/piloto
architect/arquitecto
artist/artista
astronaut/astronauta
athlete/atleta
author/autor
ballerina/bailarina
banker/banquero
bus driver/conductor de autobús
camera operator/operador de
    cámara
carpenter/carpintero
cashier/cajero
chef/jefe de cocina
computer technician/técnico en

    computación
cosmetologist/cosmetólogo
dancer/bailarín
dentist/dentista
doctor/doctor
electrician/electricista
engineer/ingeniero
farmer/granjero
firefighter/bombero
forest ranger/guardabosques
lawyer/abogado
manicurist/manicurista
musician/músico
nurse/enfermera
paramedic/paramédico
photographer/fotógrafo
police officer/policía
postal worker/empleado postal
real estate agent/corridor de
    bienes raíces
refuse collector/recolector de
    basura
reporter/reportero
school crossing guard/guarda
    escolar
server/mesero
ship captain/capitán de barco
singer/cantante
skater/patinador
teacher/maestro
truck driver/conductor de camión
veterinarian/veterinario
weaver/tejedora

Structures

adobe/casa de adobe
airplane hangar/hangar de avión
airport/aeropuerto
apartment building/edificio de
    departamentos/edificio de pisos
arena/arena
art museum/museo de arte
bakery/panadería
bank/banco
barn/granero
bridge/peunte
bus shelter/parada cubierta
city hall/ayuntamiento
clothing store/tienda de ropa
condominium/condominio
courthouse/tribunal
covered bridge/puente cubierto
dam/presa
dock/muelle
drawbridge/puente levadizo
duplex/dúplex
fire station/estación de bomberos
flower shop/floristeria
garage/garaje
gas station/gasolinera
gazebo/mirador
grain elevator/elevador de granos
grocery store/supermercado
hospital/hospital
house/casa
library/biblioteca
log cabin/cabaña de madera
marina/marina
monument/monumento
movie theater/cine
opera house/teatro de la ópera
palace/palacio

parking garage/estacionamiento
pizza shop/pizzaría
police station/estación de policía
power plant/central eléctrica
pyramid/pirámide
restaurant/restaurante
school/escuela
shelter house/albergue
shopping mall/centro comercial
skyscraper/rascacielos
stadium/estadio
swimming pool/alberca/piscina
tent/tienda
toy store/juguetería
train station/estación del tren
windmills/molino de viento

Transportation

airplane/avión
bicycle/bicicleta
bus/autobús
canoe/canoa
car/coche
four-wheel-drive vehicle/coche con
    doble tracción
helicopter/helicóptero
hot air balloon/globo de aire
    caliente
kayak/kayac
moped/ciclomotor
motor home/casa motora
motorboat/lancha motora
motorcycle/motocicleta
pickup truck/camioneta
rowboat/bote de remos
sailboat/velero
school bus/camión escolar

semitrailer truck/camión con semi-
    remolque
ship/barco
submarine/submarino
subway/metro
taxi/taxi
train/tren
van/furgoneta

Learning Trajectories for Math

Children follow natural developmental progressions in learning. Curriculum research has revealed sequences of activities that are effective in guiding children through these levels of thinking. These developmental paths are the basis for *Building Blocks* learning trajectories.

Learning Trajectories for Primary Grades Mathematics

Learning trajectories have three parts: a mathematical goal, a developmental path along which children develop to reach that goal, and a set of activities matched to each of the levels of thinking in that path that help children develop the next higher level of thinking. The **Building Blocks** learning trajectories give simple labels, descriptions, and examples of each level. Complete learning trajectories describe the goals of learning, the thinking and learning processes of children at various levels, and the learning activities in which they might engage. This document provides only the developmental levels.

The following provides the developmental levels from the first signs of development in different strands of mathematics through approximately age 8. Research shows that when teachers understand how children develop mathematics understanding, they are more effective in questioning, analyzing, and providing activities that further children's development than teachers who are unaware of the development process. Consequently, children have a much richer and more successful math experience in the primary grades.

Each of the following tables, such as "Counting," represents a main developmental progression that underlies the learning trajectory for that topic.

For some topics, there are "subtrajectories"—strands within the topic. In most cases, the names make this clear. For example, in Comparing and Ordering, some levels are "Composer" levels and others involve building a "Mental Number Line." Similarly, the related subtrajectories of "Composition" and "Decomposition" are easy to distinguish. Sometimes, for clarification, subtrajectories are indicated with a note in italics after the title. For example, Parts and Representing are subtrajectories within the Shape Trajectory.

Frequently Asked Questions (FAQ)

1. Why use learning trajectories? Learning trajectories allow teachers to build the mathematics of children—the thinking of children as it develops naturally. So, we know that all the goals and activities are within the developmental capacities of children. Finally, we know that the activities provide the mathematical building blocks for success.

2. When are children "at" a level? Children are at a certain level when most of their behaviors reflect the thinking—ideas and skills—of that level. Most levels are levels of thinking. However, some are merely "levels of attainment" and indicate a child has gained knowledge. For example, children must learn to name or write more numerals, but knowing more numerals does not require more complex thinking.

3. Can children work at more than one level at the same time? Yes, although most children work mainly at one level or in transition between two levels. Levels are not "absolute stages." They are "benchmarks" of complex growth that represent distinct ways of thinking.

4. Can children jump ahead? Yes, especially if there are separate subtopics. For example, we have combined many counting competencies into one "Counting" sequence with subtopics, such as verbal counting skills. Some children learn to count to 100 at age 6 after learning to count objects to 10 or more, some may learn that verbal skill earlier. The subtopic of verbal counting skills would still be followed.

5. How do these developmental levels support teaching and learning? The levels help teachers, as well as curriculum developers, assess, teach, and sequence activities. Through planned teaching and encouraging informal, incidental mathematics, teachers help children learn at an appropriate and deep level.

6. Should I plan to help children develop just the levels that correspond to my children's ages? No! The ages in the table are typical ages children develop these ideas. (These are rough guides only.) These are "starting levels" not goals. We have found that children who are provided high-quality mathematics experiences are capable of developing to levels one or more years beyond their peers.

Developmental Levels for Counting

The ability to count with confidence develops over the course of several years. Beginning in infancy, children show signs of understanding numbers. With instruction and number experience, most children can count fluently by age 8, with much progress in counting occurring in kindergarten and first grade. Most children follow a natural developmental progression in learning to count with recognizable stages or levels. This developmental path can be described as part of a learning trajectory.

Age Range	Level Name	Level	Description
1–2	Precounter	1	At the earliest level a child shows no verbal counting. The child may name some number words with no sequence.
1–2	Chanter	2	At this level, a child may sing-song or chant indistinguishable number words.
2	Reciter	3	At this level, the child may verbally count with separate words, but not necessarily in the correct order.
3	Reciter (10)	4	A child at this level may verbally count to 10 with some correspondence with objects. He or she may point to objects to count a few items, but then lose track.
3	Corresponder	5	At this level, a child may keep one-to-one correspondence between counting words and objects—at least for small groups of objects laid in a line. A corresponder may answer "how many" by recounting the objects.
4	Counter (Small Numbers)	6	At around 4 years of age, the child may begin to count meaningfully. He or she may accurately count objects in a line to 5 and answer the "how many" question with the last number counted. When objects are visible, and especially with small numbers, the child begins to understand cardinality (that numbers tell how many).
4	Producer (Small Numbers)	7	The next level after counting small numbers is to count out objects to 5. When asked to show four of something, for example, this child may give four objects.
4	Counter (10)	8	This child may count structured arrangements of objects to 10. He or she may be able to write or draw to represent 1–10. A child at this level may be able to tell the number just after or just before another number, but only by counting up from 1.
5	Counter and Producer—Counter to (10+)	9	Around 5 years of age, a child may begin to count out objects accurately to 10 and then beyond to 30. He or she has explicit understanding of cardinality (that numbers tell how many). The child may keep track of objects that have and have not been counted, even in different arrangements. He or she may write or draw to represent 1 to 10 and then 20 and 30, and may give the next number to 20 or 30. The child also begins to recognize errors in others' counting and is able to eliminate most errors in his or her own counting.

Age Range	Level Name	Level	Description
5	Counter Backward from 10	10	Another milestone at about age 5 is being able to count backward from 10 to 1, verbally, or when removing objects from a group.
6	Counter from N (N+1, N–1)	11	Around 6 years of age, the child may begin to count on, counting verbally and with objects from numbers other than 1. Another noticeable accomplishment is that a child may determine the number immediately before or after another number without having to start back at 1.
6	Skip Counting by 10s to 100	12	A child at this level may count by 10s to 100 or beyond with understanding.
6	Counter to 100	13	A child at this level may count by 1s to 100. He or she can make decade transitions (for example, from 29 to 30) starting at any number.
6	Counter On Using Patterns	14	At this level, a child may keep track of a few counting acts by using numerical patterns, such as tapping as he or she counts.
6	Skip Counter	15	At this level, the child can count by 5s and 2s with understanding.
6	Counter of Imagined Items	16	At this level, a child may count mental images of hidden objects to answer, for example, "how many" when 5 objects are visible and 3 are hidden.
6	Counter On Keeping Track	17	A child at this level may keep track of counting acts numerically, first with objects, then by counting counts. He or she counts up one to four more from a given number.
6	Counter of Quantitative Units	18	At this level, a child can count unusual units, such as "wholes" when shown combinations of wholes and parts. For example, when shown three whole plastic eggs and four halves, a child at this level will say there are five whole eggs.
6	Counter to 200	19	At this level, a child may count accurately to 200 and beyond, recognizing the patterns of ones, tens, and hundreds.
7	Number Conserver	20	A major milestone around age 7 is the ability to conserve number. A child who conserves number understands that a number is unchanged even if a group of objects is rearranged. For example, if there is a row of ten buttons, the child understands there are still ten without recounting, even if they are rearranged in a long row or a circle.
7	Counter Forward and Back	21	A child at this level may count in either direction and recognize that sequence of decades mirrors single-digit sequence.

Learning Trajectories for Math

Developmental Levels for Comparing and Ordering Numbers

Comparing and ordering sets is a critical skill for children as they determine whether one set is larger than another in order to make sure sets are equal and "fair." Prekindergartners can learn to use matching to compare collections or to create equivalent collections. Finding out how many more or fewer in one collection is more demanding than simply comparing two collections. The ability to compare and order sets with fluency develops over the course of several years. With instruction and number experience, most children develop foundational understanding of number relationships and place value at ages four and five. Most children follow a natural developmental progression in learning to compare and order numbers with recognizable stages or levels. This developmental path can be described as part of a learning trajectory.

Age Range	Level Name	Level	Description
2	Object Corresponder	1	At this early level, a child puts objects into one-to-one correspondence, but may not fully understand that this creates equal groups. For example, a child may know that each carton has a straw, but does not necessarily know there are the same numbers of straws and cartons.
2	Perceptual Comparer	2	At this level, a child can compare collections that are quite different in size (for example, one is at least twice the other) and know that one has more than the other. If the collections are similar, the child can compare very small collections.
3	First-Second Ordinal Counter	3	At this level the child can identify the "first" and often "second" object in a sequence.
3	Nonverbal Comparer of Similar Items	4	At this level, a child can identify that different organizations of the same number are equal and different from other sets (1–4 items). For example, a child can identify ••• and •••• as equal and different from •• or •••.
4	Nonverbal Comparer of Dissimilar Items	5	At this level, a child can match small, equal collections of dissimilar items, such as shells and dots, and show that they are the same number.
4	Matching Comparer	6	As children progress, they begin to compare groups of 1–6 by matching. For example, a child gives one toy bone to every dog and says there are the same number of dogs and bones.

Age Range	Level Name	Level	Description
4	Knows-to-Count Comparer	7	A significant step occurs when the child begins to count collections to compare. At the early levels, children are not always accurate when a larger collection's objects are smaller in size than the objects in the smaller collection. For example, a child at this level may accurately count two equal collections, but when asked, says the collection of larger blocks has more.
4	Counting Comparer (Same Size)	8	At this level, children make accurate comparisons via counting, but only when objects are about the same size and groups are small (about 1–5 items).
5	Counting Comparer (5)	9	As children develop their ability to compare sets, they compare accurately by counting, even when a larger collection's objects are smaller. A child at this level can figure out how many more or less.
5	Ordinal Counter	10	At this level, a child identifies and uses ordinal numbers from "first" to "tenth." For example, the child can identify who is "third in line."
6	Counting Comparer (10)	11	This level can be observed when the child compares sets by counting, even when a larger collection's objects are smaller, up to 10. A child at this level can accurately count two collections of 9 items each, and says they have the same number, even if one collection has larger blocks.
6	Mental Number Line to 10	12	As children move into this level, they begin to use mental images and knowledge of number relationships to determine relative size and position. For example, a child at this level can answer which number is closer to 6, 4 or 9 without counting physical objects.
6	Serial Orderer to 6+	13	At this level, the child orders lengths marked into units (1–6, then beyond). For example, given towers of cubes, this child can put them in order, 1 to 6.
7	Place Value Comparer	14	Further development is made when a child begins to compare numbers with place value understanding. For example, a child at this level can explain that "63 is more than 59 because six tens is more than five tens, even if there are more than three ones."
7	Mental Number Line to 100	15	Children demonstrate the next level when they can use mental images and knowledge of number relationships, including ones embedded in tens, to determine relative size and position. For example, when asked, "Which is closer to 45, 30 or 50?" a child at this level may say "45 is right next to 50, but 30 isn't."
8+	Mental Number Line to 1,000s	16	At about age 8, children may begin to use mental images of numbers up to 1,000 and knowledge of number relationships, including place value, to determine relative size and position. For example, when asked, "Which is closer to 3,500—2,000 or 7,000?" a child at this level may say "70 is double 35, but 20 is only fifteen from 35, so twenty hundreds, 2,000, is closer."

Developmental Levels for Recognizing Number and Subitizing (Instantly Recognizing)

The ability to recognize number values develops over the course of several years and is a foundational part of number sense. Beginning at about age two, children begin to name groups of objects. The ability to instantly know how many are in a group, called *subitizing,* begins at about age three. By age eight, with instruction and number experience, most children can identify groups of items and use place values and multiplication skills to count them. Most children follow a natural developmental progression in learning to count with recognizable stages or levels. This developmental path can be described as part of a learning trajectory.

Age Range	Level Name	Level	Description
2	Small Collection Namer	1	The first sign occurs when the child can name groups of 1 to 2, sometimes 3. For example, when shown a pair of shoes, this young child says, "two shoes."
3	Maker of Small Collections	2	At this level, a child can nonverbally make a small collection (no more than 4, usually 1 to 3) with the same number as another collection. For example, when shown a collection of 3, the child makes another collection of 3.
4	Perceptual Subitizer to 4	3	Progress is made when a child instantly recognizes collections up to 4 and verbally names the number of items. For example, when shown 4 objects briefly, the child says "4."
5	Perceptual Subitizer to 5	4	This level is the ability to instantly recognize collections up to 5 and verbally name the number of items. For example, when shown 5 objects briefly, the child says "5."
5	Conceptual Subitizer to 51	5	At this level, the child can verbally label all arrangements to about 5, when shown only briefly. For example, a child at this level might say, "I saw 2 and 2, and so I saw 4."
5	Conceptual Subitizer to 10	6	This step is when the child can verbally label most arrangements to 6 shown briefly, then up to 10, using groups. For example, a child at this level might say, "In my mind, I made 2 groups of 3 and 1 more, so 7."
6	Conceptual Subitizer to 20	7	Next, a child can verbally label structured arrangements up to 20 shown briefly, using groups. For example, the child may say, "I saw 3 fives, so 5, 10, 15."
7	Conceptual Subitizer with Place Value and Skip Counting	8	At this level, a child is able to use groups, skip counting, and place value to verbally label structured arrangements shown briefly. For example, the child may say, "I saw groups of tens and twos, so 10, 20, 30, 40, 42, 44, 46…46!"
8+	Conceptual Subitizer with Place Value and Multiplication	9	As children develop their ability to subitize, they use groups, multiplication, and place value to verbally label structured arrangements shown briefly. At this level, a child may say, "I saw groups of tens and threes, so I thought, 5 tens is 50 and 4 threes is 12, so 62 in all."

Learning Trajectories for Math

Developmental Levels for Composing (Knowing Combinations of Numbers)

Composing and decomposing are combining and separating operations that allow children to build concepts of "parts" and "wholes." Most prekindergartners can "see" that two items and one item make three items. Later, children learn to separate a group into parts in various ways and then to count to produce all of the number "partners" of a given number. Eventually children think of a number and know the different addition facts that make that number. Most children follow a natural developmental progression in learning to compose and decompose numbers with recognizable stages or levels. This developmental path can be described as part of a learning trajectory.

Age Range	Level Name	Level	Description
4	Pre-Part-Whole Recognizer	1	At the earliest levels of composing, a child only nonverbally recognizes parts and wholes. For example, when shown 4 red blocks and 2 blue blocks, a young child may intuitively appreciate that "all the blocks" includes the red and blue blocks, but when asked how many there are in all, the child may name a small number, such as 1.
5	Inexact Part-Whole Recognizer	2	A sign of development is that the child knows a whole is bigger than parts, but does not accurately quantify. For example, when shown 4 red blocks and 2 blue blocks and asked how many there are in all, the child may name a "large number," such as 5 or 10.
5	Composer to 4, then 5	3	At this level, a child knows number combinations. A child at this level quickly names parts of any whole, or the whole given the parts. For example, when shown 4, then 1 is secretly hidden, and then shown the 3 remaining, the child may quickly say "1" is hidden.
6	Composer to 7	4	The next sign of development is when a child knows number combinations to totals of 7. A child at this level quickly names parts of any whole, or the whole when given parts, and can double numbers to 10. For example, when shown 6, then 4 are secretly hidden, and then shown the 2 remaining, the child may quickly say "4" are hidden.
6	Composer to 10	5	This level is when a child knows number combinations to totals of 10. A child at this level may quickly name parts of any whole, or the whole when given parts, and can double numbers to 20. For example, this child would be able to say "9 and 9 is 18."
7	Composer with Tens and Ones	6	At this level, the child understands two-digit numbers as tens and ones, can count with dimes and pennies, and can perform two-digit addition with regrouping. For example, a child at this level may explain, "17 and 36 is like 17 and 3, which is 20, and 33, which is 53."

Developmental Levels for Adding and Subtracting

Single-digit addition and subtraction are generally characterized as "math facts." It is assumed children must memorize these facts, yet research has shown that addition and subtraction have their roots in counting, counting on, number sense, the ability to compose and decompose numbers, and place value. Research has also shown that learning methods for addition and subtraction with understanding is much more effective than rote memorization of seemingly isolated facts. Most children follow an observable developmental progression in learning to add and subtract numbers with recognizable stages or levels. This developmental path can be described as part of a learning trajectory.

Age Range	Level Name	Level	Description
1	Pre +/−	1	At the earliest level, a child shows no sign of being able to add or subtract.
3	Nonverbal +/−	2	The first sign is when a child can add and subtract very small collections nonverbally. For example, when shown 2 objects, then 1 object being hidden under a napkin, the child identifies or makes a set of 3 objects to "match."
4	Small Number +/−	3	This level is when a child can find sums for joining problems up to 3 1 2 by counting with objects. For example, when asked, "You have 2 balls and get 1 more. How many in all?" the child may count out 2, then count out 1 more, then count all 3: "1, 2, 3, 3!"
5	Find Result +/−	4	**Addition** Evidence of this level in addition is when a child can find sums for joining (you had 3 apples and get 3 more; how many do you have in all?) and part-part-whole (there are 6 girls and 5 boys on the playground; how many children were there in all?) problems by direct modeling, counting all, with objects. For example, when asked, "You have 2 red balls and 3 blue balls. How many in all?" the child may count out 2 red, then count out 3 blue, then count all 5. **Subtraction** In subtraction, a child can also solve take-away problems by separating with objects. For example, when asked, "You have 5 balls and give 2 to Tom. How many do you have left?" the child may count out 5 balls, then take away 2, and then count the remaining 3.

Age Range	Level Name	Level	Description
5	Find Change +/–	5	**Addition** At this level, a child can find the missing addend (5 + _ =7) by adding on objects. For example, when asked, "You have 5 balls and then get some more. Now you have 7 in all. How many did you get?" The child may count out 5, then count those 5 again starting at 1, then add more, counting "6, 7," then count the balls added to find the answer, 2. **Subtraction** A child can compare by matching in simple situations. For example, when asked, "Here are 6 dogs and 4 balls. If we give a ball to each dog, how many dogs will not get a ball?" a child at this level may count out 6 dogs, match 4 balls to 4 of them, then count the 2 dogs that have no ball.
5	Make It +/–	6	A significant advancement occurs when a child is able to count on. This child can add on objects to make one number into another without counting from 1. For example, when told, "This puppet has 4 balls, but she should have 6. Make it 6," the child may put up 4 fingers on one hand, immediately count up from 4 while putting up 2 fingers on the other hand, saying, "5, 6," and then count or recognize the 2 fingers.
6	Counting Strategies +/–	7	This level occurs when a child can find sums for joining (you had 8 apples and get 3 more…) and part-part-whole (6 girls and 5 boys…) problems with finger patterns or by adding on objects or counting on. For example, when asked "How much is 4 and 3 more?" the child may answer "4…5, 6, 7. 7!" Children at this level can also solve missing addend (3 + _ = 7) or compare problems by counting on. When asked, for example, "You have 6 balls. How many more would you need to have 8?" the child may say, "6, 7 [puts up first finger], 8 [puts up second finger]. 2!"
6	Part-Whole +/–	8	Further development has occurred when the child has part-whole understanding. This child can solve problems using flexible strategies and some derived facts (for example, "5 + 5 is 10, so 5 + 6 is 11"), can sometimes do start-unknown problems (_ + 6 = 11), but only by trial and error. When asked, "You had some balls. Then you get 6 more. Now you have 11 balls. How many did you start with?" this child may lay out 6, then 3, count, and get 9. The child may put 1 more, say 10, then put 1 more. The child may count up from 6 to 11, then recount the group added, and say, "5!"

Age Range	Level Name	Level	Description
6	Numbers-in-Numbers +/–	9	Evidence of this level is when a child recognizes that a number is part of a whole and can solve problems when the start is unknown (_ + 4 = 9) with counting strategies. For example, when asked, "You have some balls, then you get 4 more balls, now you have 9. How many did you have to start with?" this child may count, putting up fingers, "5, 6, 7, 8, 9." The child may then look at his or her fingers and say, "5!"
7	Deriver +/–	10	At this level, a child can use flexible strategies and derived combinations (for example, "7 + 7 is 14, so 7 + 8 is 15") to solve all types of problems. For example, when asked, "What's 7 plus 8?" this child thinks: 7 + 8 = 7 [7 + 1] = [7 +7] + 1 = 14 + 1 = 15. The child can also solve multidigit problems by incrementing or combining 10s and 1s. For example, when asked "What's 28 + 35?" this child may think: 20 + 30 = 50; + 8 = 58; 2 more is 60, and 3 more is 63. He or she can also combine 10s and 1s: 20 + 30 = 50. 8 + 5 is like 8 plus 2 and 3 more, so it is 13. 50 and 13 is 63.
8+	Problem Solver +/–	11	As children develop their addition and subtraction abilities, they can solve by using flexible strategies and many known combinations. For example, when asked, "If I have 13 and you have 9, how could we have the same number?" this child may say, "9 and 1 is 10, then 3 more makes 13. 1 and 3 is 4. I need 4 more!"
8+	Multidigit +/–	12	Further development is shown when children can use composition of 10s and all previous strategies to solve multidigit +/– problems. For example, when asked, "What's 37 – 18?" this child may say, "Take 1 ten off the 3 tens; that's 2 tens. Take 7 off the 7. That's 2 tens and 0…20. I have one more to take off. That's 19." Or, when asked, "What's 28 + 35?" this child may think, 30 + 35 would be 65. But it's 28, so it's 2 less…63.

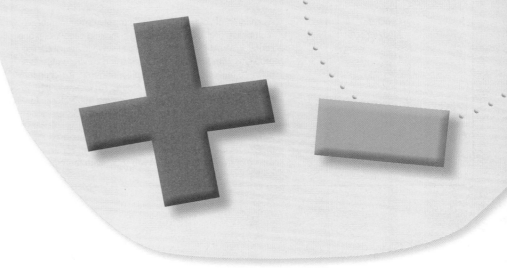

Developmental Levels for Multiplying and Dividing

Multiplication and division build on addition and subtraction understanding and are dependent upon counting and place-value concepts. As children begin to learn to multiply, they make equal groups and count them all. They then learn skip counting and derive related products from products they know. Finding and using patterns aid in learning multiplication and division facts with understanding. Children typically follow an observable developmental progression in learning to multiply and divide numbers with recognizable stages or levels. This developmental path can be described as part of a learning trajectory.

Age Range	Level Name	Level	Description
2	Non-quantitative Sharer "Dumper"	1	Multiplication and division concepts begin very early with the problem of sharing. Early evidence of these concepts can be observed when a child dumps out blocks and gives some (not an equal number) to each person.
3	Beginning Grouper and Distributive Sharer	2	Progression to this level can be observed when a child is able to make small groups (fewer than 5). This child can share by "dealing out," but often only between 2 people, although he or she may not appreciate the numerical result. For example, to share 4 blocks, this child may give each person a block, check that each person has one, and repeat this.
4	Grouper and Distributive Sharer	3	The next level occurs when a child makes small equal groups (fewer than 6). This child can deal out equally between 2 or more recipients, but may not understand that equal quantities are produced. For example, the child may share 6 blocks by dealing out blocks to herself and a friend one at a time.
5	Concrete Modeler ×/÷	4	As children develop, they are able to solve small-number multiplying problems by grouping—making each group and counting all. At this level, a child can solve division/sharing problems with informal strategies, using concrete objects—up to 20 objects and 2 to 5 people—although the child may not understand equivalence of groups. For example, the child may distribute 20 objects by dealing out 2 blocks to each of 5 people, then 1 to each, until the blocks are gone.
6	Parts and Wholes ×/÷	5	A new level is evidenced when the child understands the inverse relation between divisor and quotient. For example, this child may understand "If you share with more people, each person gets fewer."

Age Range	Level Name	Level	Description
7	Skip Counter ×/÷	6	As children develop understanding in multiplication and division, they begin to use skip counting for multiplication and for measurement division (finding out how many groups). For example, given 20 blocks, 4 to each person, and asked how many people, the children may skip count by 4, holding up 1 finger for each count of 4. A child at this level may also use trial and error for partitive division (finding out how many in each group). For example, given 20 blocks, 5 people, and asked how many each should get, this child may give 3 to each, and then 1 more.
8+	Deriver ×/÷	7	At this level, children use strategies and derived combinations to solve multidigit problems by operating on tens and ones separately. For example, a child at this level may explain "7 × 6, five 7s is 35, so 7 more is 42."
8+	Array Quantifier	8	Further development can be observed when a child begins to work with arrays. For example, given 7 × 4 with most of 5 × 4 covered, a child at this level may say, "There are 8 in these 2 rows, and 5 rows of 4 is 20, so 28 in all."
8+	Partitive Divisor	9	This level can be observed when a child is able to figure out how many are in each group. For example, given 20 blocks, 5 people, and asked how many each should get, a child at this level may say, "4, because 5 groups of 4 is 20."
8+	Multidigit ×/÷	10	As children progress, they begin to use multiple strategies for multiplication and division, from compensating to paper-and-pencil procedures. For example, a child becoming fluent in multiplication might explain that "19 times 5 is 95, because 20 fives is 100, and 1 less five is 95."

Developmental Levels for Measuring

Measurement is one of the main real-world applications of mathematics. Counting is a type of measurement which determines how many items are in a collection. Measurement also involves assigning a number to attributes of length, area, and weight. Prekindergarten children know that mass, weight, and length exist, but they do not know how to reason about these or to accurately measure them. As children develop their understanding of measurement, they begin to use tools to measure and understand the need for standard units of measure. Children typically follow an observable developmental progression in learning to measure with recognizable stages or levels. This developmental path can be described as part of a learning trajectory.

Age Range	Level Name	Level	Description
3	Length Quantity Recognizer	1	At the earliest level, children can identify length as an attribute. For example, they might say, "I'm tall, see?"
4	Length Direct Comparer	2	In this level, children can physically align 2 objects to determine which is longer or if they are the same length. For example, they can stand 2 sticks up next to each other on a table and say, "This one's bigger."
5	Indirect Length Comparer	3	A sign of further development is when a child can compare the length of 2 objects by representing them with a third object. For example, a child might compare the length of 2 objects with a piece of string. Additional evidence of this level is that when asked to measure, the child may assign a length by guessing or moving along a length while counting (without equal-length units). For example, the child may move a finger along a line segment, saying 10, 20, 30, 31, 32.
6	Serial Orderer to 6+	4	At this level, a child can order lengths, marked in 1 to 6 units. For example, given towers of cubes, a child at this level may put them in order, 1 to 6.
6	End-to-End Length Measurer	5	At this level, the child can lay units end-to-end, although he or she may not see the need for equal-length units. For example, a child might lay 9-inch cubes in a line beside a book to measure how long it is.
7	Length Unit Iterater	6	A significant change occurs when a child iterates a single unit to measure. He or she sees the need for identical units. The child uses rulers with help.
7	Length Unit Relater	7	At this level, a child can relate size and number of units. For example, the child may explain, "If you measure with centimeters instead of inches, you'll need more of them because each one is smaller."
8+	Length Measurer	8	As a child develops measurement ability, they begin to measure, knowing the need for identical units, the relationships between different units, partitions of unit, and the zero point on rulers. At this level, the child also begins to estimate. The children may explain, "I used a meterstick 3 times, then there was a little left over. So, I lined it up from 0 and found 14 centimeters. So, it's 3 meters, 14 centimeters in all."
8+	Conceptual Ruler Measurer	9	Further development in measurement is evidenced when a child possesses an "internal" measurement tool. At this level, the child mentally moves along an object, segmenting it, and counting the segments. This child also uses arithmetic to measure and estimates with accuracy. For example, a child at this level may explain, "I imagine one meterstick after another along the edge of the room. That's how I estimated the room's length to be 9 meters."

Developmental Levels for Recognizing Geometric Shapes

Geometric shapes can be used to represent and understand objects. Analyzing, comparing, and classifying shapes help create new knowledge of shapes and their relationships. Shapes can be decomposed or composed into other shapes. Through their everyday activities, children build both intuitive and explicit knowledge of geometric figures. Most children can recognize and name basic two-dimensional shapes at four years of age. However, young children can learn richer concepts about shape if they have varied examples and nonexamples of shape, discussions about shapes and their characteristics, a wide variety of shape classes, and interesting tasks. Children typically follow an observable developmental progression in learning about shapes with recognizable stages or levels. This developmental path can be described as part of a learning trajectory.

Age Range	Level Name	Level	Description
2	Shape Matcher—Identical	1	The earliest sign of understanding shape is when a child can match basic shapes (circle, square, typical triangle) with the same size and orientation.
2	Shape Matcher—Sizes	2	A sign of development is when a child can match basic shapes with different sizes.
2	Shape Matcher—Orientations	3	This level of development is when a child can match basic shapes with different orientations.
3	Shape Recognizer—Typical	4	A sign of development is when a child can recognize and name a prototypical circle, square, and, less often, a typical triangle. For example, the child names this a square. ☐ Some children may name different sizes, shapes, and orientations of rectangles, but also accept some shapes that look rectangular but are not rectangles. Children name these shapes "rectangles" (including the nonrectangular parallelogram).
3	Shape Matcher—More Shapes	5	As children develop understanding of shape, they can match a wider variety of shapes with the same size and orientation.
3	Shape Matcher—Sizes and Orientations	6	The child matches a wider variety of shapes with different sizes and orientations.
3	Shape Matcher—Combinations	7	The child matches combinations of shapes to each other.
4	Shape Recognizer—Circles, Squares, and Triangles	8	This sign of development is when a child can recognize some nonprototypical squares and triangles and may recognize some rectangles, but usually not rhombi (diamonds). Often, the child does not differentiate sides/corners. The child at this level may name these as triangles.
4	Constructor of Shapes from Parts—Looks Like *Representing*	9	A significant sign of development is when a child represents a shape by making a shape "look like" a goal shape. For example, when asked to make a triangle with sticks, the child may create the following: △ .

Age Range	Level Name	Level	Description
5	Shape Recognizer—All Rectangles	10	As children develop understanding of shape, they recognize more rectangle sizes, shapes, and orientations of rectangles. For example, a child at this level may correctly name these shapes "rectangles."
5	Side Recognizer *Parts*	11	A sign of development is when a child recognizes parts of shapes and identifies sides as distinct geometric objects. For example, when asked what this shape is, the child may say it is a quadrilateral (or has 4 sides) after counting and running a finger along the length of each side.
5	Angle Recognizer *Parts*	12	At this level, a child can recognize angles as separate geometric objects. For example, when asked, "Why is this a triangle," the child may say, "It has three angles" and count them, pointing clearly to each vertex (point at the corner).
5	Shape Recognizer—More Shapes	13	As children develop, they are able to recognize most basic shapes and prototypical examples of other shapes, such as hexagon, rhombus (diamond), and trapezoid. For example, a child can correctly identify and name all the following shapes:
6	Shape Identifier	14	At this level, the child can name most common shapes, including rhombi, without making mistakes such as calling ovals circles. A child at this level implicitly recognizes right angles, so distinguishes between a rectangle and a parallelogram without right angles. A child may correctly name all the following shapes:
6	Angle Matcher *Parts*	15	A sign of development is when the child can match angles concretely. For example, given several triangles, the child may find two with the same angles by laying the angles on top of one another.

Age Range	Level Name	Level	Description
7	Parts of Shapes Identifier	16	At this level, the child can identify shapes in terms of their components. For example, the child may say, "No matter how skinny it looks, that's a triangle because it has 3 sides and 3 angles."
7	Constructor of Shapes from Parts—Exact Representing	17	A significant step is when the child can represent a shape with completely correct construction, based on knowledge of components and relationships. For example, when asked to make a triangle with sticks, the child may create the following:
8	Shape Class Identifier	18	As children develop, they begin to use class membership (for example, to sort) not explicitly based on properties. For example, a child at this level may say, "I put the triangles over here, and the quadrilaterals, including squares, rectangles, rhombi, and trapezoids, over there."
8	Shape Property Identifier	19	At this level, a child can use properties explicitly. For example, a child may say, "I put the shapes with opposite sides that are parallel over here, and those with 4 sides but not both pairs of sides parallel over there."
8	Angle Size Comparer	20	The next sign of development is when a child can separate and compare angle sizes. For example, the child may say, "I put all the shapes that have right angles here, and all the ones that have bigger or smaller angles over there."
8	Angle Measurer	21	A significant step in development is when a child can use a protractor to measure angles.
8	Property Class Identifier	22	The next sign of development is when a child can use class membership for shapes (for example, to sort or consider shapes "similar") explicitly based on properties, including angle measure. For example, the child may say, "I put the equilateral triangles over here, and the right triangles over here."
8	Angle Synthesizer	23	As children develop understanding of shape, they can combine various meanings of angle (turn, corner, slant). For example, a child at this level could explain, "This ramp is at a 45° angle to the ground."

Learning Trajectories for Math

Developmental Levels for Composing Geometric Shapes

Children move through levels in the composition and decomposition of two-dimensional figures. Very young children cannot compose shapes but then gain ability to combine shapes into pictures, synthesize combinations of shapes into new shapes, and eventually substitute and build different kinds of shapes. Children typically follow an observable developmental progression in learning to compose shapes with recognizable stages or levels. This developmental path can be described as part of a learning trajectory.

Age Range	Level Name	Level	Description
2	Pre-Composer	1	The earliest sign of development is when a child can manipulate shapes as individuals, but is unable to combine them to compose a larger shape.
3	Pre-Decomposer	2	At this level, a child can decompose shapes, but only by trial and error.
4	Piece Assembler	3	Around age 4, a child can begin to make pictures in which each shape represents a unique role (for example, one shape for each body part) and shapes touch. A child at this level can fill simple outline puzzles using trial and error.
5	Picture Maker	4	As children develop, they are able to put several shapes together to make one part of a picture (for example, 2 shapes for 1 arm). A child at this level uses trial and error and does not anticipate creation of the new geometric shape. The children can choose shapes using "general shape" or side length, and fill "easy" outline puzzles that suggest the placement of each shape (but note that the child is trying to put a square in the puzzle where its right angles will not fit).
5	Simple Decomposer	5	A significant step occurs when the child is able to decompose ("take apart" into smaller shapes) simple shapes that have obvious clues as to their decomposition.

Age Range	Level Name	Level	Description
5	Shape Composer	6	A sign of development is when a child composes shapes with anticipation ("I know what will fit!"). A child at this level chooses shapes using angles as well as side lengths. Rotation and flipping are used intentionally to select and place shapes.
6	Substitution Composer	7	A sign of development is when a child is able to make new shapes out of smaller shapes and uses trial and error to substitute groups of shapes for other shapes in order to create new shapes in different ways. For example, the child can substitute shapes to fill outline puzzles in different ways.
6	Shape Decomposer (with Help)	8	As children develop, they can decompose shapes by using imagery that is suggested and supported by the task or environment.
7	Shape Composite Repeater	9	This level is demonstrated when the child can construct and duplicate units of units (shapes made from other shapes) intentionally, and understands each as being both multiple, small shapes and one larger shape. For example, the child may continue a pattern of shapes that leads to tiling.
7	Shape Decomposer with Imagery	10	A significant sign of development is when a child is able to decompose shapes flexibly by using independently generated imagery.
8	Shape Composer— Units of Units	11	Children demonstrate further understanding when they are able to build and apply units of units (shapes made from other shapes). For example, in constructing spatial patterns, the child can extend patterning activity to create a tiling with a new unit shape—a unit of unit shapes that he or she recognizes and consciously constructs. For example, the child may build Ts out of 4 squares, use 4 Ts to build squares, and use squares to tile a rectangle.
8	Shape Decomposer — Units of Units	12	As children develop understanding of shape, they can decompose shapes flexibly by using independently generated imagery and planned decompositions of shapes that themselves are decompositions.

Developmental Levels for Comparing Geometric Shapes

As early as four years of age, children can create and use strategies, such as moving shapes to compare their parts or to place one on top of the other, for judging whether two figures are the same shape. From Pre-K to Grade 2, they can develop sophisticated and accurate mathematical procedures for comparing geometric shapes. Children typically follow an observable developmental progression in learning about how shapes are the same and different with recognizable stages or levels. This developmental path can be described as part of a learning trajectory.

Age Range	Level Name	Level	Description
3	"Same Thing" Comparer	1	The first sign of understanding is when the child can compare real-world objects. For example, the children may say two pictures of houses are the same or different.
4	"Similar" Comparer	2	This sign of development occurs when the child judges two shapes to be the same if they are more visually similar than different. For example, the child may say, "These are the same. They are pointy at the top."
4	Part Comparer	3	At this level, a child can say that two shapes are the same after matching one side on each. For example, a child may say, "These are the same" (matching the two sides).
4	Some Attributes Comparer	4	As children develop, they look for differences in attributes, but may examine only part of a shape. For example, a child at this level may say, "These are the same" (indicating the top halves of the shapes are similar by laying them on top of each other).
5	Most Attributes Comparer	5	At this level, the child looks for differences in attributes, examining full shapes, but may ignore some spatial relationships. For example, a child may say, "These are the same."
7	Congruence Determiner	6	A sign of development is when a child determines congruence by comparing all attributes and all spatial relationships. For example, a child at this level may say that two shapes are the same shape and the same size after comparing every one of their sides and angles.
7	Congruence Superposer	7	As children develop understanding, they can move and place objects on top of each other to determine congruence. For example, a child at this level may say that two shapes are the same shape and the same size after laying them on top of each other.
8+	Congruence Representer	8	Continued development is evidenced as children refer to geometric properties and explain with transformations. For example, a child at this level may say, "These must be congruent because they have equal sides, all square corners, and I can move them on top of each other exactly."

Developmental Levels for Spatial Sense and Motions

Infants and toddlers spend a great deal of time learning about the properties and relations of objects in space. Very young children know and use the shape of their environment in navigation activities. With guidance they can learn to "mathematize" this knowledge. They can learn about direction, perspective, distance, symbolization, location, and coordinates. Children typically follow an observable developmental progression in developing spatial sense with recognizable stages or levels. This developmental path can be described as part of a learning trajectory.

Age Range	Level Name	Level	Description
4	Simple Turner	1	An early sign of spatial sense is when a child mentally turns an object to perform easy tasks. For example, given a shape with the top marked with color, the child may correctly identify which of three shapes it would look like if it were turned "like this" (90 degree turn demonstrated), before physically moving the shape.
5	Beginning Slider, Flipper, Turner	2	This sign of development occurs when a child can use the correct motions, but is not always accurate in direction and amount. For example, a child at this level may know a shape has to be flipped to match another shape, but flips it in the wrong direction.
6	Slider, Flipper, Turner	3	As children develop spatial sense, they can perform slides and flips, often only horizontal and vertical, by using manipulatives. For example, a child at this level may perform turns of 45, 90, and 180 degrees. For example, a child knows a shape must be turned 90 degrees to the right to fit into a puzzle.
7	Diagonal Mover	4	A sign of development is when a child can perform diagonal slides and flips. For example, children at this level may know a shape must be turned or flipped over an oblique line (45 degree orientation) to fit into a puzzle.
8	Mental Mover	5	Further signs of development occur when a child can predict results of moving shapes using mental images. A child at this level may say, "If you turned this 120 degrees, it would be just like this one."

Developmental Levels for Patterning and Early Algebra

Algebra begins with a search for patterns. Identifying patterns helps bring order, cohesion, and predictability to seemingly unorganized situations and allows one to make generalizations beyond the information directly available. The recognition and analysis of patterns are important components of young children's intellectual development because they provide a foundation for the development of algebraic thinking. Although prekindergarten children engage in pattern-related activities and recognize patterns in their everyday environment, research has revealed that an abstract understanding of patterns develops gradually during the early childhood years. Children typically follow an observable developmental progression in learning about patterns with recognizable stages or levels. This developmental path can be described as part of a learning trajectory.

Age Range	Level Name	Level	Description
2	Pre-Patterner	1	A child at the earliest level does not recognize patterns. For example, a child may name a striped shirt with no repeating unit a "pattern."
3	Pattern Recognizer	2	At this level, the child can recognize a simple pattern. For example, a child at this level may say, "I'm wearing a pattern" about a shirt with black and white stripes.
4	Pattern Fixer	3	At this level the child fills in missing elements of a pattern, first with ABABAB patterns. When given items in a row with an item missing, such as ABAB_BAB, the child identifies and fills in the missing element (A).
4	Pattern Duplicator AB	4	A sign of development is when the child can duplicate an ABABAB pattern, although the children may have to work alongside the model pattern. For example, given objects in a row, ABABAB, the child may make his or her own ABABAB row in a different location.
4	Pattern Extender AB	5	At this level the child extends AB repeating patterns. For example, given items in a row—ABABAB—the child adds ABAB to the end of the row.
4	Pattern Duplicator	6	At this level, the child is able to duplicate simple patterns (not just alongside the model pattern). For example, given objects in a row, ABBABBBABB, the child may make his or her own ABBABBBABB row in a different location.
5	Pattern Extender	7	A sign of development is when the child can extend simple patterns. For example, given objects in a row, ABBABBBABB, he or she may add ABBABB to the end of the row.
7	Pattern Unit Recognizer	8	At this level, a child can identify the smallest unit of a pattern. For example, given objects in a row with one missing, ABBAB_ABB, he or she may identify and fill in the missing element.

Developmental Levels for Classifying and Analyzing Data

Data analysis contains one big idea: classifying, organizing, representing, and using information to ask and answer questions. The developmental continuum for data analysis includes growth in classifying and counting to sort objects and quantify their groups. Children eventually become capable of simultaneously classifying and counting; for example, counting the number of colors in a group of objects. Children typically follow an observable developmental progression in learning about patterns with recognizable stages or levels. This developmental path can be described as part of a learning trajectory.

Age Range	Level Name	Level	Description
2	Similarity Recognizer	1	The first sign that a child can classify is when he or she recognizes, intuitively, two or more objects as "similar" in some way. For example, "that's another doggie."
2	Informal Sorter	2	A sign of development is when a child places objects that are alike in some attribute together, but switches criteria and may use functional relationships as the basis for sorting. A child at this level might stack blocks of the same shape or put a cup with its saucer.
3	Attribute Identifier	3	The next level is when the child names attributes of objects and places objects together with a given attribute, but cannot then move to sorting by a new rule. For example, the child may say, "These are both red."
4	Attribute Sorter	4	At the next level the child sorts objects according to given attributes, forming categories, but may switch attributes during the sorting. A child at this stage can switch rules for sorting if guided. For example, the child might start putting red beads on a string, but switches to spheres of different colors.
5	Consistent Sorter	5	A sign of development is when the child can sort consistently by a given attribute. For example, the child might put several identical blocks together.
6	Exhaustive Sorter	6	At the next level, the child can sort consistently and exhaustively by an attribute, given or created. This child can use terms "some" and "all" meaningfully. For example, a child at this stage would be able to find all the attribute blocks of a certain size and color.

Age Range	Level Name	Level	Description
6	Multiple Attribute Sorter	7	A sign of development is when the child can sort consistently and exhaustively by more than one attribute, sequentially. For example, a child at this level can put all the attribute blocks together by color, then by shape.
7	Classifier and Counter	8	At the next level, the child is capable of simultaneously classifying and counting. For example, the child counts the number of colors in a group of objects.
7	List Grapher	9	In the early stage of graphing, the child graphs by simply listing all cases. For example, the child may list each child in the class and each child's response to a question.
8+	Multiple Attribute Classifier	10	A sign of development is when the child can intentionally sort according to multiple attributes, naming and relating the attributes. This child understands that objects could belong to more than one group. For example, the child can complete a two-dimensional classification matrix or form subgroups within groups.
8+	Classifying Grapher	11	At the next level the child can graph by classifying data (e.g., responses) and represent it according to categories. For example, the child can take a survey, classify the responses, and graph the result.
8+	Classifier	12	A sign of development is when the child creates complete, conscious classifications logically connected to a specific property. For example, a child at this level gives a definition of a class in terms of a more general class and one or more specific differences and begins to understand the inclusion relation.
8+	Hierarchical Classifier	13	At the next level, the child can perform hierarchical classifications. For example, the child recognizes that all squares are rectangles, but not all rectangles are squares.
8+	Data Representer	14	Signs of development are when the child organizes and displays data through both simple numerical summaries such as counts, tables, and tallies, and graphical displays, including picture graphs, line plots, and bar graphs. At this level the child creates graphs and tables, compares parts of the data, makes statements about the data as a whole, and determines whether the graphs answer the questions posed initially.